PRAISE FOR

The Hidden Ear of God

"We do not see or hear with the ear of God when we pray. Thus at the heart of Christian practice in prayer, and not at its margins, lies a reserve, an openness to a transcendent universal we can never grasp. On this basis, Stephen Headley attempts a Christian theological anthropology of prayer in other faiths. By combining anthropology in both the doctrinal and ethnographic senses, he offers us nothing less than a new sort of non-secular universalism for which it is Christian specificity itself that opens to the universal in a different way. What a sensitive, subtle, and remarkable achievement."

    —JOHN MILBANK, author of *Theology and Social Theory*, co-author of *The Politics of Virtue*

"Prayer can be said to be common to all religions. Such a statement, however, can be misleading, for prayer may take many forms, and there was a tendency in the last century to privilege interior, 'mystical' prayer in the belief that here all religions converge. Fr. Stephen Headley writes as both a social anthropologist and an Orthodox priest: these qualifications lead him to explore the experience and practice of prayer in different religious traditions in all their particularity. His background in social anthropology lends acuteness of empirical observation, while his vocation as priest means that prayer is approached with a rare empathy. This book constitutes an astonishing achievement, leading to hard-won insights into the variety of prayer, as well as the characteristic genius of the religions discussed."

    —FR. ANDREW LOUTH, author of *The Origins of the Christian Mystical Tradition* and *Introducing Eastern Orthodox Theology*

"Stephen Headley has had a long and distinguished career as one of Southeast Asian studies' most accomplished scholars of religion in general and Islam in particular. Over the course of his career as an anthropologist, he has also been a priest and respected scholar of Christian orthodoxy, working from a ministerial base outside of Paris. Those of us who have known him personally have long understood that, even as he provided gifted analyses of ritual, prayer, and religious imaginaries across history and cultures, his engagement involved more than representing religion's reality as a simple social construction. In this new book, Headley brings all of his impressive intellectual breadth and originality to bear on what he aptly describes as a 'Christian anthropology of prayer.' The approach is comparative, moving across Judaism, Islam, Christianity, Hinduism, and Buddhism. In each instance, Headley aspires to treat religion and prayer 'in their own right,' exploring both not as the product of secular powers or social disciplines, but something deeper and more transformative because oriented toward what a prayer petitioner hopes to become. The range and depth of erudition Headley displays in engaging each prayer and faith tradition are breathtaking. In an age in which anthropologists and other scholars of religion have begun to put aside the shibboleths of modernist social science, this is a welcome work of astonishing originality and spiritual beauty. It is also a work that should be read by all anthropologists, scholars of comparative religion, and anyone intrigued by the challenge and reward of standing within a faith-tradition so as to more deeply understand another."

—ROBERT W. HEFNER, Professor of Anthropology and Global Affairs, Pardee School of Global Affairs, Boston University

The Hidden Ear of God

The Hidden Ear
of God

A COMPARATIVE ANTHROPOLOGY
OF PRAYER IN
Christianity, Judaism,
Islam, Hinduism, and Buddhism

(*A Theological Anthropology, vol. I*)

STEPHEN C. HEADLEY

Angelico Press

First published in the USA
by Angelico Press 2018
Copyright © Stephen C. Headley 2018

For information, address:
Angelico Press, Ltd.
169 Monitor St.
Brooklyn, NY 11222
www.angelicopress.com

pb: 978-1-62138-404-5
cloth: 978-1-62138-405-2
ebook: 978-1-62138-406-9

Book and cover design
by Michael Schrauzer
Cover image:
Study for a fresco of the Creation (Genesis),
by Anne Everett, in pastel and egg tempera:
Vézelay, France (2007)

CONTENTS

Where Motivations Lead to Methods

THIS MODEST INTRODUCTION TO A CHRISTIAN'S VIEW of the prayers of other faiths was born out of two sources: first, some thirty-five years of successive visits to central Java, where I did ethnographic research on village rituals and their invocations; second, my work as a parish priest and teacher of Christian anthropology and ascetics in an Orthodox seminary near Paris. I was prompted to write this volume because I could find nothing like it to recommend to my students. My work as an anthropologist and a priest convinced me that social science and theology had been enemies too long and that they could collaborate, even if this involved violation of their own axioms. If ethno-musicologists are often musicians, why should not anthropology of prayer be undertaken by someone who is used to praying? St Paul had a kaleidoscopic, complementary view of the multiplicity of faiths in first-century Athens. Preaching on the Areopagus, Paul said,

> Therefore the One whom you worship without knowing Him I proclaim to you: God who made the world and everything in it, since He is the Lord of heaven and earth, does not dwell in temples made with hands.... And He has made from one blood every nation of men to dwell on all the face of the earth, and has determined their pre-appointed times and the boundaries of their dwellings, so that they should seek the Lord, in the hope that they might grope for Him and find Him, though He is not far from each of us; for in Him we live and move and have our being.... (Acts of the Apostles 17:23–28)

I had already tried to mix the methodology of anthropology and theology in a previous book, *Christ after Communism: Spiritual Authority and its Transmission in Moscow Today* (2010). The comparative dimension that anthropology brings to the topic it researches need not deny the uniqueness of a revelation, and, where similarities or differences appear between rituals of prayer, pointing them out can only render them more comprehensible. On a personal level, I have always listened to the invocations of other religions with increasing respect as I was drawn into the sobriety and meaningfulness with which I initially was unfamiliar. Daily prayer is a fundamental building block of humanity's life worldwide, and its diversity only further demonstrates its capacity for a primordial meaningfulness.

Matthew the Poor, in closing the preface to his book *Orthodox Prayer Life: The Interior Way*, stated, "For I consider writing on prayer as prayer *per se*. This is what I have learned and what God has taught me."

The study of prayer outside monasteries has only a recent history. This "scientific" approach, *Religionswissenschaft*, appears at the end of the nineteenth century, sponsored by the likes of the Dutch professor at Leiden, Cornelius Tiele (1830–1902), and a French Protestant minister, Augusta Sabatier (1839–1901), first dean of the Faculté Protestante in Paris which he helped to found. Other German and French liberal Protestants sought to describe prayer outside of dogmatic theology. One of these was Friedrich Heiler, a Lutheran convert from Catholicism, whose book *Das Gebet*, published in 1918 (English translation: *Prayer, A Study in the History and Psychology of Religion*, 1932), initially attempted a phenomenological approach to religion stepping off from prayer. For Heiler, ritual was associated with primitive magic, while prayer, especially mystical prayer, by being individual, was always prior to the social. If, in England, Max Müller, W.H.R. Rivers, and Robert Marett placed prayer at the end of a religious evolution, after earlier stages using incantations and magic, Heiler's reliance on personal experience found less favor with Marcel Mauss and Emile Durkheim's periodization based on an evolutionary model. In their science, all religion was derived from projections onto the cosmos arising out of a given sociology, its social morphology.

Empirically speaking, this was an advance in the effort to disengage religion from European "Christian" categories, where culture was segmented into law, economics, religion, etc.[1] Custom in non-European societies usually embraced all of these, however, which explains why there is often no word for religion. The ancient Near Eastern template of a unified, controlled cosmos, a divine justice underlying all of life, was both foreign to much of the rest of the world and an impediment to any effort at description of their "religion." Society, structured by the cosmos, was isomorphic with the cosmological values as hierarchized by local custom. Having gained access to empirical descriptions of non-"Western" religion, the sociological approach developed by Durkheim's followers gradually lost any interest in describing monotheistic rituals and the prayers developed there. Nonetheless, if, as Mauss insisted (1909), prayer

1 Maurice Bloch has recently discussed the role of the state in Europe's "disembedding" of religion.

is a social act with social content, people learn how to pray through the practices they are taught. Only in the course of the twentieth century did the individual's role in creating prayers and interpreting them become better recognized. Following such classics as *Do Kamo* (1947) by Maurice Leenhardt (1878–1954), the co-founder of the Société des Océanistes and the Musée de l'Homme, it was at the end of the twentieth century that recent anthropological studies of Christianity in non-European contexts appeared, stressing the impact of local culture on the expression of the Christian faith.[2] What characterizes these recent anthropological descriptions is that the exceptional is privileged; the norms of Christian belief are not valued. The reasons behind the choice of these approaches are varied: indifference and ignorance of any Christian religious experience, and therefore interest in bringing to light their sociological content; dislike of the universalistic pretenses of monotheistic revelations; and finally, and this is perhaps the most disturbing, a view of "religion" where anthropology rejects any apologies of authenticity.

Approaching Persons Who Are Listening, Both God and Man

I have previously written three books and (co-)edited four[3] dealing with prayer. In this volume, I try to gain a better perspective on prayer in four traditions by viewing them through the prism of Christian theology. I have tried to be light-handed, letting the non-Christian prayers speak for themselves. The reason behind this change of approach from the earlier volumes is that, in doing so, I find new insights, often just those subjective and personal dimensions that the Durkheim tradition wanted to set aside. My approach encounters obstacles that are inevitable. An example: to study, indeed to enjoy, say, the

---

2 Some examples from Southeast Asia are: Webb Keane, *Signs of Recognition: Powers and the Hazards of Representation in an Indonesian Society* (1997) and *Christian Moderns: Freedom and Fetish in the Mission Encounter* (2007); Lorraine Aragon, *Fields of the Lord: Animism, Christian Minorities and State Development in Indonesia* (2000); Fanella Cannell, *Power and Intimacy in the Christian Philippines* (1999). Other examples: Robert Hefner (ed.), *Conversion to Christianity* (1993); Fanella Cannell (ed.), *The Anthropology of Christianity* (2006); Adeline Masquelier, *Prayer has Spoiled Everything: Possession, Power and Identity in an Islamic Town of Niger* (2001); Isabelle Nabokov, *Religion Against the Self: An Ethnography of Tamil Rituals* (2000); Sam D. Gill, *Sacred Words: A Study of Navajo Religion and Prayer* (1981); T.M. Luhrmann, *When God Talks Back: Understanding the American Evangelical Relationship with God* (2012).

3 *Christ after Communism: Spiritual Authority and its Transmission in Moscow Today*; *Durgā's Mosque: Cosmology, Conversion and Community in Central Javanese Islam*; *From Cosmogony to Exorcism in a Javanese Genesis: The Spilt Seed.* Edited volumes: *Moitiés d'hommes*; *Islamic Prayer Across the Indian Ocean: Inside and Outside the Mosque*; *Vers une anthropologie de la prière: études ethnolinguistiques javanaises*; *Anthropologie de la prière: rites oraux en Asie du Sud-Est.*

Bengali Râmprasâd's (1718–1775) songs to Kālī (M. Lupsa, 1967) without hearing them *sung* there, by leaving their melodies aside, is to risk experiencing them as dry and boring. And many of the great poets of South India were as much musicians as hymnographers. The hymnography, poetry, and melodies used in religious traditions need to be experienced orally in the mosque, on the banks of the Ganges, in the temples with thousands of devotees present. My idea here is not to try to identify fully with the experience of others but only to approach the fervor that brings so much beauty up from their hearts and out of their mouths. This endeavor is not just an aesthetic one; it also offers a critical approach to Christian theology, whose horizons could stand to be broadened. The opposition between monotheism and polytheism does not have to shut all the doors of mutual understanding. In India, the communion that visual apprehension of the temple deities brings, the "reciprocal eye" contact that Hindu worshippers say dissolves the frontiers between humanity and the deity when one "takes *darshan*," when the camphor flame on an *ârâti* is waved before the icon and one's offering of prayer is "shown," can also be addressed. After bringing forth food and incense during *pûjâ* (offerings), the return of these gifts, of *prasâda*, is a form of communion, of thanksgiving that can be partially grasped by a Christian through his experience of the Eucharist.[4] He will see both the difference and the similarity, and in neither case will he be indifferent to the seriousness with which one approaches the temple.

It is necessary not to overplay the role of empathy in observing prayer elsewhere, but it is even more important not to exaggerate the role of social hierarchies when we analyze people's motivation. Such social science approaches result in an abusive ascription of control of other people, of "relations of power," to explain almost all rituals. Some people participate in prayer in order to legitimate their own very private dilemmas, to identify their own personal frontier between inner and outer, a point of contact that is also the site of coalescence between two domains of experience that are as much related as they are opposed, "matching public and private worlds in order for them to meet," merge, and fuse. In this perspective, Isabelle Nabokov reminds her reader that the Tamil word for God (*katavul*) derives from just this movement of crossing, exceeding, and surpassing, and refers to the masking and unmasking of divinity, a cosmological personage, through an investment in a very personal relation with the deity.[5]

It is for these reasons that, in the following five chapters, ethnology, social anthropology, and theology will be marshaled to embrace a view of prayer that attempts to be as varied as its manifestations.

4 See Chapter 4 in this volume for Goodall on Tantric prayer.
5 *Religion Against the Self: An Ethnography of Tamil Rituals* (New York: OUP, 2000), 8.

What Theology; What Anthropology?

This is not a book of synthetic theology, in the sense that I have not incorporated non-Christian perspective into Christian prayer. Although that might be a worthwhile endeavor, for me, it raises too many unanswered questions; one needs to proceed slowly, as the practitioners of prayer usually claim. Thus Francis X. Clooney states in *Seeing Through Texts*:

> We were therefore choosing not to engage in a kind of research which would separate scholarship from questions of personal commitment.... Surely...research ought not to be undertaken as the means of personal fulfillment, personal concerns must be disciplined by a commitment to understanding...reflection on what one brings to the reading of religious texts and what one gets from that reading.[6]

That paradoxical way of avoiding narrow dogmatism is repeated by Clooney in a more recent book, *His Hiding Place is Darkness: A Hindu-Catholic Theopoetics of Divine Absence*, when he states that God is real enough to be absent, for such absence is a formidable site of encounter. He goes on to say that

> we need first of all to be grounded in the specificity and particularity in our own enduring love.... No matter how universal the truth, what we say is still the tale of the comings and goings of a beloved whose presence cannot be conceptualized as simply universal. To speak to the truth and love central to our faith bears with it an acute awareness of the failures and gaps that make claims to faith more fragile, vulnerable—and only in that way more convincing.[7]

While Clooney tries to speak for our times ("Ours is an era that both celebrates and tames religious diversity. It privatizes religion and shifts the deepest experiences to the realm of inner life"), the dichotomy between too much or too little religious commitment is a profoundly anti-monastic one. Universality is an abstract, but religious prayers are addressed to a "person," whatever that may mean. In the Christian ascetical tradition, "You shall have no other gods before me" (Exodus 20:3) is understood as a personal address

---

6 *Seeing Through Texts: Doing Theology among the Srīvaisnava of South India* (Albany, NY: SUNY, 1996), 247.

7 Francis X. Clooney, SJ, *His Hiding Place is Darkness: A Hindu-Catholic Theopoetics of Divine Absence* (Stanford: Stanford University Press, 2014), ix–x.

to those who had been baptized through the passage from death to life (in the crossing of the Red Sea). This jealous God shows "mercy to thousands, to those who love me and keep my commandments" (Exod. 20:6). Clooney's reserve over monotheism's exclusiveness (overly confident rhetoric about God's presence) is certainly not shared by the Indian poets and by the European Christian authors he enjoys reading, where the beloved is hidden for us in each text and only discovered by a determined ascetical exploit of one's pointedness of mind. Exclusivity is inherent to that intimate relationship. What to do with Clooney's vision of comparative theology, other than to admit to my own preference for the penitential approach of the ascetics at prayer, for whom the acute awareness of their distance from God, their longing for reconciliation, is the proof that God is coming toward them?[8]

This is, of course, not to say that broad theological questions are not germane to my approach. To give only one example of a question, but one that is difficult to answer: what is the relation between Jewish and Muslim monotheism (*tawhīd*), the Trinitarian monad of three persons in one Godhead in Christian revelation, a non-dualistic theology (*advaita* Vedanta), and Vedanta's qualified dualism, as per Rāmānuja? In the most general way, any reflection on the relationship between God and man poses the issue of the distance that separates them. Christology is preoccupied by the formulation of the anomaly, the philosophical puzzle, the *aporia*, of the total distinction and the full proximity of the incarnate Logos to humanity, who turns to him in prayer. In Indian philosophy, the tension is over the transcendence of the Absolute Lord, which inspires a debate over whether to know the Lord is to lose the Self in that mystery.

One cannot address this issue, however briefly, and not include in the discussion India's notion of *avatar,* which would seem to invalidate monotheism. Geoffrey Parrinder provides a useful summary of twelve characteristics of avatars.[9] Avatars most famously appear in the Indian epics of the Mahabharata and the Rāmayana. There is a pre-history to these narratives; for example, in the earlier *Shatapatha Brāhmana* (8th to 6th centuries BC), Vishnu is a dwarf. But, in the epics, this figure will later become a great mediator, a great Pervader, god of many avatars. If the Lord exists beyond all illusory becoming, his *māyā,* his incompressible *sakti,* allows him to make the impossible an event by *just this māyā.* Even if avatars may be repetitive, like reincarnation, these interventions in the lives of mankind are historical, for history is taken to be

---

8 Cf. St John of the Ladder (step seven) on spiritual tears in John Chryssavgis, *Ascent to Heaven,* chapter 5.

9 *Avatar and Incarnation: Wilde Lectures* (London: Faber & Faber, 1970), 120–27.

a linear, singular, and unique series of events. Parrinder lists the following characteristics of avatars. They are real and not docetic appearances; avatars have human parents. Rāma, for instance, has a childhood, a marriage, suffers and triumphs over evil through his avatars, and finally dies once they have accomplished their mission. While animal avatars are clearly mythological, human avatars are taken to be historical. The repetition of avatars tends to give their interventions into human history a mythological quality, yet, in Hindu Dharma, they are very important to both morality and religion, for they teach and create harmony. The monist vision of the world denies its objectivity, but the divine power of *māyā* is shown to live in that same world, thus guaranteeing divine revelation in a special way in a world where there is some general revelation to be found among mankind. These special revelations indicate that the Lord responds to human beings by using divine speech and through a "personality," an avatar. Rāmānuja, in his commentary on the *Bhagavad Gita*, claimed that, by his avatar, the Lord "can be seen by the eyes of all men." God needs worshippers to reveal his grace. While avatars are proper to Vishnu, Shivā appears in a visible way to men through other divine manifestations.

To return briefly to the issue of monotheism and monism raised above, what sort of isomorphism exists between these paramount theological debates of Christian and Indian philosophy over divine unity? The controversy in Christian Trinitarian theology matches Indian debates over monism in its complexity. The Trinitarian God is one in three persons. Over the centuries, an adequate vocabulary to express this revelation was debated, especially during and after the Council at Chalcedon (AD 451) proposed to clarify it. The single personhood of Christ in a single (*mia phusis*) or dual nature had proved a stumbling block for the oriental Syriac-speaking Christians when they translated the Greek of the Ecumenical Councils into their own terminology. They had been accustomed by the Antiochian School's theologians, Diodore of Tarsus (330–394), Theodore of Mopsuestia (ca. 350–428) and Nestorius of Constantinople (ca. 386–450), to speaking of the Word of God as having assumed, put on, the human nature of Jesus Christ. Cyril of Alexandria (ca. 376–444) insisted that the Word of God and Christ were the same person, but with two natures. The Council of Chalcedon tried to express the Antiochian distinction of the two natures while avoiding the notions of assumption or inhabitation of the Logos in mankind. This they did by using four adjectives describing the relation of the two natures in the one person of Christ: without confusion, without change, without division, without separation. For the Syrians, this precluded the description of human nature as the temple or the vestment of the divinity. If the formulation of one hypostasis in two natures was rejected by the Syrians, it was because they translated *hypostasis* (person) by *qnoma,* which also meant, in Syriac, the concrete and individual nature (*kyana*). So, for Severus of Antioch, a single hypostasis meant a single nature, i.e., two natures would be reflected in two hypostases.

Even today, these difficulties of vocabulary remain a deeply valued distinction among Oriental Orthodox Christians. Nonetheless, all Orthodox liturgies are Syriac, Semitic, by their origin and remain so by the tonality of their hymnography, even if their Greek rhetorical forms are Hellenistic.[10] And this is why they are all "Orthodox," Western and Eastern. By the incorporation of Semitic praise poetry into the Eucharistic canons of the "Greek" liturgies of St John Chrysostom and St Basil of Caesarea, a devotional path was traced where the ascesis of meditation serves as a yardstick for divinization. However, in Indian devotion (*bhakti*) after the fifth century A D,[11] despite the presentation of devotional poetry to a theistic "Lord" (Isvara), the element of self-apotheosis of these poets via their extraordinary piety can only be contrasted to the self-transformation of Christ[12] in his incarnation. Let me explain.

In Chapter 4, we briefly present the figure of the poet Nammâlvâr, a fervent devotee of Vishnu. Since the words of revelation he receives are pre-ordained, they are eternal, and, while Nammâlvâr's humanity is preserved through his

10 Cf. Louis Bouyer, *Eucharist: Theology and Spirituality of the Eucharistic Prayer,* trans. Charles Underhill Quinn (Notre Dame: University of Notre Dame Press, 1968).

11 Around the end of the Gupta and Harsha Empire, the disintegration of central power led to a regionalization of religiosity. As regional cults and languages gained in importance, the influence of the ritualistic Hinduism of the Brahmans diminished. Among the rural devotional movements, Shaivism, Vaishnavism, Bhakti, and Tantra competed for recognition by the local raja.

12 *Self and Self-Transformation in the History of Religions,* edited by D. Shulman and G. Stroumsa (Oxford and New York: Oxford University Press, 2002), 5, 8, 14. The experimental basis of ascetics is a quest for understanding, a *credo ut intelligam* stepping off from self-transformation in gradual ascetic or meditative praxis. But Jesus Christ's Incarnation required a new anthropology, a new theology. This is not a self-apotheosis of South India poets like Annamayya at Tirupati, who was elevated to the level of avatars of deities, which these authors described as an expansive, fluid, yet coherent, bounded self-model around an empty core.

In a personal communication from Fr Radu Marasescu: what might be important about the relation between *tawhîd* and Chalcedonian theology, at least as far as my personal queries go, is probably the meaning of Incarnation ... beyond the mystical path to union, common to both, the positive meaning of creation (and, ultimately, the part man is to play in it as "co-creator"). . . . Do we have, in Christianity, more than anywhere else, the seeds of such a take on creation, the rather essentialistic way we define (and even pray) Christ (and even the Father) ... slightly idolatric (every Jew would tell us so!)? Would a more Syrian/Semitic theology allow more "flexibility" in this respect? Syrian hymnology surely taps into such a dialogue between the Formless and the form? Someone like Henri Corbin used to think so.

passionate devotion, in one sense, he has neither beginning nor end. The perfection of his poem the *Tiruvaymoli*, and indeed the entire collection of the *Divya Prabadham*, is a "disembodied voice."[13] The Lord composes, and the poets lend their voices. Untouched by any human or worldly substance, Nammâlvâr is a paradigmatic seer for the Indian women and lower castes. People who do not wear the sacred thread that Hindu twice-born castes are allowed to wear can, without social discrimination, learn the Tamil Veda and can do so in the temple. God in his mercy becomes audible and visible.[14] The Christians' view of deification is totally different from that of these Indian ascetics, because here it is not man who enters the divine but God who enters all mankind, and He does so for all time and not simply through one or another avatar, be it a statue or a sacred text (*arcâvatâra*).

The New Comparative Theology[15]

Many methods are available today to study prayer comparatively. Both the *Journal of Comparative Theology* and the *Journal of Hindu-Christian Studies*

13   Vasudha Narayanan, *The Vernacular Veda: Revelation, Recitation, and Ritual* (Columbia, SC: South Carolina University Press, 1994), 137.

14   Ibid., 144.

15   Certain reservations concerning the "new" comparative theology are dealt with in Samuel J. Youngs's book review of *The New Comparative Theology,* a recent book edited by Francis Clooney. I will paraphrase Youngs's review below. The editor has included in this volume a wide variety of approaches under the rubric of a new comparative theology, all of which include sympathy with, and some understanding of, Christianity as well as detailed knowledge of non-Christian faith.

In the first chapter, James Fredericks defines comparative theology as dialectical, theological, non-soteriologically focused, and rooted in "experiments" in comparison that enable it to be non-theorizing. Youngs wonders in what sense there would be any theology left if all comparative theology were to avoid such theory, i.e., the notion of salvation, justification, liberation, and enlightenment. He also asks how Fredericks's recreation of identity through encounter, using the eyes of faith to imagine the great Other (what Derrida called an "unreserved hospitality"), could serve as a method for constructing any kind of desirable understanding.

In the next chapter of *The New Comparative Theology*, A. Bagus Laksanan claims that comparative theology is a pilgrimage, a process, and a hermeneutic bridge to the Other. The Orthodox follow the Cappadocian fathers' understanding of the difference (*diaphorà*) separating persons as the *sine qua non* allowing for communion and participation. In short, there is more to communion than bridges.

Closer to my approach is the chapter by Kristin Beise Kiblinger, which presents the challenge of an anti-theology of religion. Older forms advocating inclusivism or permitting pluralism in comparative religion studies have been discredited. The perspective of a real theology of religion is a necessary part of methodological honesty, of a self-disclosure of one's own faith that makes comparative theology more respectful, making all our presuppositions clear.

propose different kinds of comparisons between Christian and non-Christian prayer. To take one example: Francis Clooney's own approach is to "surrender" to several texts, as he does in the concluding chapter of *Seeing Through Texts*, his book on practicing theology among the Srivaisnavas of South India. Personally (and Clooney allows for this option), I find that one cannot surrender to a succession of texts from different religious traditions without losing something of one's "unconsolation," one's dissatisfaction with oneself as one prays over the distance separating oneself from the Lord. Personally, by changing the texts one meditates on, and broadening one's surrender to several of them, one risks losing just this "unconsolation," one's humility.

For Hugh Nicholson (chapter 4), comparative theology is a corrective to post-Enlightenment hegemonic discourse; one must depoliticize the us-them opposition by a dialogical encounter, by small modest comparisons, and by being honest about one's faith commitments. Nevertheless, isn't my own personal experience always going to be paramount, unless, indeed, I have none?

David Clairmont (chapter 5) uses a description of a sixteenth-century encounter between a Ceylonese Buddhist king and a Portuguese Franciscan monk to illustrate that our struggle to live up to our own religious ideals affects our dialogues. This implies that a devotional outlook can be characterized by an intellectually reserved and historically gradual approach to other religions, characterized by a sorrow and solidarity. Youngs asks whether such an approach toward comparative theology, while personally and relationally desirable, is not too closely identified with a particular ethical and spiritual outlook.

In chapter 6, Daniel Joslyn-Siemiakoski criticizes "supercessionist" Christian approaches, i.e., those assuming that, because Christianity follows after Israel, the first Testament is an old one. He reverses the question of Christology by asking whether the Son and Logos was the active agent of the revelation on Sinai and, if so, was Jesus obedient to the Torah that he himself revealed? Why are there not more inter-Abrahamic comparisons of Judaism, Christianity, and Islam, instead of a preference for comparisons with Indian and Chinese traditions?

Like Aloysius Pieris, Peter Phan, and Sathianathan Clarke, Tracy Sayuki Tiemeier (chapter 8), inspired by Asian liberation theologies, claims that the new comparative theologians, by looking for new theological goods, are new imperialists. Since Christianity is inevitably entangled with other faiths historically, its theology always has a cultural context. But then why should revelation or theology be value free?

Jeffrey Long (chapter 9), writing on Sri Rāmakrishna, develops a hybrid system by blending Neo-Vedanta, the Jain philosophy of *nayavada* (a doctrine of perspective which allows the fusion of truth claims into a religious pluralism), and Whitehead's process thought into an open system. He feels that, while topical comparisons broaden dialogue, more abstract comparisons expand and co-ordinate our understanding, as in, for instance, the relation of karma to atonement.

John Sheveland (chapter 12) uses a polyphonic conceptual space as an analogy for comparative theology, since it allows religious distinction to form a unity. It amplifies the aesthetic dimensions of hearing, providing a new metaphor for a global theological community. He treats St Paul, Vedanta Desika, and Santideva. Isn't this overly analogical thinking, i.e., analogy foregoing truth claims by providing a tonality of dialogue? Theological contradiction is not always dissonance or the suppression of heterodox voices.

My understanding of a Christian approach to non-Christian prayer is different from that of Clooney. His *His Hiding Place is Darkness* compares the Hindu *Holy Word of Mouth* (*Tiruvaymoli*) with the Hebrew *Song of Songs* (*Shir ha-Shirim*) by reading the two poems conjointly, thereby increasing their mutual understanding. This is his fourth essay in comparative theology after *Seeing Through Texts*; *Divine Mother, Blessed Mother: Hindu Goddesses and the Virgin Mary* (2005); and *Beyond Compare: St. Francis de Sales and Srî Vedânta Desika on Loving Surrender to God* (2008). Other currents in comparative theology are found in the articles of the Harvard Divinity School's *Journal of Comparative Theology*.

Clooney's approach, given the amount of work he has put in on the philological side (texts and commentaries in Sanskrit and Tamil) and his serious spiritual training, requires that one define one's own. Perhaps his approach has an immediate echo in the American context. It seems to me (but am I right?) that the evolution of Catholicism in America since the Second Vatican Council and the importance of Pentecostal and Evangelical understandings of Christianity remain relatively absent from Europe. There is also the fact that, in America, since the 1950s, a Buddhist movement has arisen with its own way of dealing with modernity.[16] In any case, not having lived in America for fifty years, yet having been educated there,[17] I seem to have kept moving east, which has unconsciously reflected a certain alienation. First, I went to France, where I studied and worked from 1973 to 2006. Further travels have taken me to Java, India, Russia (2006–2010), and Greece. Through this, I became a small part of the Slavic and Greek expressions of the Orthodox Christian faith in Western Europe. While Francis Clooney will want to speak to the cultural milieu where he teaches, New England, I find that American post-modern culture leaves me ill at ease with its understanding of narrativity and reflectivity, and, in a general way, with what one can do when one starts thinking about texts. My subject here is personal prayer, which is pre-eminently an I–Thou relationship, not in the sense of Mikhail Bahktin's dialogics but in the sense that one's sincerity and subjectivity are constantly subject to the loss of humility, which destroys communion and participation in the words of prayer.

In *Divine Mother, Blessed Mother*, Clooney studies the Akathistos ("Standing") hymn that is so popular in the Orthodox churches. Yet, when I recall

---

16   Cf. David L. McMahan, *The Making of Buddhist Modernism* (New York: OUP, 2008), 9–14. Rick Fields, *How the Swans Came to the Lake: A Narrative History of Buddhism in America* (Boston: Shambhala Publications, 1992).

17   Cf. D. Oliver Herbel, *Turning to Tradition: Converts and the Making of an American Orthodox Church* (New York: OUP, 2014).

that poem in my mind's eye, I see and hear a group of Greek women in a small monastery near Brussels, singing their hearts out to God late into the night. They need no text, for they pray by rote, transforming a poem, which, instead of losing so much in translation from Greek, *in situ,* becomes a vibrant sacrifice of praise.

Perhaps Indians and Americans will not share it, but, for me, there is an ambience of alienation that creeps into otherwise admirable efforts to compare prayers of different traditions. I have been deprived by the printed word, and all the work that has gone into putting it on paper, of the source of prayer, that elusive opening of the heart whose sensitivity has to be cultivated to bring it to speak to the Lord. Outside of active prayer, the word "God" may mean nothing to a reader. As Clooney has been telling us, faith and hope are largely the experience of absence, what I call "de-consolation," for, while our faith reaches out to the Lord, God's grace alone may partially reveal him to us in the *logos,* which is certainly not a text. As the anaphor of the Eucharist of St Basil puts it:

> Oh Master of all, Lord of heaven and of earth, and of all creation both visible and invisible, who sits on a throne of glory, and sounds the depths, who art without beginning, invisible, incomprehensible, uncircumscribed, immutable, the Father of our Lord Jesus Christ, a great God and Savior, our hope, who is the image of Thy goodness, the seal of faithfully reproducing yourself, in Himself showing forth Thee, the Father, the Living Word, true God. . .

While I have no reason to be suspicious of Clooney's enterprise, I find it culturally distant, even though I live in a profoundly de-Christianized country, France, where the gospel of *laïcité* is pervasive. Perhaps this secularization has cleared the playing field here for Christianity over the last hundred years. There is no heritage of Unitarianism here. Few find their Christian faith enriched by an oriental religion, even if some do become Buddhists. Many travel to India and observe the fervor with which Hindus pray, but, usually, they go East only to visit, and remain rooted in the West. In any case, the proximity of the Christian martyrs of Eastern Europe provides another kind of apostolic succession, written in blood as well as revealing the presence of the Spirit. Persecution opened the doors to a kind of ecumenism that has stripped down our relations with Jews and Buddhists, Lutherans and Baptists, to the genuine *kenosis* of Christ. It is striking that, in the early Church, Christ's victory, His Resurrection, His Pascha was preached by St

Peter (Acts 2:22–24, 29–32; 13:34–37) and all the early hymnographers as His descent into hell, which he conquered, raising the dead with him to life eternal.[18] Here, theophany is self-emptying, or *kenosis*. For me, the practice of prayer requires a concentration that others may find exclusivist, but which the desert fathers associated with deep humility that produces another kind of openness, silent tranquility (*hèsychia*). As St John Climacus (ca. 579–648), hermit at wadi el-Tlah, later abbot at Mt Sinai, says in the seventh rung of his *Ladder*, the only way to describe what separates us from the Lord is to weep.

—Vézelay, May 2015

---

18 Cf. Hilarion Alfeyev, *Christ the Conqueror of Hell: The Descent into Hades from an Orthodox Perspective* (Crestwood, NY: St Vladimir's Seminary Press, 2009).

CHAPTER 1

Approaching Prayer beyond Christianity through Verbal Icons and Iconic Words

Prayer is the only way to name God.

—Fr Boris Bobrinskoy[1]

The Name of God is the ontological foundation of prayer, its substance, power, and justification.

—Fr Sergei Bulgakov[2]

A cry covers the tumult: "there is no God".... The musings of the psalmist do not cease to illumine the essential by affirming that there is only one gratuitous and perfect murder on the terrible borderland between death and life: that of the innocent one. Riveted to his anxiety... the sole nostalgia of the reprobate remains the forever-impossible murder: deicide.

—André Chouraqui[3]

ST EPHREM THE SYRIAN (AD 306–373) DESCRIBED GOD AS listening to man's prayers through his "hidden ear." He attests to the truth that God alone can "hear" a man's prayers—nobody else may truly listen to what a man says in prayer or to how God responds. For social scientists studying the phenomenon of prayer across different religious traditions, this poses some problems. First of all, if prayer concerns a relationship with the divine, how can it ever really be fully grasped or described, let alone studied in detail?

---

1 Boris Bobrinskoy, *The Compassion of the Father* (Crestwood, NY: St Vladimir's Press, 2003).

2 Sergius Bulgakov, *Icons and the Name of God*, trans. Boris Jakim (Grand Rapids, MI: Wm. B. Eerdmans, 2012), 165.

3 André Chouraqui, "Liminaires" (trans. S.C. Headley), *Le Cantique des Cantiques suivi des Psaumes* (Paris: PUF, 1970), 89.

Perhaps a secular approach to prayer will always fall short. But what of a Christian approach? Might it be possible to develop a Christian "anthropology of prayer" that may help us, as Christians, to approach the prayer traditions of other religions with deeper understanding? Such an approach, which both takes seriously the truths believed by Christians and respects the reality of deep spiritual traditions in non-Christian religions, is one way forward—a way that safeguards respect for the deeply held beliefs of all believers, without reducing them to secular and superficial categories. In our current political situation, this respectful—but honest—approach to interfaith dialogue and study is needed more than ever.

This book describes a Christian anthropology of prayer. In this first chapter, I will present the foundations of this approach. This will serve as the basis for the main chapters of this book, which will use the template of Christian anthropology to characterize the prayers of four other major non-Christian religions: Judaism (Chapter 2), Islam (Chapter 3), Hinduism (Chapter 4), and Buddhism (Chapter 5). In a final concluding chapter (Chapter 6), I will summarize what we have learned from each of these studies, and how this initial foray into anthropology of religions prepares us for the themes covered by subsequent volumes in this series: first, religious ritual (Volume 2), which invariably comprises individual prayers, and, finally, the situation of prayer and ritual in today's context: the nature of secularization and its impact outside of Western Europe (Volume 3). While this study, and the series in general, is broad in scope, it is, by nature, introductory in character, and interested readers are directed to the lists of further reading provided in the footnotes.

A Christian Anthropology of Prayer

Before I begin the work of defining a Christian "anthropology of prayer," a further question arises: what kind of Christianity are we talking about? Is it possible to find agreement on the nature of prayer even within our own religion?

The answer, I believe, is a resounding yes. While our local traditions may differ, the basic underlying tradition of Christian prayer holds fast across our differences. My own background is that of an Orthodox priest, educator, and anthropologist, and, as such, I will draw extensively on Orthodox sources. However, as a Westerner surrounded by Western forms of Christianity and their literatures, I have found my own views echoed in Roman Catholic and Anglican writers, and I incorporate them into my approach. Our shared tradition does indeed allow us to formulate a distinctively Christian understanding of prayer that, in turn, allows us to grow in understanding of other religions.

What, then, of our Christian anthropology of prayer? A theological approach to anthropology is unusual, both for Orthodox Christians and for social anthropologists. So it is necessary to define what we mean by such an approach. For many, this will be unfamiliar territory.

Studies in anthropology of religion generally examine all aspects of the general nature of human sociability, i.e., the way humans have created and shared the often time-resistant, stable representations of social relations, even if no two versions of any ritual invocation are identical. These concepts of sociability simultaneously situate the individual's relation to the gods, the cosmos, and his own society. For social anthropology, religion is not a category *sui generis,* but a component in a larger societal whole, in which there usually exist stable shared relations between men and their common cosmos. Thus it is society as a whole, and its inevitable power games, that becomes the focus of such studies, and the predominant reason for differences in religious practice.

Secular social scientists must also hold to the so-called "axiom of neutrality," by which they treat all manifestations of religious traditions equally and at arm's length. Relativism and tolerance are considered key. However, because such researchers are not able to treat any religious system as containing "truth"—for this would undermine their tenet of neutrality and impartiality—they must treat no religious system as containing truth. This is a further reason why studies in anthropology of religion tend to focus on superficial expressions of faith, on exterior sociability: religious prayers and rituals are viewed in a purely external way, as moves in the broader societal struggle for status, identity, and power.

Secular social scientists will thus object that any faith-specific approach to anthropology places religion outside of society as a whole, destroying any pretense of "objectivity" and of holding to the axiom of neutrality. But, as believers, we do believe that religion transcends human society and has its origins beyond us. There is little advantage in "objectivity" if it prevents us from addressing the topic of prayer in its own right. There are plenty of purely secular works on religious traditions, but they do not help believers to come to terms with other religions. To address this, a new approach is needed.

A Christian anthropology of prayer, treating religion and prayer "in its own right," questions many of secular anthropology's basic assumptions—not least the idea that religious expression is purely about power games. In any living faith tradition, "prayer in its own right" is not just a strategy for accumulating power or forming an identity, but something much deeper. Prayer is transformative; it is best understood in terms of what the praying person, the *orans,* is trying to *become* through his or her prayer. Prayer can be mapped by studying which indexes the *orans* believes in, what "gift of credit" (the underlying meaning of the Latin *credo*) he or she offers to the divinities.

Mapping this understanding onto a range of unfamiliar beliefs, through exploration of prayer in other religions, may seem like an overwhelming task, but it is an important one, and provides the premise for a comprehensive anthropology of prayer.[4] It is imperative to begin from the premise of belief: what the Jesuit scholar Michel de Certeau refers to as the "credit given to God" and which Anselm of Canterbury (d. AD 1109) characterized with the maxim *credo ut intelligam*.[5] This holds true even through the vast diversity of invocations in terms of form and content, as well as through their diverse focus, whether toward God or gods, ancestors or spirits, termite hills or guardians of the land. People who pray—and almost everyone does, in one form or another—envisage themselves in an intricately changing matrix, which makes description of their constituent qualities difficult.[6] The *orans* is trying to change his or her persona through an exchange of words. Treating this behavior as a simple matter of persuasion ("make-believe"), as do secular social scientists, denies any authenticity to the pragmatics of such

4   I have addressed this challenge in three earlier volumes with regional focus: Stephen C. Headley and David Parkin eds., *Islamic Prayer across the Indian Ocean: Inside and Outside the Mosque* (Richmond, Surrey: Curzon, 2000); Stephen C. Headley, ed., *Towards an Anthropology of Prayer: Javanese Ethnolinguistic Studies* (Aix-en-Provence: Publications de l'Université de Provence, 1996); Stephen C. Headley, "Pour une anthropologie de la prière," *L'Homme* 132 (1994), 7–14.

5   Anselm, *Proslogion* 1. Anselm's maxim expresses his belief that reason requires man to believe in God, for human rebelliousness demanded that God should become incarnate as man. (See his *Cur Deus Homo?* [*Why God Became Man*] in which he defends his conviction that Christ's atonement satisfies the offense made by Adam's fall.) Anselm concludes that *credo ut intelligam,* a variation on Augustine's *crede, ut intelligas,* "believe so that you may understand" (*Tract. Ev. Jo.,* 29.6), thereby relating faith to reason.

6   Since Marcel Mauss's long essay *On Prayer* (New York and Oxford: Durkheim Press/ Berghahn, 2003 reprint), and his article "Une catégorie de l'esprit humain: la notion de personne celle de 'moi'," *Journal of the Royal Anthropological Institute of Great Britain and Ireland* 68 (1938), 263–81, there have been numerous Christian studies of personhood, including B. Meunier, *La Personne et le Christianisme ancien* (Paris: Éditions du Cerf, 2006), Jean-Claude Larchet, *Personne et Nature: La Trinité—Le Christ—L'homme: contributions aux dialogues interorthodoxe et interchrétien contemporain* (Paris: Éditions du Cerf, 2011), as well as, of course, studies by social anthropologists, such as M. Carrithers, Steven Collins, and Steven Lukes, *The Category of the Person: Anthropology, Philosophy, History* (Cambridge: Cambridge University Press, 1985), S. Radhakrishnan and P.T. Raju, eds., *The Concept of Man: A Study in Comparative Philosophy* (London: Allen and Unwin, 1966), and, with an Indian focus, Ákos Östör, Lina Fruzzetti, and Steve Barnett, eds., *Concepts of Person: Kinship, Caste and Marriage in India* (Dehli and Oxford: Oxford University Press, 1992). These studies have shown how the culturally constituted qualities or constituents of personhood vary widely.

communication, yet it is the prevalent attitude in today's individualistic society, where public expressions of belief are not encouraged. We need to insist here that, for any anthropology of prayer, there is a ritualized exchange of words. One can understand such prayer even if its destination (spirits, gods, ancestors) escapes us.

It is this understanding of prayer and invocation as a transformative "gift of credit," founded on an initial belief, that will form the basis of our understanding of Christian anthropology. And, since prayers, as oral rites that express and embody genuine beliefs, are also theological statements, they benefit from both anthropological and theological study—hence my use of the term "theological anthropology." Methodological duality and a certain interdisciplinary focus will strengthen our conclusions.

This approach—applying a Christian understanding of invocation to other religions—has at least three significant advantages: first, it takes prayer of all kinds seriously as real communication. It is inevitable that Christians are biased: they will view Vedic hymns, or the Muslim five-daily *salāt*, primarily through their own experience of hymnography (the Psalms and Biblical canticles). Yet this bias contains advantages, for, by approaching non-Christian prayers in this way, Christians admit that Brahmins, like themselves, are also deeply implicated in saying their prayers; they are not following an elaborate set of rules for building up an empty ritual, but are engaged in what they believe is genuine invocation.

Second, it is less pretentious than a straightforwardly comparative approach. One can remain Christian in one's outlook without trying to pretend otherwise—and without pretending that one has no real experience of prayer upon which to draw. What is the point of comparing prayer traditions unless one has already grasped one's own? It would be insincere and negligent not to take one's own experience in prayer as a helpful doorway into the prayers of other religions, even though these prayers do not share a Christian foundation.

Third and finally, the approach allows us to preserve genuine differences between religious traditions. If Christian prayer is properly represented, for example, then Christian revelation may also appear distinct from the cosmo-morphic religiosities within which social scientists place all elements of religion. We are able to state that Christ, according to Christian revelation, is not simply an inevitable product of a purely human religious system, but originates beyond this. Jesus is more than another legendary mythological figure or avatar; his personality does not simply arise out of a cosmology.

Thus a Christian approach to the anthropology of religion, of prayer, is personal, rather than slanted toward concepts of exterior sociability favored by academics. It allows for increased familiarity and intimacy—a willingness, perhaps, to take other religions' assertions about their prayers at face value, while holding true to one's own faith—enabling a broader, better understanding of different kinds of prayer, even if one's primordial "ear" for invocation will always be tuned to one's own experience.

The Origins of Christian Prayer

Christians are monotheists, and understand prayer as a dialogue initiated not by man, the creature, but by God, who created man. This is part and parcel of God's "work," his creation of human beings. Prayer, as natural dialogue with God, began with creation, where Adam walked with God in the Garden of Eden—but prayer as man's natural state was lost with the Fall. For the New Testament Church, Christian prayer, or renewed dialogue with God, is only possible through the Holy Spirit, the Third Person of the Trinity: "no one can say, 'Jesus is Lord,' except by the Holy Spirit" (1 Cor. 12:3).[7] The recognition of Christ—and therefore the very possibility of true Christian prayer—is itself a gift from God, God's gift of his own presence within us.

The Church Fathers attest to man's natural state of dialogue with God, made possible through God's own "gift" of the Holy Spirit, but also emphasize the idea that this gift of prayer is transformative. St Irenaeus of Lyon (died c. AD 202) famously said, "The glory of God is a living human being"[8]—in other words, "a human being fully alive," a person restored to the communion with God for which he was created. God's gift of prayer, His gift of Himself, allows man to be transformed—not only restored to the state Adam enjoyed before the Fall, but even further, to a divinized state of full communion with God. Thus it is that, as we recover the divine image and likeness in which we were created, we may become co-creators with God in His Creation. The creation and restoration of humanity, and humanity's own part in this, is an ongoing process that continues through the revelation of God's Logos and Messiah in the hearts of men. This Logos, the Word of God, is at once both man's Creator and man's partner, communing with the creature He created. He initiates prayer, and yet He is also a communicative presence much too dense, complete, and saturating to be grasped by the single word "prayer." As the Letter to the Hebrews puts it, "the

7 When a quoted author is citing the Bible, I will leave whatever text that author uses, because, for the Old Testament, some authors prefer the Septuagint versions to the translations from the Masoretic text for their own interpretation. My own quotations from the Bible will be taken from the New International Version (NIV), unless otherwise specified.

8 *Against Heresies*, 4.20.7.

word of God is living and active" and "sharper than any double-edged sword" (Heb. 4:12). This "living and active" reality places the Word simultaneously at the root of all our prayer, our transformation, as cause, and also utterly beyond any simple attempts at definition. Silent prayer thus becomes the ineffable verbal interface of this relationship. St Augustine of Hippo (AD 354–430) wrote, "Through him you sought us when we were not seeking you, but you sought us that we might begin to seek you."[9] Christ is the active one, freely giving us the possibility of prayer and inner transformation. And the incarnation of the Messiah awaited by Israel was not a single temporal or even a cosmic event, but the arrival of an enduring presence in the hearts of the faithful.

Well before any of the affirmations made by early Christian writers, prayer is described in Scripture as having been placed on man's lips by God when Moses, before the burning bush, insisted that, to speak to God, he needed to be given his name (Exod. 3:13–14). This is the first and most ancient evidence that Christians understand prayer fundamentally differently from the way in which social scientists do. For Christians, prayer exists "in its own right" as a "gift," an invocation that comes from beyond ourselves. The Old Testament revelation that man is created in God's image (Gen. 1:26–27) recurs in the New Testament (e.g., in 1 Cor. 11:7), but in a new light. Here it is primarily Christ who comes in the likeness of God (2 Cor. 4:4, Col. 1:15), and it is through him that we undergo transformation to grow into that same image: "to be conformed to the likeness of his Son," as St Paul says (Rom. 8:29), and "we, who with unveiled faces all reflect the Lord's glory, are being transformed into his likeness with ever-increasing glory" (2 Cor. 3:18). This creation is qualified as a renewed creation (see Titus 3:5, "rebirth," *paliggenesia*, literally a re-naissance) that retrieves the original creation of man out of nothing. As the Orthodox theologian Fr Andrew Louth puts it, being in God's image is indeed the hallmark of what it is to be human, even if everything that we are comes from God.[10] St Paul reformulates this in a baptismal metaphor when he says that the Christian has "put on the new self, which is being renewed in knowledge in the image of its Creator" (Col. 3:10). Christ in his incarnation thus projects, "images" forth, so that man can recover the resemblance of God lost by Adam.

The creation of the universe did not end on the sixth day. Rather, it is an ongoing process whose major medium is gifted prayer, our transformation through dialogue with God. The Nicene Creed (AD 325) states of Christ that "through him all things were made." As Louth points out, this makes more sense when we realize that, in Greek, "likeness" (*homoiōsis*) is a process and

9 Augustine, *Confessions* 11:4.
10 See Andrew Louth, *Introducing Eastern Orthodox Theology* (London: SPCK, 2013), ch. 6.

not a state. John the Evangelist implies as much in his first epistle: "Dear friends, now we are children of God, and what we will be has not yet been made known. But we know that when he appears, we shall be like him, for we shall see him as he is" (1 John 3:2). Growing into the likeness of God takes time and spiritual effort.

Yet where exactly in us do we find this "likeness" and creation "in the image of God"? According to St Athanasius (AD 296–373), our likeness to God lies in our capacity for rational thought. He says that God

> created human beings not simply like all the irrational animals upon the earth, but making them according to his own image, and giving them a share of the power of his own Word, so that having as it were shadows of the Word and being made rational, they might be able to abide in blessedness, living the true life, which is really that of the holy ones in paradise.[11]

Thus, for Athanasius, it is through man's rationality that he is enabled to return to the state of paradise. For John of Damascus (AD 676–749), this rationality includes both intelligence and free will: "The 'according to the image' is manifest," he says, "in intelligence (*noeron*) and free will (*autexousion*)."[12]

Louth unpacks these statements further. If the image of God is in Christ, then we cannot understand the Word of God apart from his incarnation. For early Greek-speaking Christians, it was participation in the Logos that designated being "according to the image (*to kat'eikona*)" of God. Above and beyond the capacity for rationality and free will, Louth insists that this participation in the Logos is vital. It is participation in the Logos that ultimately gives man the capacity for expressing meaning that allows him to participate in the lives of others and that of God—in other words, it creates the very possibility of prayer and communion.[13]

A further consequence: we can only know Christ incarnate if we already understand what it is to be human. So Christ's miracles are not proof of his divinity but of his humanity. For a person to be "in the image" of God means to have a grace-given affinity to God. Put in simpler terms, it means being able to pray. When Christ says to Philip, "Anyone who has seen me has seen the Father" (John 14:9), this implies that Philip can recover the boldness (*parrhesia*) of Adam, who was able to speak with God as he walked with him in the

11 Athanasius, *On the Incarnation*, 3, cited in Louth, *Eastern Orthodox Theology*, 85.
12 John of Damascus, *On the Orthodox Faith*, 26.
13 Louth, *Eastern Orthodox Theology*, 86.

garden of paradise. This return to the "natural" state of man, in turn, implies that all Christians are becoming members of the body of Christ, united to him (1 Cor. 12:26–27). Just as Eve is Adam's companion, so Christ's Church is his bride (Eph. 5:25–32 and Rev. 21–22). As St Paul puts it, we are "sons of God through faith" (Gal. 3:26); through faith, we come to share in what Christ is by nature. This union, however, nonetheless preserves genuine diversity, for difference (*diaphorà*) is necessary for communion and participation in the life of another.[14]

Because our individual unity with Christ is bound up in a higher unity—the unity of Christ with the Church—our identity is defined by a "catholic" (*kath'holon*), holistic sharing in humanity as a whole. This sharing in humanity must begin with a self-emptying, a *kenosis*. We abandon our narrow and selfish definitions of what it means to be human in order to encompass the whole catholicity and fullness of humanity, founded on a truth that concerns all of us both individually and collectively. Recreated in the Spirit and set free, we discover our humanity and recognize such a personhood as a response both to God and to one another. Thus, in Orthodox Christian piety, to open ourselves out in prayer for the love of God is initially to love the image, the *eikōn*, of God, of Christ who underwent *kenosis* and self-emptying for the sake of humanity. By restoring in us His image, He places words on our lips for prayer.

This understanding of prayer as kenotic is inevitably bound up with such a Christian understanding of transcendence. Self-emptying, *kenosis*, leads one face to face with the abyss of one's own nothingness, which—if one can accept, can relinquish any pretense of consolation in the presence of God—leads to an experience of silence and of revelation beyond words. Abandoning our free will is only possible when we realize that God believes in us and can guide us toward him, placing his own words on our lips to enable us to call upon him. This prayer, in turn, leads us to the freedom that comes from accepting that Christ suffers for us; to attain this freedom, we practice prayer, which is an act of obedience, of faith, of self-denial, which paradoxically gives us the confidence to embrace who we really are, as creatures created out of nothingness and conformed to the image of God our creator. In His image and likeness (Gen. 1:26), we are able to cross through the abyss of non-being to a fullness of being that is at once poor and rich—rich in the silence where the "hidden ear of God" is attentive to our plight. Its symbol is that of Moses standing barefoot before the burning bush. Verbal prayer and invocation ultimately lead to silence before God. And while, viewed

---

14 For a discussion of difference (*diaphorà*), division (*diairesis*) in the space (*diàstéma*) that characterizes creation *ex nihilo*, see the introduction to John Zizioulas, *Communion and Otherness* (London: T&T Clark, 2006).

from the outside, this state may seem like a "dumb silence," it is, in fact, the silence of deep communion that enriches a person who draws near to God.

However, the question of silence before God continued to stir up skepticism in the twentieth century, as we will see in the controversy presented next.

A Recent Point of Departure:
Bulgakov's Theology of the Name of God

Surprisingly, during the almost 1,300 years of theological reflection and ascetical theology that stand between St John of Damascus and our own day, very little energy was spent to further develop this Christian anthropology. It is not until the twentieth century that we find serious renewed attempts at answering the question of humanity's place in the world. This development is found, *inter alia*, in Fr Sergei Bulgakov's theological discussions of Orthodox Christian prayer and anthropology.

Bulgakov's reflections were sparked by controversy. In 1907, a Russian monk named Ilarion (Domratchev) published a work entitled *On the Caucasus Mountains* that presented his experience of monastic prayer. It contained the surprising belief that "the Name of God is God himself and can work miracles."[15] Ilarion's ideas found support in the Russian Andreyevsky skete on Mt Athos where another monk, Antonii (Bulatovich), promoted Ilarion's book—until 1912, when the Holy Synod in St Petersburg banned it for heresy. The ensuring controversy, known as the "onomatodox," *Imiaslavie* or "Name of God" (*imya bozhie*) heresy, came to be centered on the Russian monastery of St Panteleimon on Mt Athos (1910–1918).[16]

The "heresy" grew out of the monastic experience of praying the Jesus Prayer, which focuses on repeating the name of Christ. When mixed with the Platonic idea that the name or idea of an object always exists before the object itself does, this experience led monks to a belief that the name of God itself must be pre-eternal and miraculous. Many monks took up the idea, and, in 1913, a supporter of the movement was elected hegumen of the Andreyevsky skete. The wider church took action: the Patriarch of Constantinople proclaimed their

15 Hilarion Domratchev, *Sur les Monts de Caucase* (Paris: Syrtes, 2017).

16 Hilarion Alfeev, *Le Nom Grand et Glorieux* (Paris: Cerf, 2007); the Russian version is more complete. Bulgakov's *Imya Bozhie* was recently reprinted in Russian with the sixth chapter (written in 1940 and published in Russian in Paris in 1953), and is available in English in Jakim's translation *Icons and the Name of God*. When, in 1942, Bulgakov finally finished the sixth and final chapter of his *Philosophy of the Name*, begun some thirty-five years earlier, it came too late for the controversy that had broken out in 1907; it was, however, still a major contribution to the theology of invocation of the divinity.

teaching to be pantheism, and that summer, on the orders of Tsar Nicholas II, Russian troops violently evicted more than 600 monks from the monastery. As part of a drive for a full theological response, the 1917–1918 local synod of the Russian Orthodox Church tasked Fr Sergei Bulgakov with the philosophical and theological clarification of the status of the name of God in monastic prayer. His resulting study was published in 1920 as the book *The Name of God*.

Bulgakov begins his opening chapter by asking what it is that allows a word to be a word. As just said following Plato, the onomatodox based their belief on the fact that the names of objects precede objects themselves. Yet, says, Bulgakov, if it is not so—if objects are the cause of names, rather than vice versa—the very possibility of prayer is undermined, since prayer proceeds from inside us. Thus, to avoid this dilemma, and come to a clear understanding of what a name is, it is important to clarify what words themselves are. One possibility is that a word, or word-idea, is a psychological "representation": it is a mark or a sign of something else. However, a word-idea still lacks full meaning, since there is no thought without words, and there are no words without thought. For Bulgakov, words "speak" us. Our mind is the arena of an *"auto-ideation* of the universe."* Adam, he says, as a man and microcosm, as bearer of the divine Logos, as image of God, has within himself a force for the *ideation* of the world. In this sense, the world is born in him.[17] Thus, for Bulgakov, while the creation of words is a subjective psychological process in the form of its existence, it is cosmic by its essence—a cosmos uttered by a micro-cosmos. This implies the existence of a junction between the cosmic and the elemental, between meaning and sound, between essence and sign, and this junction constitutes what Bulgakov calls a symbol. Words—and therefore names—are symbols that are born, not invented, and active with a life-creating energy. Yet, since words still find their origin in human psychology, they are therefore ultimately "created," just as man himself is created. Onomatodoxy is refuted.

Bulgakov wrote in response to a specific context: he replied to the Council's request to clarify the status of the name of God in Orthodox theology. He did not intend to state the philosophical possibilities of transcendental nomination. Rather, he took his cues from nearly 2,000 years of reflection on Christian revelation through the practices of prayer described above, and from ideas developed by St Maximus the Confessor (ca. AD 558–662) about

17 A somewhat similar understanding is found in certain Indian schools of philosophy: see Madeleine Biardeau, *Théorie de la Connaissance et Philosophie de la Parole dans le brahmanisme classique* (Paris: Mouton, 1964); and André Padoux, *Vāc: The Concept of the Word in Selected Hindu Tantras*, trans. Jacques Gontier (Albany: State University of New York Press, 1990).

man as a microcosm.[18] It is in the context of this tradition that Bulgakov's originality is seen most clearly.

For us, Bulgakov's argument is of particular interest for its reflections on Christian anthropology. He asks the very question at the root of anthropology: how is religion possible? He argues, "Man is endowed with the image of God not only in his soul (*esprit*), but also in his nature (*ousia*) and in his relation to the world."[19] Thus man, in his very created state, reflects and mirrors God's relation to the world as creator. Bulgakov sees in humanity an innate freedom, a creative self-positioning: "one's personal consciousness carries in it the breath of freedom." God's creation of a personal consciousness is different from the creation of the rest of the universe because humankind, created in the uncreated image of God, contains the seeds of divinization. Put more simply, God is man's prototype and metaphysical *in-originality*. Bulgakov explains,

> In this free admission of consisting of nothing more than an image of Another, the first Image, is born the love for the Other, that is to say of God, a love that is like the seal of the Logos, of divine sonship. The Son loves the Father and, loving God, man sees himself only as the image of his Creator, from whom he holds his being. As he freely affirms himself as image, he accomplishes a kenotic act of love. . . . This godlike "I" is also for man a divine "Thou," given to him in his human "I," and he is called to listen to him. Thus his creaturely "I" contemplates himself through prayer in the absolute "I".[20]

Bulgakov's description of how prayer becomes possible is a good expression of the founding Christian belief in humanity's creation out of nothingness according to the image and likeness of God.[21] But what about the Fall? Is this "likeness of God" not lost? Bulgakov proposes that the "likeness of God" in us "is the free realization by man of his image."[22] Together, both God and man

18 See Lars Thunberg, *Microcosm and Mediator: The Theological Anthropology of Maximus the Confessor* (Chicago: Open Court, 1995).

19 Sergei Bulgakov, *Le Verbe Incarné: l'Agneau de Dieu* (Paris: Aubier, 1943), 66–67; trans. Stephen C. Headley. See Georges Florovsky, "The Analysis of the Context of Bulgakov's Return from Religious Philosophy to Theology," in *Les Voies de la Théologie Russe*, ed. Georges Florovsky (Lausanne: l'Age d'Homme, 2001), 434.

20 Bulgakov, *Le Verbe Incarné*, 66–67.

21 Image (*eikōn*) and likeness (*homoiōsis*) mean much the same thing in the Greek of the LXX (Septuagint); but, in Plato (*Theaetetus* 176b), likeness is used to mean "to be assimilated" to God, which the early Greek Church fathers Irenaeus, Clement, and Origen will develop.

22 Bulgakov, *Le Verbe Incarné*, 67.

are free to engage in prayer. And this realization is indeed possible—although perhaps more difficult—after Adam's disobedience.

Bulgakov's vision of man's condition and his capacity to pray does not limit itself to human actors alone. God, as Augustine realized in the early centuries of Christian belief, is always drawing closer to his creatures. Thus redemption, a restoration of dialogue and communion between God and man, is an emancipation that leads us to the state of becoming children of God. Beginning as an infant "without words" (Latin, *infans*), man is totally inexperienced and ignorant of himself, since he has not yet tested his ability to communicate, to commune. His nature (*ousia*), perched on the metaphysical brink of the abyss, is in danger until he grows to recognize his own resemblance to God, the image of God natural to him.

As we have said repeatedly, this requires that man see God as his prototype, and thus that he see in himself that which is "unoriginate," without origin. Yet is it not a logical contradiction to say that God's creation of man in his image and likeness is "without origin"? Pavel Florensky (1882–1937) analyzed this antinomy and proposed that Christian revelation occurs in three stages:

1. Truths are revealed that contradict our reason, in the sense that they are counterintuitive to our original understanding of selfhood.
2. We grow in awareness that created humanity is always oriented toward its Creator. This gradually eradicates any division between sacred and profane, between heaven and earth. As Metropolitan Anthony of Sourozh argued, the ineffable being of God is identifiable in the human "non-consolation" of our non-being. Such an outlook justifies the adage *credo ut intelligam*—we believe in the Creator in order to penetrate the incomprehensibility of his presence in his creatures.
3. The heroic and free abandonment of our non-being leads us to the third stage of faith: the realization that being without God is no "being" at all. This is the joyous knowledge in which our understanding becomes faith: *intelligo ut credam*.[23]

---

23 See Pavel Florensky, *The Pillar and Ground of Truth*, trans. Boris Jakim (Princeton: Princeton University Press, 1997), 110–14; 411–12, and the discussion in Christoph Schneider, "Au-delà des limites de la raison: réflexions sur l'ouvrage de Paul Florensky *La Colonne et la Fondement de la Vérité* (1914)," in *Contacts. Revue orthodoxe de théologie et de spiritualité* 65 (2013), 89–100, esp. 94–97. For a critique of Florensky's understanding of antinomy, see Florovsky, *Théologie Russe*, 435–37; and see André Bloom, "Technique et Contemplation," *Etudes Carmélitaines* (1940), 49–67.

What is revealed here is a new logical order of co-existence; the principle of the excluded middle (or *tertium non datur*, i.e., no third possibility is given) is violated in the Otherness and successive identification of the persons of the Holy Trinity. It is just this threefold "mutual indwelling" or "circumincession" of Father, Son, and Holy Spirit, in which is grounded man's creation in the image and likeness of the Trinity, that establishes human personhood. Pavel Florensky presented this logical paradox of the relation between the three Persons of the Trinity as follows: the divine subject is both A (the Father) and non-A, while B (the Son) is also both B and non-B, for there is a third personal partner and component, C (the Holy Spirit).[24] "In the other of C, in its non-C, A finds itself as A. 'A' receives by return for its rejection of self."[25] Having overcome the obstacle of the excluded middle (for each proposition p, both p and non-p are true), a participative ontology becomes possible. In a manner that defies definition but founds the possibility of prayer between man and God, the relations of the three persons of the Trinity are the paradigm of communion between God and man.

Mikhail Nesterov's *Philosophers* (1917), Pavel Florensky and Sergei Bulgakov: Invoking the Other

24 Schneider, "Au-delà des limites de la raison," 94–97.
25 Ibid., 96.

Any anthropology of prayer is an attempt to describe the soul's awareness of the divine. Above, I have tried to describe the movement from God's presence and humanity's personal encounter with him to the verbal formulations used in prayer. We use words to prolong our awareness of God's presence in the world. In prayer, we follow a common Christian tradition bequeathed to us by the desert fathers: the anchorites of northern Egypt, the coenobitic tradition of Pachomius, St Sabas of the Judean desert, and St John Climacus in Sinai. We are thus not alone, not trapped in a subjective understanding of prayer. Nor is our grasp of prayer abstract and impersonal, for, as one prays, personal consciousness is proper to every soul—each of us has our own personality.[26] It is written that, when God created Adam, He "breathed into his nostrils the breath of life; and the man became a living being [literally, 'soul']" (Gen. 2:7). An impersonal soul would be a contradiction. Even the Hindu concept of the person as "illusion" (*māyā*) lets one "imagine" that one is a person, that one has a personal reality (see Chapter 4).

The objectivity of the personal soul or spirit is based on this personal consciousness that allows one to say one's own name, and to say it to another person. This naming is an initiative that begins with God's revelation to Moses of his own name—how Moses is to address him (Exod. 3:14). Later, when Moses remained on Mt Sinai forty days and forty nights and once more heard the Lord speak, Moses knew Him to be God because he had been given His name (Exod. 24). Without a name, one cannot know whom one speaks to. Having a name—"Adam," for instance—is indicative of the unity of one's personal consciousness and one's nature, one's being alive.[27] This is true of mankind, but is also true of the angels and of God. The consequence of God being God is recovered in the meaning of his name, when he said, through the burning bush, "I am who I am."

God, the divine spirit, is, however, unique, for He has one nature in three Persons or *hypostases,* each with its own personal life. The relation of the Persons of the Trinity is the highest form of relationship and dialogue—indeed, of "prayer," if prayer is understood as dialogue and communion.[28]

---

26 Bulgakov, *Le Verbe Incarné,* 6. This point is developed in his book on the possibility of religion, *The Unfading Light,* trans. Thomas Allen Smith (Grand Rapids: Eerdmans, 2012), ch. 3, section 6.

27 In Hebrew, the noun *ādām* means simply man (ἄνθρωπος) whereas transcribed as *Adam* it is a proper name. See Marguerite Harl, trans. and ed., *La Genèse. La Bible d'Alexandrie. Traduction du texte grec de la Septante. Introduction et Notes* (Paris: Éditions du Cerf, 1986), 95, and note to ch. 1, 26.

28 As a noun, it appears in one of the early writings of St Maximus the Confessor, while, as a verb (περιχορέω, "perichoreō" in Greek), Gregory of Nazianzus and John of

Having summarized the traditional Orthodox understanding of prayer, and considered Bulgakov's development of these ideas, we are in a position to turn to the prayers of other religions and document the similarities and differences found there. However, before we do so, I would like first to test the strength of Bulgakov's position by comparing it with other Christian viewpoints. For this, I will turn to a modern academic movement in Anglican and Roman Catholic theology, known by the general term "Radical Orthodoxy." This group would appreciate the fact that Bulgakov, in stepping off from Immanuel Kant, almost accomplishes a "linguistic turn" in his theology. It is Radical Orthodoxy's semantic and rhetorical approach that makes it the best comparison to Bulgakov.[29]

Creating a Space of Audition for the Roman Eucharist

While the Radical Orthodoxy movement is not necessarily representative of all Roman Catholic or Anglican theology, their broad foundations and desire to return to traditional Western Christianity make its adherents interesting dialogue partners—especially since they also discuss prayer "in its own right." Catherine Pickstock, in particular, develops a theory of liturgical invocation that echoes and supplements our earlier conclusions, emphasizing the nature of prayer as "gift" and dialogue.

In chapter 4 of her *After Writing*, Pickstock proposes a semantic, or rhetorical, analysis of the medieval Latin Eucharist, in which she proposes that the eucharistic rite configures language as being *simultaneously* gift and sacrifice.[30] For Pickstock, prayers alone can properly consummate believers' subjectivity, for these semiotic signs are both things in themselves and figures of something else; they are more than they seem. Genuine relational individuality is made possible through humanity's return to God. This return requires that the praying person, the *orans*, set aside his or her own self in order to confess and worship God in prayer. What does this entail? The medieval eucharistic rite, with its de-centered *ordo* and repetitions, readily admits a constitutive, positive, and analogical distance between God and man—what might be

---

Damascus use it for the relationship between the divine and human natures of Christ. The latter also employs it for the "interpenetration" of the three Persons of the Trinity, which later became commonplace. See Harl, ed., *La Genèse*.

29 See Adrian Pabst and Christoph Schneider, "Introduction: Transfiguring the World Through the Word," in *Encounter Between Eastern Orthodoxy and Radical Orthodoxy: Transfiguring the World Through the Word*, ed. Pabst and Schneider (London and New York: Routledge, 2016).

30 Catherine Pickstock, *After Writing: On the Liturgical Consummation of Theology* (Oxford: Blackwell, 1998), 169–219.

termed humanity's apophatic reserve from God. This distance constitutes our freedom as creatures to distance ourselves from the Creator, our freedom to exist as individuals, but also our freedom to turn away from the resemblance to God in which we were created—our potential for sin. So, Pickstock argues, we must stammer, we must make incomplete, small, and repeated attempts at prayer, in order to learn how to pray.

It is through this de-familiarizing of normal, secularized human language that our subjectivity moves away from mental representations of the outside world and we are enabled to receive the gifts of God, Who always transcends our concepts of Him. If we consciously try to manipulate these images, we unconsciously deprive ourselves of the experience of otherness. The very shape of the liturgy arises from this struggle to articulate itself among the plethora of human opinions since the Fall. It is only Christ's resurrection, the restoration of God's image in which we were created, which renders humanity once again capable of hearing with clarity the angelic doxologies, as we see in the image of the nativity story, when the shepherds of Bethlehem heard angels praising the incarnation.

Pickstock emphasizes the centrality of reiteration in the Latin Eucharist. One of the strongest examples is the repeated invocation of the Name of God in three persons, the Trinity—Father, Son, and Holy Spirit.[31] Reiteration also characterizes the central eucharistic act itself: we call upon God to bless the bread and wine He has *already* offered us, says Pickstock. This she calls a giving of the elements to themselves. Thus we offer what is sacrificed for others by Christ at the Last Supper. The elevation of these offerings, and accompanying prayers, introduces a radical expansion of subjectivity, both in human terms (including those present in the church, but also the departed, the saints and believers who have gone before us) and in divine terms, as we perpetually re-enter God's presence through this repeated invocation.

The reiteration—of both the invocations and the eucharistic offering—serves to emphasize that liturgy is a time for purification. As Pickstock puts it, we pray that we might be able to pray. We constantly need fresh beginnings, through confession and absolution, to re-prepare ourselves for prayer and communion with God. Yet how exactly does the Eucharist invoke the invisible God? Pickstock argues that one of the pragmatic devices is

---

31 John Zizioulas, *The One and the Many*, ed. Gregory Edwards (Alhambra, CA: Sebastian Press, 2010), 10–11 (notes 20 and 23) makes a distinction that Pickstock seems to ignore, namely, that the anaphora prayers of the Liturgy of St Basil and St John Chrysostom are both addressed to the Father (as cause) because he is the "God and Father of our Lord Jesus Christ." This is not the Augustinian position identifying the concept of God with "essence."

the use of the so-called "apostrophic" voice, i.e., speech to an imaginary or absent person or idea, where the speaker addresses them as he or she would a present person. In French, "*apostrophier*" still means "to call someone down."

All failure of the *orans*'s liturgical action is due to the fact that the subject, originally created in the image of God, has since lost his or her resemblance. This state can be linked to the Cartesian dichotomy of subject and object that penetrates everyday language through the praxis of the "trope of nominaliza- tion." Whereas liturgical discourse substitutes the figure of apostrophe for such mundane designations, this nominalization or vocative address "turns away" from daily presences to address an absent, deceased, or wholly other person. Its vocal, exclamatory, dramatic, apostrophic voice calls out to be heard (as we see later in Chapter 2 on the Psalms). Pickstock identifies two liturgical types: 1) invocation, pleading to be before and with God, and 2) gratuitous and spontaneous apostrophic exclamations, identifying His gifts for what they are.

Liturgy is the opposite of any trope of nominalization, says Pickstock, "for it transcends the ideal spatiality of immanentism by 'temporalizing' and restoring personhood to the abstrusely 'absent'... spatialization, in its post-modern consummation, renders absent every present, while apostrophe in the hope of further calling renders present every absent."[32]

So apostrophe, as a rhetorical figure, can be said to problematize the cat- egory of the real. "Apostrophic address reveals the object's character as 'sign,' pointing away from itself... restoring to time and physicality that which cannot be seen."[33] In an immanent epistemology, reality is that which *appears and is appropriated* by the subject. Still, "without liturgy there can be no sub- ject, without self-dispossessing apostrophic abasement before the ultimate absent, there can be no subject at all."[34]

This apostrophic calling upon God, however, is not just a calling upon God in worship. It is also an opportunity for humility and repentance before God, before the gulf separating us from Him. Pickstock writes, "The agony of apostrophic striving... bespeaks its own appalling distance from God, in a stammer which abruptly shifts from a mode of passionate doxology to melancholia...." This striving is clear in the central Vespers Psalms 141, 142, 130: "O Lord, I call to you; come quickly to me. Hear my voice when I call to you." Our very act of invocation shows us how far we are from God.

By design, the immanent subject is self-identical, self-objectified, and, in a certain sense, erased, for self-identity results in evaluative indifference.

32 Pickstock, *After Writing*, 194.
33 Ibid., 195.
34 Ibid., 196.

Identity must open outward and up to restore the subject. This is where a liturgical negotiation of the resemblance to the image in which one was created arises. This negotiation occurs notably through repetitions (*anaphorae*) and supplementations that gradually navigate the distance between God and us. In liturgy, one's personhood is transformed, so that being Christian becomes a process. As one evolves, as one desires to pray, one exceeds and goes beyond one's earlier "identity." And so does the manner in which one identifies God. For instance, Pickstock takes the chant "Gloria in excelsis Deo" as continually remaking itself, repeatedly switching from a *constative* rhetorical mode (i.e., glory being given up to God), to an *optative* mode (a wish to offer God glory), to a *performative* one (instantiating the offering), to an *impersonation*—by the celebrant—of the angelic worship.[35]

Beyond such distinctions between dialogical, performative, and monological constative modes, the Trinitarian relations are articulated by combining co-ordination and subordination in a triangular perspective. Linear modification becomes more complex when anaphoric relations refer back to an earlier reference.

This leads to what Pickstock calls a semantic consummation. By this, she means that it is simultaneously anamnetic, looking back, and anticipatory, looking forward, i.e., it recalls a preceding fragment that allows the *orans* to proceed further. This is the liturgical doxological figure in Psalm 63:1, "thirsting" for God, and simultaneously involves thanksgiving, confession, dissemination, invocation, theophany, anticipation, and repetition.

To do all this, the *orans* borrows names in a process of putting aside of self: the "I" in the Eucharist "realizes" itself by the self-dispossessing of doxological impersonation. For Pickstock, this is not arbitrary mimicry but a redemptive mimesis, a pilgrimage advancing by the emulation of others. By beginning every prayer "in the name of the Father, the Son, and the Holy Spirit," one speaks for oneself, but, even more so, one speaks in the name of an as-yet-undisclosed Other, using the authentic un-fallen, other-worldly voice of the angels—for such impersonation foresees our own authentic voice. A Christian synthesis of angelic hierarchy and human equality allows us to become ourselves. Through this redemptive and mimetic invocation, we recover our original likeness to our Creator.

Pickstock recalls that our request for God to turn toward us is preceded by the journey of the Logos to the Father. The *orans*'s character is not dissipated or separated from its subject but is rather intensified, transfigured by its

---

35 Ibid., 203.

desire; and the litanies of the saints re-order subjectivity. We find ourselves in a different company, in which what is spoken about suddenly speaks to the subject as one of us.

To enter this new realm is to become "alike," to be re-figured to the one whom one addresses. This is done through the assumption of the diverse voices contained in the liturgical narrative. It is the plethora of different voices that allows Pickstock to characterize this narrative as a kind of liturgical satire, for, in Latin, *satura* originally meant a diversity of rhetorical genres and had an incantatory function.[36] She uses this meaning to explore the reversibility of seer and what is seen, of speaker and what is spoken. Divinely permutated, the vocal locus is de-centered. Liturgy's diverse genres articulate different voices: dialogue, antiphon, monologue, apostrophe, doxology, oration, invocation, citation, supplementation, and entreaty.

"We," in the context of prayer, is founded on and includes difference, for God's *fiat* as he creates us is the non-alienating gift of difference. In Christian prayer, by de-centering the strategic voice, one restores the subject in the hope that there might be a psalm, a liturgy, even a prayer. While admitting one's vocal or doxological inadequacy, one de-secularizes and de-familiarizes language to prevent its return as a mechanical, humiliating repetition of pious clichés that dissolve the subject into secularized space.

The drama that liturgical space requires has an eschatological reserve. By acknowledging the impossibility of prayer, one combats *acédia*, the boredom of *ascesis*. As Pickstock reminds us, the prophetic stammering of prayer is an ancient theme harking back to the "slow tongue" of Moses, the unclean lips of Isaiah, the demure Jeremiah, and the mute Ezekiel.[37] But now what lies on the altar is the Gospel of the Word of God. As uttered to the Father in the eucharistic canon, the voice of Christ continues to be heard in the breath of the Spirit. The performance of the liturgy encourages renewal; its enunciation in what Pickstock characterizes as erotic, ecstatic language separates and purifies us from everyday speech and permits a total sacrifice of meaning that makes prayer a "now."[38] We are purified by a Gospel event, and participate in eternity.

Pickstock does well with her attempt at explaining prayer "in its own right." She manages a comprehensive study of the Latin rite in terms of semantic and rhetorical figures, and manages to make from this a theory of prayer, of man's approach to God. Yet, when compared to Bulgakov, we see that her purely semantic approach to the Eucharist, focusing on rhetorics, is simply

36 Ibid., 213.
37 Ibid., 215–16.
38 Ibid., 218.

neither as forceful nor as all-encompassing as Bulgakov's "Name of God" theology provoked by the monastic prayer crisis on Mt Athos. Asceticism follows the vortex, the path into the depths of the *orans*'s heart, wherein lies the grace of the image in which he was created. We will now return to Bulgakov and synthesize his iconic approach to prayer into a way forward for our exploration of the prayers of world religions.

Verbal Icons and Iconic Words

To remain in line with the traditional theological vocabulary of Christian revelation and scripture—especially in words like *logos* and *eikōn*—I present here a different kind of description of invocation.[39] Christian prayer and worship is at its root "iconic"—not only in the physical images so essential to Orthodox Christianity but also in the words of prayer themselves, and especially in the Name of God as invoked in prayer. Our invocation of God creates a verbal icon of him whenever we call upon his name, and it is this link between iconic words and invocation that mediates plurality in Christian prayer. There can be no discussion of the partnership which prayer implies if the *orans* is an individual with an isolated identity. To show the uniqueness of this approach, let us compare it to the two other prevalent understandings of personhood.

First, in the rituals of traditional societies, custom articulates plurality through ascriptive roles. These traditional cosmologies inscribe human diversity into a totality, a whole society. Understandings of the cosmos as a whole dictate a close relationship between human beings and a "socialized" cosmos. Man's anthropology, his place in society, is defined by his place within a cosmic morphology.[40] By contrast, in modern secular society, where the whole is not considered greater than the sum of its parts, plurality comes to be used as an *ersatz* for the whole—"representation" in the modern sense. Diversity is made to fit around individualism.

39 The use of these two words to characterize the human person in Christian theology is developed in Meunier, *La Personne*; and in Larchet, *Personne et Nature* (2011), as well as in Michael J. Christensen and Jeffery A. Wittung, eds., *Partakers of the Divine Nature: The History and Development of Deification in the Christian Traditions* (Grand Rapids, MI: Baker Academic, 2008). Their approach favors an understanding of participative ontology and a theology of difference integral to communion.

40 See Stephen C. Headley, "From Cosmos to Hierarchy in Dionysios the Areopagite (sixth century) & Maximos the Confessor (580–662)," in *La cohérence: Volume en honneur de Daniel de Coppet*, ed. André Itéanu (Paris: Les Éditions de la Maison des Sciences de l'Homme, 2010), 283–313.

The Christian understanding of the recapitulation in Christ, of salvation, entails an entirely different experience of diversity. The experience of createdness leads to transcendence, through the source of image and likeness in which man is created by God. A person is no longer simply defined by his place within the cosmos, but neither is he cast adrift—as in individual univocal ontologies—into a vision of personhood devoid of communion between self and other. Rather, the Christian understanding of personhood is based on the concept of "being through communion."[41]

Without resorting to revelation and theology, but simply by looking at Indo-European etymologies for the term "belief," Michel de Certeau claimed the dialogue of prayer must begin by its gift, its "donation." Belief is the "gift of credit" as in the Latin *cred-do*, found in the same morphology in Sanskrit, *srad-dha*, where *srad* means credit and *dha* is cognate with the Latin *do, dare*, to give.[42] By waiting for God to speak, by "crediting" God with the desire to communicate to man in the words of prayer, man inscribes God in man's near future, a time of waiting and listening. This expectation creates "credit with God," a deficit for man, who anticipates that it will be repaid when God answers him. So the words of prayer have two sides: that of the loss of one's present time as one waits for God's reply in the near future and that of the promise of the return to one's words in the form of an answer. A prayer makes sense, for, by a sacrifice (*sacer-facere*), this credit is created; what is owed to oneself will be redeemed at a moment of divine restitution, the visitation of grace.

Bulgakov's conceptualization of prayer is more theological than that of de Certeau.[43] As stated above, Bulgakov's repeated claim was that the names of God are verbal icons of Divinity.[44] As an icon, Divinity and the human power of speech are united here without separation and without confusion. Before man speaks and names, that which he names is given and revealed

---

41 See John Zizioulas, *Being as Communion* (Crestwood, NY: St Vladimir's Seminary Press, 1985); ibid., *Communion and Otherness*. See also John Milbank, *The Future of Love: Essays in Political Theology* (Eugene, OR: Cascade Books, 2009); and his "Only Theology Saves Metaphysics," in *Belief and Metaphysics*, ed. Peter Candler and Conor Cunningham (London: SCM, 2007), 452–500. For the conflict between Christian and secular ideas of personhood, see John Milbank's lecture "Programmatic Address: Faith, Reason and Imagination: the Study of Theology and Philosophy in the 21st century," modified January 8, 2007, http://theologyphilosophycentre.co.uk/online-papers/, 17.

42 Michael de Certeau, "Une pratique sociale de la différence: croire," in *Faire Croire* (Rome: École Française de Rome, Palais Farnèse, 1981), 363–83, esp. 365–66. See also Émile Benveniste, *Le vocabulaire des institutions indo-européennes* (Paris: Éditions de Minuit, 1969), vol. 1, 177.

43 Hilarion Alfeyev, *Le Nom grand et glorieux* (Paris, Éditions du Cerf, 2007), ch. 5.

44 Bulgakov, *Icons and the Name of God*, passim, and 115-77.

to him. Before presenting Bulgakov's analysis, let us set this treatment of Christian prayer in a wider context.

How is the inherent plurality of peoples' expressions of faith mediated in Christian worship? As we just said, a Christian understanding of personhood, based in "being through communion," entails a different experience of diversity. So not all forms of prayer are comparable. Failed prayers do not bring with them communion any more than prayers repeated mindlessly. And even if the condescension of the *bodhisattva* resembles that of Christ, we have here two understandings of personhood, to say the least.

If one admits that liturgy mediates pluralism, that multitudes of prayers with different motivations and destinations locate both Divinity and the created universe as a unifying backdrop for iconic words and verbal icons, then one begins to understand how prayers reintegrate mankind and divinity. St Ephrem the Syrian distinguished the "visible ear of humanity" from "the hidden ear of God." In his twentieth *Hymn on Faith*, he describes the "visible ear of humanity" as something that is transfigured by penetration from what is, by definition, apophatic: the ineffable transcendent relation with God for which there are no words. [45] Rather, a "luminous inner chamber" of the mind where "silence is (his) cry" is the way downward and forward in prayer.

Another example of prayer stretching out to reach the hidden ear of God is found in the writings of St Symeon the New Theologian (AD 949–1022):

> Do not say that it is impossible to receive the Spirit of God. Do not say that it is possible to be made whole without him. Do not say that one can possess him without knowing it. Do not say that God does not manifest himself to man. Do not say that men cannot perceive the divine light, or that it is impossible in this age! Never is it found to be impossible, my friends. On the contrary, it is entirely possible when one desires it. [46]

While many of the Greek fathers of the Church have said that the unknown nature of God could never be described, St Symeon is adamant that prayer, animated by deep desire, is the one thing that can reduce the distance that separates us from God.

45 *The Syriac Fathers on Prayer and Spiritual Life*, ed. and trans. Sebastian Brock (Kalamazoo, MI: Cistercian Publications, 1987), 33–35.

46 This prayer serves as a preface to the Hymns of St Symeon the New Theologian: *Syméon le nouveau théologien. Hymnes*. Ed. Johannes Koder, trans. Joseph Paramelle and Louis Neyrand. Sources Chrétiennes 156 (Paris: Éditions du Cerf, 1969), 150–55. See also St Isaac the Syrian, *Homily 65*, trans. J. Touraille, *Oeuvres Spirituelles: Les 86 discours ascétiques, Les lettres Isaac le syrien* (Paris: Desclée de Brouwer, 1981), 342.

Even if certain recent films have tried to portray invocation *in situ* (e.g., *The Island* [*Ostrov*] by Pavel Longuin, 2006), one cannot present, penetrate, and describe the internal subjective experience of prayer, so it is better to present and compare the prayers and faith displayed. Let us return to Bulgakov's formal style of presenting invocation.

As we have seen above, Bulgakov claims that every judgment or opinion gives rise to a naming and every judgment can become a name.[47] In this, he also echoes Dionysius the Areopagite, writing in the sixth century.[48] For example, saying, "God is holy" gives rise to the name "the Holy One." A whole series of predicate names arises since, as St Paul wrote, God revealed himself to men "at many times and in various ways" (Heb. 1:1). Bulgakov says that predicates, as subjects, act *pars pro toto*, so, as a subject, there is an indeterminate number of names flowing from the essence of God.[49] Predicates are an immanent disclosure; these revelations are names of God whose meanings can be revealed to man yet more deeply through contemplation. However, Bulgakov continues, a noun such as God is not exhausted by its predicates, since it is both transcendent and immanent. The subject *kat' exochen* (par excellence), the subject of all predicates, receives, in every subsequent theophany, a new name for the unnameable and ineffable. Although man names God by analogy with the other occasions he has for naming things, it is God who himself names himself in man. By his revelation through man, he enables men to practice the moral exploits of contemplation and scientific insights through the creativity of human life.

If, as per Feuerbach, man creates God in his own image, as an objective projection of himself, for Bulgakov, it is because the naming of God is accomplished in man and through man as a realization of the image of God in man. So, finally, this is not a linguistic issue but an anthropological one. The revelation of God as creator of man is the foundation of all invocations. Divinity is self-sufficient, yet practices self-depletion through his divine energies. We call these energies the wisdom revealed by God. Intramundane or cosmic transcendence expresses the relation of the attributes to their subject, while supra-mundane is apophatic. God is the negation of all naming, as Dionysius the Areopagite repeatedly insists. Bulgakov, who here is clearly indebted to Dionysius, wrote:

47 Bulgakov, *Icons and the Name of God*, 155.
48 Pseudo-Dionysius the Areopagite, *On the Divine Names*, trans. into French by M. de Gandillac, *Oeuvres completes du Pseudo-Denys l'Aréopagite* (Paris: Aubier, 1943), 68ff.
49 Bulgakov, *Icons and the Name of God*, 116.

> It is not man who names things but they speak themselves through man,
> and this constitutes the ontologism of the word.... God, in his revealing
> himself in the world through man, bears witness about Himself in man's
> consciousness, names Himself, even if it is with man's lips: the naming
> is an act of God in man; it is man's answer to this act, a manifestation of
> Divine energy... both different from this energy and inseparable from
> it.... The difference between Divinity and the world with its things
> lies not in this element of transcendence-immanence of every subject
> in relation to its predicates, but in a metaphysical hierarchy.[50]

By the word "hierarchy," a term invented by Dionysius, he meant a relationship articulated of values and being where those "higher up" enrich and
help those "lower," which is ultimately an expression of God's mercy.

This brings us to icons, or rather verbal icons. Bulgakov's understanding
of prayer is foreshadowed in the pronouncement of the Seventh Ecumenical
Council (Nicaea II, 787) that "an icon is like its prototype not according to
essence but only according to name (*kata to onoma*)...."[51] And again, "The
cross onto which Christ was raised is called this also because of the significance of the name as well as because of the nature of the life-giving wood.
Its image (*ektupoma autou*) is called the cross only because of the significance
of the naming, not because of the nature of the life-giving wood, since the
image of the cross can be made of different material. But nevertheless it
participates in the name of the prototype and therefore in the reverence
and the 'veneration' offered to this name."[52] So, for Bulgakov, "the true icon
of the Divinity is his name," which brings us back to the controversy in the
early twentieth century that he was asked to clarify.[53] What is it about the
name of God that makes prayer possible?

Just as icons differ in the degree of their venerability or intensities, so
there is an analogy with the living icon of man: "an icon is only a place of
the presence of God's power, but not the power itself." The names of God are
verbal icons of divinity, just as the canonical icons of the Eastern Christian
Churches are non-verbal icons.[54] As in an icon, man speaks and names, but

---

50 Ibid., 118.

51 J.-P. Migne, ed., *Patrologiae cursus completus. Series Graeca*, vol. 99 (Paris: 1857), 361.

52 Bulgakov, *Icons and the Name of God*, 120, 123.

53 Ibid., 124–25.

54 See Stephen C. Headley, "Liturgically Mediated Plurality: Transformative Contem-
plation in St Basil's *Eucharistic Canon* and in St Maximos's *Mystagogy*," in *Seeing Through the
Eyes of Faith: New Approaches to the Mystagogy of the Church Fathers*, ed. Paul J.J. van Geest
(Leuven-Dudley: Peeters, 2016), 401–22.

that which he names is given and revealed to him![55] It is here that we find a statement of paramount importance for our anthropology of prayer, and for the very possibility of a Christian approach to the prayers of other religions. Bulgakov, discussing "pagan" religions, natural piety, and natural revelation, admits that God's ways are "unfathomable." Yet the commandment against naming pagan gods in Exodus 23:13 ("Do not invoke the names of other gods; do not let them be heard on your lips") implies that these names, too, may be "iconic." Surprisingly, Bulgakov agrees and believes one thing is certain: "an onomastically skeptical attitude is inapplicable even to the names of the pagan gods."[56] He thus goes so far as to say that pagans, in some way, may well be naming God. This bold statement should, however, be qualified by his discussion in the treatise *Unfading Light* on comparative "religion," where he discusses the "impotent" names of transcendental illusion as atheism and philosophical immanentism. Bulgakov is quite capable of stating that it is man who pronounces prayers. He writes, "in a certain sense it is man who names God, feeling in himself his revelation and responding with the name-creating faculty of his spirit," but this does not change the fact that "the name of God is not only a cognitive, theoretical judgment, but also a means of invoking God in prayer"; it is "an acoustic icon."[57] Thus God's own presence and assistance is necessary for true prayer:

> Just as it is impossible to be saved by human power, so it is impossible to pray to God by human power.... Prayer becomes prayer to God and objectively signifies the union of man with God precisely through the presence of God in the prayer itself.... The Name of God is the onto-logical foundation of prayer, its substance, power, and justification.[58]

What Bulgakov says here applies to non-verbal manifestations, such as revelations of God on his cross or on Mount Tabor: "in all these cases the predicate 'is God' does not by any means establish an identity with God's hypostatic essence...." Nevertheless, it is the verbal utterance that is primordial. Concerning this, Bulgakov says: "The name Jesus is not just one of the names of God but his proper name, the name of God, the self-naming divinity."[59]

55 Bulgakov, *Icons and the Name of God*, 126.
56 Ibid., 128–29.
57 Ibid., 130, 144.
58 Ibid., 159, 164–65.
59 Ibid., 148.

Approaching Prayer beyond Christianity

An Orthodox Christian understanding of prayer is that prayer is a dialogue and communion with God that is itself only possible through God's gift to us. Prayer is based on the invocation of divine names, including that of the Trinity and the Name of Christ.

A Christian anthropology of prayer cannot *a priori* understand invocation as it is found in various forms in other religious traditions, but it does provide a fresh and intriguing point of departure. We will develop our anthropology by moving first through those religions traditionally closest to Christianity. We will turn first to Judaism, and then, in Chapter 3, to Islam, before progressing to religious practices from farther afield (Hinduism in Chapter 4 and Buddhism in Chapter 5). This gradual exploration will help us hone our methods as we progress.

In all cases, however, we must remember that any description of prayer is a delicate task because invocation is an intimate activity of one's soul. In order to preserve our integrity as Christians, we must proceed with a clear grasp of our own faith, and of Christ's own example of respectful humility.

CHAPTER 2

The Hebrew Psalter: God's Name on Man's Lips

WE BEGIN OUR EXPLORATION OF THE PRAYERS OF THE other monotheist religions with the religion closest to Christianity: Judaism. While it may be more difficult for Christians to find common ground in, say, Hindu prayers, at least with the Hebrew Bible, we are on more familiar territory. While Jewish and Christian theology remains strongly "out of tune," we can at least agree that we attempt to address the same God: the God of Abraham, of Isaac, and of Jacob. Within both Judaism and Christianity, the most ancient prayers still in use are found in the biblical Psalms.[1] In fact, we could say that Christians and Jews simply cannot pray without using the Psalms, but it is not for that reason that we should launch into a comparison of how each hears them. The Psalms are about crying out to God for his mercy, and, once that is said, the rest should be left to the discretions of each person's heart. Yet an analysis of the prayers themselves reveals many striking similarities with the anthropology of prayer we developed in the previous chapter.

We will begin with an overview of the Psalter's formation and of the Psalms' context in biblical history. Following this initial orientation, we will proceed to describe how Israel prays the Psalms. We will then focus in on a single prayer among the Psalms—the joint "hymn" of Pss. 42–43—for a detailed study of the variety of themes and modes present in a single psalm. From there, we will step back to take a broader look at the Psalter as a whole, and the repeating theological and anthropological themes and concerns common to the whole Psalter.

---

1 We will follow the Masoretic (Hebrew) numbering of the Psalms, used by Protestant Christians and in recent Catholic official texts. The Greek Septuagint numbering, used by the Orthodox Church and by the Catholic Church until 1969, is the same as the Masoretic for Psalms 1–8 and 148–150, but is one less than the Masoretic for Psalms 11–113 and 117–146. Other Psalms are split differently: Greek Ps. 9 is Masoretic Pss. 9–10, Greek Ps. 113 is Masoretic Pss. 114–15, Masoretic Ps. 116 is Greek Pss. 114–15, and Masoretic Ps. 147 is Greek Pss. 146–47.

These themes reveal the Psalms' distinctive anthropology and call to prayer that informs our own experience as Christians.

Historical Origins of the Psalms

In the Hebrew Bible, the Psalter is the first of the books of the third section called *Ketûbîm* (writings), what the Greek Septuagint calls the didactic writings, which underlines the primary fact that reciting the Psalms teaches us how to pray, that is to say, to express ourselves to God through these phrases. In Hebrew, the Psalter is designated by the word *tehillîm,* from the root *hâlal,* to praise, which, in fact, corresponds to only one of the genres of Psalms, the hymns. The word "psalm" in Hebrew is *mizmor* (from *zâmar,* to sing with an accompanying instrument, often a *psalterion* or harp of David). This collection of hymns is often dated roughly to the post-exilic period of the Second Temple (ca. 520 BC). But many if not most of the Psalms are of an earlier date, as can be shown, for example, by their parallels with Ugaritic hymns. A pre-exilic date, with some psalms even composed during the Davidic period, can thus be envisaged. Psalms 120–134, for example, are designated for the procession up to Jerusalem.[2] A few psalms are also specifically assigned to events in the life of King David: for example, his moment of penitence after his transgression with Bathsheba (Ps. 51), his flight from Absalom (Ps. 3), and his flight from Saul (Pss. 7, 18, 34, 56, 59, 62, 142).

While we see, therefore, that the Psalms themselves were written at different times and for different contexts, it is important to note that they developed hand-in-hand with Israel's cultic worship in general. A review of Israel's cultic evolution is therefore a good starting point to establish the role and significance of the Psalms within Jewish worship.[3] This is of particular importance because the Psalms do not occupy the same place in Jewish worship as they do in Christian worship, where, especially in monastic services, they form the very basis of daily prayer.[4]

2 The Greek Septuagint adds many such indications that may have been originally translated from Hebrew but have since disappeared.

3 A.Z. Idelsohn, *Jewish Liturgy and its Development* (New York: Holt, 1932; reprinted by Dover, 1995), 3–25.

4 For a brief presentation of the Orthodox Christian re-reading of the Psalms, see Placide Deseille, *Les Psaumes, prières de l'Eglise: le psautier des septante* (Paris: YMCA Press, 1979), 5–22. For a general historical overview of the Psalms through Western Christian eyes, see Bruce K. Waltke, James M. Houston, and Erika Moore, *The Psalms as Christian Worship: A Historical Commentary* (Grand Rapids, MI/Cambridge: William B. Eerdmans, 2010). For early Christian interpretations of the Psalms, see Brian E. Daley, SJ and Paul R. Kolbet, eds., *The Harp of Prophecy: Early Christian Interpretation of the Psalms* (Notre

Israel's cult of sacrifices at the altar was initiated by the patriarch Abraham (Gen. 17:5). Abraham, the "father of a multitude" (Gen. 17:5), already calls upon the name of the Lord (Gen. 15, 18:16–33, 20:17), and his obedience to God is such that he is prepared to sacrifice his son Isaac (Gen. 22). Through this, Abraham comes to realize that God wants not human sacrifices but the fear of him that arises out of love of his commandments. While Leviticus squarely prohibits human sacrifices (Lev. 18:21, 20:2–5), nonetheless, the Tophet "altar" near Jerusalem, used for sacrificing children, was only destroyed much later, in the time of King Josiah (reigned 641–609 BC).

While the prophet Samuel is famous for having insisted firmly that "to obey is better than sacrifice" (1 Sam. 15:22), and the prayers and blessings of the patriarchs are often described without any reference to sacrifice, the burning of sacrificial meat on altars was an enduring feature of their prayers. Nonetheless, right from Abraham's time, respect was granted to the intercessor (*mithpallel*), and worshipping with words alone became an integral part of prayer: "And Abraham prayed (Hebrew, *vayithpallel*)" (Gen. 20:17). There exists a link between the Hebrew root *pallal*, which as a reflexive (*hithpallel*) means to judge oneself, and its other meaning, the concept of cutting oneself in worship—self-mutilation as a form of sacrifice. So, as early as Abraham, a patriarch or prophet could intercede (*mithpallel*) by his prayer. Moses, the savior from Egypt and the lawgiver, was also known as the great intercessor (Exod. 32:9–14). Although he never prayed during the sacrifices that we know of, we do know that God "used to speak to Moses face to face, as a man speaks to his friend" (Exod. 33:11); He says of Moses, "With him I speak face to face, clearly and not in riddles; he sees the form of the LORD" (Num. 12:8).

Yet, as Abraham Idelsohn states, from Moses until the time of the First Temple, it was rare for priests to be asked to intercede with God on behalf of the people.[5] While verbal prayer could be linked to the act of sacrifice, as in Psalm 141, "May my prayer be set before you like incense" (Ps. 141:2), it was still considered something separate. Traditionally, it is King David (ca. 1040–970 BC) who founded Israel's tradition of *tefillā* psaltery prayer (2 Sam. 7:18–29)—some 74 of the 150 canonical psalms are attributed to his authorship—but Idelsohn argues that "the singing of Psalms and the chanting of prayers during services dates back to the very beginnings of Israel": fixed daily worship seems to have already existed in the early sanctuaries at Beth-El, Shiloh, and Gibeon, with Sabbaths and holy days observed with

---

Dame, IN: University of Notre Dame Press, 2015).

5 Idelsohn, *Jewish Liturgy*, 6.

peace offerings on local communal altars.[6] During troubled periods, repentance, fasting, and public confession were practiced regularly (Judg. 20:26; 1 Sam. 7:6). Furthermore, Idelsohn claims that Levitical singers of prayers must have been active well before the building of the First Temple in Jerusalem, since they were present when David moved the Ark of the Covenant from Gibeon to Jerusalem (1 Chron. 16:36–42).[7] Thus Psalms, as oral sung prayers, already occupied a central role in Israel's cult.

Margaret Barker has revealed new perspectives on the theology of the worship in the First Temple from 980 BC onward.[8] Restricting ourselves to the theme of oral sung prayer, we find that the invocation for dedicating the new temple in Jerusalem attributed to Solomon (even if it was composed centuries later) is of lasting significance. Jerusalem will always be the mount from which Jews pray long after its temples were destroyed—witness, for example, the western "wailing" wall.

> May your eyes be open toward this temple night and day, this place
> of which you said, "My Name shall be there," so that you will hear the
> prayer your servant prays toward this place. (1 Kings 8:29)

Many of the rituals that took place in the First Temple of Jerusalem (tenth century BC to 587 BC) took place in silence. At the earliest stage, one finds, in addition to the temple sacrifices, formulae for oaths, curses, blessings and prophecy, and individual prayers using not formal language but everyday speech patterns incorporating vivid exchanges between the Israelite and his God. There are, *inter alia*, the Psalms. Initially, there existed a tension between sacrifice at the temple and the worship of prayer.[9]

After the seventy years of Babylonian exile, from the period of the Second Temple (517 BC onward), the temple came to be used more frequently—not just for sacrifices but also for communal activity by men and women. The priests were more active in education and politics. Nonetheless, the temple ritual remained essentially a silent one, and there existed no communal liturgy outside the temple using standardized prayers. Only in the later Apocrypha

---

6 See Num. 28.

7 Idelsohn, *Jewish Liturgy*, 9.

8 Margaret Barker, *The Great Angel: A Study of Israel's Second God* (London: SPCK, 1992); ibid., *On Earth as it is in Heaven: Temple Symbolism in the New Testament* (Edinburgh: T&T Clark, 1995); ibid., *Temple Theology* (London: SPCK, 2004); ibid., *The Hidden Tradition of the Kingdom* (London: SPCK, 2007).

9 Stefan C. Reif, *Judaism and Hebrew Prayer: New Perspectives on Jewish Liturgical History* (Cambridge: Cambridge University Press, 1993), 50.

and pseudepigraphal material do we find those "scriptural" practices that were to become associated with rabbinic traditions in the period of the Tannaim (AD 10–220). There was still no fixed liturgy, but there were more benedictions, hymns, and praises. The *She'ma Israel* ("Hear, O Israel," Deut. 6:4), which would become the leitmotif of Jewish morning and evening prayer, appeared and came into individual use, and Philo and Josephus attest that individual Jews and assemblies prayed and studied together in various situations.

During the last centuries of the Second Temple, synagogues (a Greek name for the *Beith Haknesseth*), which had appeared in the period of exile, became common not only in Jerusalem but throughout the neighboring areas, which were divided into twenty-four sectors.[10] Organized by lay representatives, each synagogue sent representatives to Jerusalem to conduct the prescribed prayers and sacrifices for two weeks every year. It was as if the whole synagogue had gone up to Jerusalem, for, at that time, the same prayers were being said at the local synagogue as were being said by their representatives in Zion. As Idelsohn puts it,

> Here we have the nucleus for a regular daily service, though only for two weeks of the year. This practice was then extended for the whole year.... The reason for this institution was the demand of the people to share in the cult. With the increase of knowledge of the prophetic teachings among the people, it became clear to them that it is not only the priest who has access to God.... The sages taught the people that it is even the duty of every man to pray daily, for which purposes fixed patterns of benedictions and prayers were created, which are claimed to date back to Ezra's Assembly.[11]

The developing synagogue practice was aided by the Deuteronomic reforms of King Josiah (reigned in Judah 640–609 BC) after the return of exiles to Jerusalem. The insistence on only eating *kosher* sacrificed meat ("having poured out the blood like water," see Deut. 12:20–25) led to a decrease in animal sacrifice. Even more importantly, when offering the first fruits of a harvest, henceforth the layman (Deut. 14:22–29) could himself invoke the Lord directly without the assistance of a priest. If the prophet Ezekiel had taught the exiles how to ask for a word from God and how to obey his moral code, Daniel, Ezra, and Nehemiah already give examples of instruction in the pattern of public prayer, creating the first assemblies.

10 Idelsohn, *Jewish Liturgy*, 24–25.
11 Ibid., 24.

Further, the Babylonian exile had influenced the invocation employed by the Levitical chanters without compromising their monotheism: the *ordo* of prayer used by the priests after the building of the Second Temple shows the increasing importance of benedictions.[12] These took the place previously occupied by the Psalms. Variations on the recitation of the Eighteen Benedictions, which date from the Second Temple period and are the central Jewish prayer, repeated three times a day, become ever stronger in the nascent synagogues, where the study of the Torah and prayer did not entail sacrificial rituals.

At the same time, the customary reading from the Scriptures also developed, as Idelsohn describes:

> There continued to flourish the free improvised mediations . . . even the fixed prayers were only patterns, frames, into which every man could pour his soul's expressions. They were transmitted orally and recited in public worship by intercessors who were learned men and well-versed in the teachings and imbued with the ideals and hopes of the people.[13]

Thus temple ritual was gradually displaced by the new practices of the synagogue, in which verbal prayer became the main form of worship. And synagogues were not the only place of liturgical innovation: evidence from the Qumran scrolls shows an even more "progressive" attitude to temple ritual. The Qumran liturgies were completely detached from temple norms and instead imitated those of the angels. The community had their own prayers for the Sabbath and the high holy days, employing formulae and notions that will appear in later rabbinic services.

Despite the growing importance of synagogue worship in the Second Temple period, it was only with this temple's destruction in A D 70 that the individual home and its "dining room" table became a place of prayer.[14] In addition, houses sprang up for the study of the Bible, which were also used for praising, thanking, and imploring God. The focus shifted once more not only to the level of the synagogue but to the level of the family, and even the individual believer.

Thus the Hebrew Bible predates the Hebrew prayer book, the *Siddur*, by well over a thousand years. Personal prayer is found in some of the writings that have come down to us, especially in prophetic books beginning with

---

12 Ibid., 22–23.

13 Ibid., 25.

14 See Reuven Kimelman, "The Shema and the Amidah: Rabbinic Prayer," in *Prayer from Alexander to Constantine: A Critical Anthology*, ed. Mark Kiley (Abingdon and New York: Routledge, 1997), 108–23.

Hosea, but it is, above all, in the sung poetry of the Jewish Psalter (*tehillîm* or praises) that personal prayer finds its fullest expression.

We can summarize the development of this personal prayer as a mirror of the development of Judaism from its origins as a patriarchal cult focused on sacrifices. The emphasis on cult rather than prayer is seen in the first book of the Torah, the book of beginnings (*Bereishit*, Genesis), where God speaks more to man than man speaks to God. Initially, this same focus made the memory of the exodus (*Pésach*) across the Red Sea as much adoration as thanksgiving. With the advent of Moses, however, God begins to be shown as seeking a mediator, and thus religion begins the journey to becoming a personal affair.

From the eighth century BC onward, the insufficiency of cultic practice is emphasized, as Amos and Hosea in Israel and Isaiah and Micah in Judah inveigh against the practices of royalty, while, for Jeremiah, Nahum, Zephaniah, and Habakkuk in the seventh century and Ezekiel during the Babylonian exile, the very conception of personhood changes, as is indicated by these prophets' theophoric names. The central theme of dialogue with Yahweh becomes the mystery of his election of Israel. Yet it is the lamentations of the "weeping" prophet Jeremiah, even before the destruction of the First Temple in 586 BC, which first interiorize the Covenant into a personal religion where man, searching with his whole heart, may find God. Thus Jeremiah may be said to be the founder of the authentic prayer of God's poor ones (*anawim*), a key theme of the Psalms as a whole.

The Psalms in Jewish Prayer

We have seen that the Psalms were used as prayers throughout the history of Israel's worship, and that their context—where and how they were prayed—changed and developed over time. The Psalms, or their precursors, were originally sung in the cultic space in front of the tabernacle. Then, once King Solomon built the First Temple, psalms were sung by the Levites on the steps leading up to the temple. Despite this public setting, the Psalms were also historically meant to enable the individual or collective *orans* to have the courage to speak with the Lord, to explain where they were *vis à vis* their God. [15] Yet how are the Psalms now prayed most commonly within Judaism since the destruction of the Second Temple?

---

15 Sometimes the titles of the Psalms give instructions about when they are to be sung. On liturgical singing in ancient Israel and Greece, see Hilarion Alfeev, *Orthodox Christianity Volume III: The Architecture, Icons and Music of the Orthodox Church* (Crestwood, NY: St Vladimir's Seminary Press, 2014), 245–62.

One constant in the use of the Psalms in Jewish worship is that they are always part of a service that post-dates their original composition; they are surrounded by a multitude of other psalms and prayers. Yet, if we look at the *ordo* determining the use of the Psalms in daily services, it is less illuminating than one might have expected. The theology of their prayer is to be found at a level above the place of given psalms. The first of the five sections of the Jewish Morning Prayer, the *pesukei dezimra* section, includes Psalms 30, 100, and 145–150. At the end of the morning service, a "psalm of the day" (*Shir shel yom*) is read. The introduction to the Friday night Sabbath services includes Psalms 95–99, 29, 92, and 93. One tradition that was kept in Judaism has also been preserved by the Eastern Orthodox Christians over the centuries: at a person's death, the *tehillîm* (i.e., the entire Psalter) is read over the body day and night until burial.

The Psalms are not simply read aloud. They are also accompanied by a rocking back and forth of the body. This involves timing, both concerning when to say the Psalms and when to adopt certain postures. In the morning, the *Amidah* prayers of the Eighteen Benedictions are said standing (the Hebrew *Amidah* literally translates to "standing"), feet kept together, facing Jerusalem—adopting the same pose as the angels Ezekiel saw at prayer, who stood straight as if they had only one leg (Ezek. 1:7). Both before and after reciting the *Amidah*, one takes three steps backward to withdraw one's attention from the mundane world and three steps forward to draw near to the Lord. At four separate moments, one bows, bending one's knees (blessing, *baruch*, is derived from knee, *berech*) at the words, "Blessed are You, O Lord." One bows at "Blessed" and straightens up at "O Lord," since, the commentary of their prayer book tells us, Psalm 146:8 says that "the Lord straightens the bent." The more these set prayers were codified, the more diversified their interpretation became.

In synagogues, the congregation normally prays the Eighteen Benedictions (*Shemoneh Esrei*)—the *Amidah*, or "Standing Prayers" (*Tefilat Ha Amidah*)—silently. Afterward, the Benedictions are repeated out loud by the reader (*chazzan*). This allows those who are illiterate to join in by answering, "Amen." Their language shows that the Benedictions date from the Mishnaic period (immediately before and after the destruction of the temple in AD 70).

On regular weekdays, faithful Jews stand before God to pray the *Amidah* three times every day, in place of the former temple sacrifices of the morning, afternoon, and evening. During the Talmudic period, there was a reluctance to make these prayers obligatory. Certain rabbis suggested adding one "new" (improvised) prayer a day. The Eighteen Benedictions begin with three blessings of praise, followed by thirteen requests: six personal, six communal, and a final request that God hear these prayers. Many of the posture codes are intended to help one's concentration, for the "service of the heart" (*avodahshebalev*) must focus one's intention (*kawwānā*) on the words, as in the silent prayer of Hannah, the mother of Samuel (1 Sam. 1:10), indicating "speaking from one's heart."[16]

We have discussed the Psalms in their original and modern prayer contexts, but it is now time to take a closer look at them. First, we will look at a single psalm in some detail, and then we will turn to an overview of the Psalms in general, and their thematic, theological, and anthropological content.

The Influence of the Ugaritic Psalter on the Hebrew Psalms: A Case Study of Psalm 42

While it is interesting to see how different Psalms reiterate similar themes, it is difficult to assess the Psalms as a whole without knowing how a single psalm stands alone. To investigate this, it is necessary to undertake a close case study of one psalm in particular. The hymn preserved in Psalm 42 is a good candidate for detailed study. The reasons for this lie in its close parallels to Ugaritic poetry, as revealed by the scholarship of Mitchell Dahood, a specialist in Ugaritic philology.[17] This, in turn, will give us a clearer understanding of the extent to which the Psalms were influenced by Israel's neighboring cults.

We know that Israel's religion was exposed to a steady stream of influence from pagan cults. Syro-Palestinian history began at the end of the third millennium BC with the destruction of the early Bronze Age urban civilization by invading ethnic groups from the Syrian desert. Abraham may have been part of this immigration. A second collapse occurred around 1200 BC when the Fertile Crescent and Egypt were overrun by various groups, including the Israelites.[18] These early Israelites brought with them their Yahweh traditions, but were in contact with Egyptian and Ataman cultures. Then, in the late Bronze Age, at about 1000 BC, King David finished his conquest of the Canaanite city-states, and Israel was exposed to the polytheistic influence of the hill stations of Canaan. Later still, King Solomon borrowed elements of his administrative system from Egypt, and his scribes were trained by copying

---

16 The Muslim *salāt* prayers discussed in Chapter 3 also speak of *niat*, intention.

17 Mitchell Dahood, trans. *Psalms I. The Anchor Bible* (Garden City, NY: Doubleday, 1965–66).

18 David Steinberg, "Ugarit and the Bible: Ugaritic Literature as an Aid to Understanding the Hebrew Bible (Old Testament)," accessed November 15 2017, http://www.houseofdavid.ca/ugarit.htm.

thirteenth-century textbooks like the book of Proverbs, which invariably contained religious themes.

From these historical facts alone, we can predict that the Psalms were strongly influenced by the cultic life of Israel's neighboring kingdoms, including the Sumerian, Assyrian, Egyptian, Canaanite, and Hittite cultures. These neighboring cults also, of course, influenced the nascent Hebrew cult in general, despite the pleas of Israel's prophets to preserve strict monotheism, and shaped not only the incense offerings and seasonal animal sacrifices but also magic practices and the royal cult, in which the king was venerated as the angel of God on earth.[19] Working through Psalm 42 will give us an insight into the workings of individual psalms in general, and of the particular influence of Ugaritic upon Israelite prayers.

Psalm 42 is a hymn punctuated by a refrain.[20] This prayer recalls not only other Hebrew scriptures but also the earlier poetic images of the polytheistic Ugaritic "Psalter."[21] Dahood's commentary emphasizes how indebted the psalmists were to this earlier hymnographic literature from the kingdom of Ugarit at the site of Ras Shamra near Latikia in northern Syria.[22] Founded in the Neolithic period (ca. 6000 BC), Ugarit came in contact with Egypt, to which it paid tribute from the second millennium BC onward. It reached its height between 1450 BC and 1200 BC, thus just before the Israelite emigration into Canaan. Ugaritic poetry illustrates one of the poetic sources of the Psalter, as do certain Egyptian hymns. While the literary influence was strong and explains some of the epithets applied to Yahweh, this did not lead to any adoption of the Canaanite polytheism that the prophet Elijah fought so strongly against in the ninth century BC.

The author of Psalm 42 has been struggling with melancholy and depression since being exiled in his own personal *shéol*. Yet his exemplary hope in God still allows him to recall God's recent proximity and the joys of his past religious experience. The psalm opens with a clear image of God as the "running," i.e., fresh, or "living" water, of which the psalmist stands in need:

19 Idelsohn, *Jewish Liturgy*, 17–20, gives a table of Babylonian and Assyrian prayers and discusses their similarities with Hebrew prayer and hymns.

20 The refrain is found at 42:5, 42:11, and 43:5. Since I have relied on Mitchell Dahood's commentary for this Psalm, for this part of the chapter, I will also use his translation and numbering: Dahood, *Psalms I*, 254–60.

21 In the Bronze Age, the Ugaritic Epic of Baal, a sky god and deity of life, epitomized the forces of fertility and renewal. Baal struggles with his brother Mot (death), and in this battle is aided by his warrior sister, Anath, and their mother, Asherah, who is the *paredra*, the consort, of the god El.

22 The Ugaritic alphabet was created around 1400 BC with 30 letters. These had phonetic value and were inscribed on clay, similar to cuneiform.

> As the deer pants for streams of water,
> so my soul pants for you, O God. (Ps. 42:1)

In some ways, this echoes phrasing found in a Ugaritic hymn: "Like the heart of a wild cow for her calf, like the heart of a ewe for her lamb, so the heart of Anath toward Baal," although it moves beyond a comparison of the affection between two animals to the basic need of an animal for external sustenance basic to survival, that of fresh water.[23] Animal metaphors were common; Dahood cites the Semitic motif of a "wild cow (who) throws her voice from the mountain." Another parallel, especially when we turn to verse 2 below, can be found in a common Ugaritic simile, "Lo, wild oxen make for the pools, like hinds make for the spring."[24]

> My soul pants for God, for the living God.
> When can I go and meet with God? (Ps. 42:2)

The expression "living God" recalls the "spring of living water" of God in Jeremiah 2:13; drinking deeply (*ra'ah*) recalls Psalm 34:8: "Taste and see that the LORD is good." The permanence of certain images is striking, for, some 2,000 years later, Eastern Christians will still be using this same image as a song to be sung while they take Holy Communion: "Taste and see that the Lord is good." As we will see later, the "presence" or "face" of God is a recurring theme throughout the psalm.

In the next part of the hymn, the soul's thirst for nourishment through encounter with the living God is contrasted with its present situation, in which the psalmist's tears provide empty nourishment:

> My tears have been my food day and night,
> while men say to me all day long, "Where is your God?"
> (Ps. 42:3)

Metaphors with tears are abundant elsewhere in the Bible (Lam. 1:2, 2:11, 2:18) but are also described as food or drink in Jeremiah 9:15: "For Yahweh our God has made us weep and has given us tears for food." This link was not uncommon in the surrounding cultural context: a Canaanite hymn makes a similar analogy, saying: "She drinks tears like wine."[25]

---

23 Dahood, *Psalms I*, 255.
24 Ibid., 256.
25 Ibid.

Psalm 42 continues with the theme of despair, but now begins to trace the anticipation of consolation and salvation:

> These things I remember, as I pour out my soul:
> how I used to go with the multitude,
> leading the procession to the house of God,
> with shouts of joy and thanksgiving among the festive throng. (Ps. 42:4)

In Job 7:19, we also find this kind of expression, "Will you never look away from me, or let me alone even for an instant [literally: 'until I swallow my saliva in grief']," and many psalms speak likewise of the posture of despair and expectation: "I will bow down towards your holy temple" (Ps. 138:2).

We come now to the first instance of the "refrain" found throughout the psalm:

> Why are you downcast, O my soul? Why so disturbed within me?
> Put your hope in God, for I will yet praise him, my Saviour and my
> God. (Ps. 42:5–6)

The Complete Jewish Bible (CJB) translates the final phrase here more literally as "I will praise him again for the salvation that comes from his presence." The theme of God's "presence" or "face" occurs earlier in Psalm 42, and in each of the three refrains throughout the hymn (Ps. 42:2, 42:5, 42:11, as well as in 43:5). Throughout the Psalter, we encounter other dialogues between man and his soul where the theme of "my presence" is introduced, although the word presence (*paniym*) need not be found (Pss. 63:3; 104:29; 116:9, 143:7). The presence of God, however, is the salvation of my "face" illumined by "your face." This notion of presence can be compared to the late Canaanite (i.e., Carthaginian) idea that Tinnit was the "presence" (power) of Baal. In this cultural universe, gods have a "presence" that you can experience.[26]

Continuing through the hymn, the psalmist turns his attention to his current situation, which is likened to the netherworld:

> My soul is downcast within me; therefore I will remember you
> from the land of the Jordan, the heights of Hermon—from Mount
> Mizar. (Ps. 42:6)

26 Ibid., 152.

What has been translated as "the land of the Jordan" is, more literally, the "land of descent," and is the poet's name for the netherworld. Being in the depths of *shéol* is as distant as one can be from his Lord, as another psalm states, likening it to "the brink/edge of the netherworld" (Ps. 61:2). This sentiment is also found in earlier Ugaritic hymns: "Be numbered with those who go down into the netherworld," and with the image, common in Ugaritic hymnography, of the place of descent into the netherworld as at the edge or rim of a mountain (as is the more literal translation of "Mount Mizar").[27] The rest of the Psalms, and the rest of the Hebrew Bible, support and expand this vision: *shéol* is described as filled with nets and snares (Ps. 18:4–5), and Jonah, crying out "from the bosom of *shéol*" (Jon. 2:2), likens this to submersion in the "heart of the seas," swallowed by waves. The parallels to the next verse of Psalm 42 are striking:

> Deep calls to deep in the roar of your waterfalls;
> all your waves and breakers have swept over me. (Ps. 42:7)

The waters beneath the waters are stirred up by the thunderbolts of Yahweh, which, in striking the seas, create the waves. Ugaritic hymnography also contains this expression of waters in two depths, but, of course, it does not mention Yahweh as the cause.

> By day the LORD [Yahweh] directs his love, at night his song is with
> me—a prayer to the God of my life. (Ps. 42:8)

By day and by night refers to the passage of days, but specifically to diurnal alternations created by the Lord whom the *orans* implores unabatedly until he experiences his wonders (Ps. 77:2, 5–12). Initially, the psalmist cries, "Will the Lord reject for ever? Will he never show his favour again?" (Ps. 77:7), but subsequently realizes, "To this I will appeal: the years of the right hand of the Most High" (Ps. 77:10).

Continuing through Psalm 42, we find further details concerning *shéol*:

> I say to God my Rock, "Why have you forgotten me?
> Why must I go about mourning, oppressed by the enemy?"
> My bones suffer mortal agony.... (Ps. 42:9–10)

27 Ibid., 258–59.

Here, the psalmist describes the terror of *shéol* in terms reminiscent of several other psalms. As in Psalm 61, *shéol* is a swamp-like place, in which one has no sure footing; one must hope for the Lord alone to provide a rock, a hard raised surface, onto which one might escape: "From the ends of the earth I call to you, I call as my heart grows faint; lead me to the rock that is higher than I" (Ps. 61:2). Other psalms show that the pain of oblivion, of being forgotten by the Lord, is proper to the torments of *shéol*: "No-one remembers you when he is dead. Who praises you from his grave?" (Ps. 6:5); it is here that death becomes one's enemy (compare the "set apart with the dead" of Ps. 88:5). In Ugaritic hymnography, death was portrayed as inhabiting the body like a sickness, hence, perhaps, the mention of a "mortal agony" within the psalmist's bones in Psalm 42.

Yet, at the end of the psalm, the psalmist returns to a position of hope:

> As my foes taunt me,
> saying to me all the day long, "Where is your God?"
> Why are you so downcast, O my soul? Why so disturbed within me?
> Put your hope in God, for I will yet praise him, my Savior and my God.
> (Ps. 42:11)

The final verse constitutes the hymn's refrain. It is notable that, while the prayer has until now been concerned with the gloom of despondency and distance from God, it nevertheless ends on a positive note of hope for salvation.[28]

Our case study of the prayer of Psalm 42 has shown us the strong poetic parallels that exist between Hebrew and Ugaritic hymnography and prayer, but a complete refusal of Ugaritic polytheism. Having seen distinctive themes uniting a whole psalm, we may now proceed to an overview and synthetic description of the Psalter in general.

The Shape of the Psalter

As mentioned above, the Psalms are grouped with the Hebrew *Ketûbîm*, didactic writings. Their Hebrew name, *tehillîm*, relates to "hymns," i.e., songs of praise, although, in fact, psalms frequently fall into many other genres, including supplications and lamentations, thanksgivings, and prayers of didactic (wisdom), royal, or messianic nature. Additionally, some psalms are collective prayers, while others are individual. Yet all these diverse prayers

---

28 Unlike the Septuagint Greek σωτήριον, "my Savior," here in verse 12 (*yešûōt*) in Hebrew is a plural of majesty and a divine name, as in Psalm 28:8. See Dahood, *Psalms I*, 257.

together make up the Psalms as a single, united biblical text. What can be said about the shape and structure of the Psalter in general?

It is possible to interpret the Psalter as a corpus of prayers divided into five books on the model of the Pentateuch.[29] Five "books" within the Psalter can be distinguished on the basis of differences in theology and address.[30] The first such "book," Psalms 1–41, is composed of non-Davidic Psalms and uses the word Yahweh to address God, while the second, Psalms 42–72, may be interpreted, as did the historians in Deuteronomy, by showing how the final Babylonian exile originated in King Solomon's laxity in the execution of his duties as king of Jerusalem.[31]

Book three, Psalms 73–89, predominantly uses the term *Elohim* to address God, reflecting the experience of this exile. For this section of the Psalter reflects the growing awareness that, having exiled his people and yet not having forgotten them, *Elohim* is the God of a diaspora and not just of Israel in the strict sense. The final series here (Pss. 85–89) uses Yahweh from an eschatological perspective, as this is the name of the God of Zion once restored. Psalm 85 is Israel's supplication for restoration. In Psalm 86—the lone Davidic psalm in this series—David's voice arises like Isaiah's servant of the Lord (vv. 2 and 4), who hopes and trusts that the Lord will answer him. And, in Psalm 87, the re-establishment of Zion is implored and hoped for in terms reflecting those of Deutero-Isaiah. The final Psalm of this book, Psalm 89, ends on this same note of hope, which is also found in Ezekiel.

Book four (Pss. 90–106) marks the end of the exile and begins with Psalm 90, the only one ascribed to Moses: "Return, O Lord, how long? . . . Let the favor of the Lord our God be upon us, and establish the work of our hands upon us, yea, the work of our hands establish thou it." Psalms 93 and 95–100 celebrate Yahweh as king. Again, as in Ezekiel and Deutero-Isaiah, Psalms 105–106 are both hymns of praise and recollection of the first gift of the land of Palestine to Israel, to which they hope to return.

The transition to book five (Pss. 107–150) is linked to this thanksgiving for, and hope in, the promise of the "new Jerusalem," with Psalm 107 constituting the third in the series of *hallel* Psalms at the end of book four (Pss. 105–106). The "Davidic" Psalms 108–110 maintain and develop the Messianic hope of

29 See further in Paul Nadim Tarazi, *The Old Testament. Vol III: An Introduction to Psalms and Wisdom* (Crestwood, NY: St Vladimir's Seminary Press, 1996).

30 Book 1: Pss. 1–41 (Doxology: Ps. 41:13); Book 2: Pss. 42–72 (Doxology: Ps. 72:18–19); Book 3: Pss. 73–89 (Doxology: Ps. 89:52); Book 4: Pss. 90–106 (Doxology: Ps. 106:48); Book 5: Pss. 107–150 (Doxology: Ps. 150:6).

31 Sigmund Mowinckel, *The Psalms in Israel's Worship*, reprinted with an introduction by R. Gnuse and D.A. Knight (Sheffield: Journal for the Study of the Old Testament, 1992), 37–40.

an eschatological "David" in the new Jerusalem, called "the Lord is there" (as in Ezek. 48:35), theme also of the long Psalm 119. The famous series of songs of ascending up to Zion in pilgrimage (Pss. 120–134) renews the implicit criticism of Solomon: "unless the Lord builds the house, those who build labor in vain" (Ps. 127:1). Those who never forgot Zion will praise him in the New Jerusalem as in the *hallel* Psalms 135–136. The new David leads onward to the city of Yahweh (Ps. 137); Psalms 138–145 are ascribed to him. And it is again David who leads the new Israel in praising the Lord forever in the final *hallel* Psalms 138–145.

Thus, as a collection, the Psalms have a distinct thematic and theological shape. We will now look more closely at these major themes and the theological vision that arises from them.

The Vision of the Psalms

From his extensive study of the Psalms, Chouraqui identifies a single comprehensive narrative, which, he argues, corresponds to Israel's shared religious experience.

For Chouraqui, the psalmist's overall concision and economy with words reflects the fact that he knows exactly what he wants to pray for: a meeting with eternity. These songs to God are the best weapon in fighting off Satan: each word of a psalm is a sword to fight the evil one, Satan (*rashá*)—who is given one hundred and twelve names, titles, and qualities in Hebrew—and the Psalter resounds with the war against him.[32] While many countries are allied against the psalmist—Edom, Moab, the Philistines, Babel, Tyre, Kedar, Amalek, the sons of Lot—it is Egypt that becomes the dominant symbol of all Israel's subsequent exiles.[33] Thus the world breaks down into two paths, and these ways demand that we choose between them: a choice for the road to darkness or the road to light.

This leads, Chouraqui argues, into the psalm's most fundamental intuition: there is only one murder, that of the innocent. There are nearly a hundred names for the innocent in the Psalms: they are the ones who walk in the light of God, the heroes, the oppressed, and the afflicted.[34] *Elohim* is their only

32 André Chouraqui, trans. *Les Psaumes: Louanges* (Paris: Éditions du Rocher, 1994), 20–21.
33 Chouraqui, *Les Psaumes*, 23–24.
34 This list would include: the oppressed, the afflicted, the despoiled, the tramp; the humble, the poor man, the brokenhearted; the faithful, the wise; the one who trembles, the upright; the stranger, the alien to the world, the beggar; God's devotee; the one who keeps watch before God's countenance, who searches for God's blessing, for his light; the innocent, the Lord's ally, the heir to eternity; the clear-sighted eye, the pure heart, the

weapon; the Psalms disdain brutal physical force, which has no purpose. The Israelite captive knows where he is on the earth, in his dark prison (Pss. 88:6; 107: 10, 14). He is being led to the valley of the shadow of death where there is no hope of life, only a valley of tears and the long agony (Ps. 88:16). The length of passing days gives the psalmist the feeling that all is perishable. He is exiled amongst his own, like the slaves in Egypt. His only *viaticum* is the *Torah*, God's words leading to eternity. The innocent exile as prisoner knows that he is a son of *Elohim*, the child of *Adonai*. He lives by and through that relationship, that incarnation of love that began with the alliance with Abraham. The *Torah* shows him his fault, giving him the desire for the word of *Adonai*, by which he enters the kingdom of innocence. The *Torah* is designated by the Psalter as that dimension of interiority by which one accedes to a perception of the real world. Spiritual realism is the condition for survival. The worship of the just is composed of prayer, meditation, fasting, and singing.[35]

Not being able to kill God, the evil one has sought out the blood of the innocent. And, even if the innocent is often killed, the evil one is always vanquished. The real shepherd of criminals is death. Nothing escapes his jurisdiction. Man is responsible for and becomes what he wants to be; what he loves is what he identifies with.

In the book of Yahweh—the *Tanakh*, the Jewish Bible—as in the world of the Psalter, everything has meaning. The night of the just is paralleled by the darkness of the criminal. The stages of the night correspond to stages of purification (Ps. 106:6–7). Responsible for his own faults, the psalmist is also responsible for the faults of his fathers. There is a solidarity between the ages that partially explains why the just does not justify himself, for he is not an individual, and, unlike Job, he merits his punishment.[36]

During this long night, the just man is speechless, deaf and blind, full of shame, humiliated and suffering. There are ten synonyms to describe this suffering. The just never protests to the Lord for long; his supplications are interwoven with patient waiting and hope. This is even more so the case in the four songs of the suffering servant of Yahweh in Isaiah (Isa. 42:1–4,

---

honest hand; herald of the word, performer of just deeds, the tree of life rooted on the river-bank of mighty waters; the strong and wise, heroic and detached, fecund and pure; clear-sighted and without self-will; dead certain of victory yet all atremble for it; lover of life, yet suffering the passion of death; exiled in gaping wounded flesh, dying from the violence of his suffering or of his ascetic combat; captive of that hope which pledges him to acts of redemption, and therefore enemy of the abyss in which non-being sparkles. See Rita Ferrone, "Praying with the Psalms," Part II; *Commonweal Magazine*, February 20, 2014.

35 Chouraqui, *Les Psaumes*, 27–30.
36 Ibid., 30.

49:1–6, 50:4–9, 52:13–53:12), where the isolation of the just, a solitary (*yahid,* martyr), is part of his condemnation.[37]

As he approaches *shéol,* the gates of death and the place of his execution, the just man nourishes and keeps up hope and love (Pss. 27:7–9, 88:16–18). *Elohim* collects his tears to change them into joy.[38] Dying, the just man is reborn in the light; as he thirsts after the presence of *Adonai,* after residing in Jerusalem, his agony marks his progress toward a dawn.[39]

To enter Jerusalem, the just man (*sadik*) needs *Adonai's* help, to which he abandons himself. For the judgment of the just assures his innocence and seals the criminal's defeat. Judgment (*mishpat*) is inescapable from justification (*sedaqa*). The care and favor (*hèsèd*) of *Adonai* is the fruit of the just man's obedience and his election. The Day of Judgment marks his astounding rehabilitation. In the Psalms, says Chouraqui, there is a continual dialectic between the individual and Yahweh. The springboard of this return to the Lord is ". . . among all the nations, whoever abandons idolatry gains access to the grace of the alliance and becomes one with Israel."[40] Yahweh's interventions in history are only images and figures of the last and final Judgment. The Hebrew exegesis insists on this eschatological character of the Psalms by interpreting them with a messianic orientation. The return of the captives of Israel (Pss. 14:7, 53:6, 85:1, 106:47, 107:3, 126:1, 147:2) from all the extremities of the earth, this conversion of the nations, is the victory of the *Elohim* of Israel. A cosmic reconciliation permits the reconstruction of Jerusalem; then the temple of David becomes the place of the real presence of *Elohim,* preparing the light of the Messiah. Psalm 2 presents the Messiah as the keystone of the Psalter. In the royal Psalms, the criminal is definitively defeated and Jerusalem becomes the center of a cosmic reconciliation. One rabbinic text (*Souka* 52 a) distinguishes the Suffering Messiah, son of Joseph, from the Glorious Messiah, son of David.[41]

The abyss separating heaven and earth is filled by redemption. Chouraqui describes this process: *Adonai* says to the king, "You are my son."[42] And the firstborn king says "My father" (Pss. 2:7, 89:26). The Messiah, the righteous King, will reign for eternity in peace and the innocent will sit at his right

37 Ibid., 31.

38 O. Odelin and R. Séguineau, eds., *Concordance de la Bible: Les Psaumes* (Paris: Desclée de Brouwer, 1980), 101–102.

39 Chouraqui, *Les Psaumes,* 32.

40 Ibid., 33–34.

41 Ibid., 35–36.

42 Ibid., 37.

hand. [43] *Elohim*'s name is *Adonai*, the lord who, in a celestial vision, conducts the liturgy of creation to its conclusion. *Elohim*, plural in form, encompasses all the infinite celestial forces. Chouraqui paraphrases Psalm 93 as follows: he manifests himself in the heart of creation, and it is he of whom creation sings. It is with his light that all creation shines and all creation sings for his transcendent love, for he illumines all with his light.

This vision is, at heart, both theological and anthropological, as we will see shortly. To summarize it into its most basic points, we could say that the Psalms are chiefly concerned with three interweaving themes:

1. Salvation: The promise of salvation which God made to mankind concerns the triumph of the just over sin. This salvation will come from Zion and the Davidic dynasty, one of whose descendants will be the Messiah. As the promise develops, the Messianic Era will become universal, and there will come a time when all the nations will come up to Zion.
2. Man: His dependence on God is expressed by his cries of distress, his feeling of abandonment.
3. Retribution: If mercy brings happiness, all unhappiness is God's punishment for evil. In Psalms 37 and 49, the defeat of justice is said to be only apparent, temporary, requiring one to wait patiently and confidently for the Lord's just retribution. The impatience of the just whose cause is unrequited is understandable, given the common assumption in the Psalms and certain prophets that life will end in *shéol*, where all are forgotten and where there is neither joy nor punishment. In some Psalms, however, we see the development of a theme of deliverance and resurrection by which the just ultimately overcome their trials:

   What gain is there in my destruction, in my going down into the pit? Will the dust praise you? Will it proclaim your faithfulness? (Ps. 30:9)

   For great is your love towards me; you have delivered me from the depths of the grave (*shéol*). (Ps. 86:13)

Furthermore, in a few passages, death is said to be incapable of separating the just from God, for he will experience neither corruption nor *shéol*:

43 Malki-Sédéq, i.e., Melchisedek of Genesis 14.

Because you will not abandon me to the grave (*shéol*),
Nor will you let your Holy One see decay. (Ps. 16:10)

But God will redeem my life from the grave;
he will surely take me to himself. (Ps. 49:15)

While the Psalter expresses a diversity of themes and voices, it is still possible to find an underlying unity, which, as we have just seen, is God's love for people, each man He has created. Pleading for God's mercy opens the heart of the oppressed, who may then see how near He is. But this return to God is, as we shall see below, a rough ascetical path.

The Psalter's Call: Can Man Return to God?

Now that we have sketched out the historical origins of the Psalms—the shape of psalms individually and within the Psalter as a whole—and their basic vision, what can we say about their vision of prayer? What do they reveal about the nature of prayer itself?

One of the most striking things to note, particularly in the light of our discussion of Christian approaches to prayer in Chapter 1, is that the Psalms insist that the initiative in prayer lies with God. The psalmist cries, "O Lord, open my lips, and my mouth will declare your praise" (Ps. 51:15). It is God who must "open" men's lips in prayer; yet, unless man stands before Yahweh, he will never truly know how to pray—he will never be given His name to utter.

This passage from silence to praying aloud needs a word of explanation. When oppressed man falls silent, he no longer has the courage to face his distress. But it is in this anguished silence that the voice of God is heard from the depths. In this crisis, words reappear. The God of the book of Genesis is a God who communicates—indeed creates—through words. His word is a *fiat*, as found in the account of creation preserved and told by the priests of the Jerusalem temple.[44] But, after that primordial moment, how can one situate the voice of God? Can God be silent, just as man is sometimes

44 Although this Elohistic account first appears in the book of Genesis (Gen. 1:1–2:3), it is later than the second Yahwistic account of creation found in 2:4–25. One should note that the name of God given to Moses on Mt Sinai (Exod. 3:14) is used in an adapted form in the Quranic account of creation (*Surah Yasin* 36:77–83) as Allah's *fiat*. The Arabic was transposed from the Hebrew *Ehyé ascher Ehyé* (I am who I am) as *kunfayakuni* (Be! And it is!). See Qur'an 36:77–83. See also A. de Libera and E. Zum Brunn, eds., *Celui qui est: Interprétations juives et chrétiennes d'Exode 3,14* (Paris: Éditions du Cerf, 1986).

reduced to silence? The prophets describe Moab and Judah, respectively, as having been reduced to silence, mute after being devastated (Isa. 15, Jer. 8:14–22). Amos (5:23) calls the northern kingdom of Israel to silence its songs in repentance. This is a silence of sorrow, of penitence. While the Psalms do describe another kind of silence—that of mute idols, "the gods of the nations" (Ps. 96:5) who are no better than the dead—and contrast this sinister silence (Ps. 135:16) with the joy of those singing in the temple, this is not the silence of prayerful repentance but something foreign to true prayer.

The Psalms also contrast this repentant silence with the natural mode of prayer, that of loud and joyful proclamation. The "joy" with which God has "filled [his] heart" (Ps. 4:7) should be vocal, proclaimed aloud for all to hear. This cultic noise is a basic value of prayer, and, when it is lacking, something is wrong, as in Psalm 32: "When I kept silent, my bones wasted away through my groaning all day long. . . . Many are the woes of the wicked, but the LORD's unfailing love surrounds the man who trusts in him. Rejoice in the LORD and be glad, you righteous" (Ps. 32:3, 10–11). And "Praise the LORD with the harp; make music to him on the ten-stringed lyre. Sing to him a new song; play skillfully, and shout for joy" (Ps. 33:2).

It is in the theophany granted to the prophet Elijah that a new under-standing of what man takes to be God's silence is first introduced, close to the stillness of a presence before whom one is both immobile and silent. This is no longer the silence of an absent, indifferent God, as some imagined. This silence is described as a "gentle whisper," a "still small voice," or "voice of thin silence" (1 Kings 19:12). Of course, this "deep" silence implies a deep listening on the part of man. This apparent silence from God is often described in the Psalms as God hiding his face from humans. Psalm 22, for example, recalls the song of the suffering servant in Isaiah 52–53, with the words

> My God, my God, why have you forsaken me? Why are you so far from saving me, so far from the words of my groaning? O my God, I cry out by day, but you do not answer, and by night, but I find no rest. ... In you our fathers put their trust; they trusted and you deliv-ered them. ... But I am a worm and not a man, scorned by men and despised by the people. (Ps. 22:1–2, 4, 6)

The irrepressible spontaneity of the faithful Israelite's heart is as unfathom-able as it is constant in the songs of the Psalms. Psalm 108 breaks the silence of the dawn: "My heart is steadfast, O God; I will sing and make music with all my soul. Awake, harp and lyre! I will awaken early with the dawn" (Ps.

108:1). And in Psalm 109 we hear the song, "O God, whom I praise, do not remain silent.... With my mouth I will greatly extol the LORD; in the great throng I will praise him. For he stands at the right hand of the needy one, to save his life from those who condemn him" (Ps. 109:1, 30–31). Within this tradition of spontaneity, certain prayers loom large: Moses led the Israelites in singing the Lord's praises on crossing the Red Sea (Exod. 15:1–18), and Miriam, the prophetess and sister of Aaron, took up her timbrel and led all the women in dances and song (Exod. 15:21).

Prayer arises in men's hearts in many different ways, and we cannot try to track spontaneity, which is only grasped by the hidden ear of God. However, as we have already mentioned, it is the famous penitential prayer of King David, Psalm 51, sung by the murderer of Uriah the Hittite and seducer of his wife Bathsheba (2 Sam. 11–12), that contextualizes why God must open the lips of mankind so that they may speak to him. Unless God takes the initiative, the distance that separates man and God—what the scriptures call man's "sin"—cannot be breached. David requests that God not cast him away from his presence or take his Holy Spirit from him. Penitence is critical, so David asks that he be washed thoroughly from his lawlessness, for his sin is always before him. "Against you, you only, have I sinned and done what is evil in your sight" (Ps. 51:4). David needs God to wash him whiter than snow, to turn his face from his sin and blot out all his transgressions. If God creates a clean heart in him and restores to him the joy of his salvation, then his tongue shall greatly rejoice in his righteousness, and "my mouth will declare your praise" (Ps. 51:15).

Another theme related to the question of whether man can pray to God at all is the psalm's theme of "saints," and the tradition of man's prayers as being echoes of the heavenly worship, as seen by Isaiah in his vision of angelic prayer around the throne of God.

To study the words of prayers as tradition has passed them on is to study their loci of experiences, and some of the words the Israelites prayed are a repetition of the prayers of the angels, awestruck by their proximity to God.[45] The description of the Holy of Holies found in 2 Chronicles 3:8–14 details its physical form, but, as a source of light—as a "burning" throne—it was really a manifestation of the glory of the presence of the Lord. When Isaiah was later called to be a prophet, in the year of the death of King Uzziah (ca. 740 BC), what he saw and what he heard (Isa. 6:1–3) became a much-repeated motif in synagogue prayer:

45 See Mowinckel, *Israel's Worship*; James Kugel, *The Idea of Biblical Poetry: Parallelism and its History* (London: Yale University Press, 1981).

I saw the Lord seated on a throne, high and exalted, and the train of his robe filled the temple. Above him were seraphs; each with six wings.... And they were calling to one another: "Holy, holy, holy is the Lord Almighty...."[46]

Those who can repeat this angelic prayer in the spirit of the prophet Isaiah, in the synagogue of the faithful, are those who can fear the holiness of the Lord, and these "saints" are evoked many times in the Hebrew Bible. "Fear the LORD, you his saints, for those who fear him lack nothing" (Ps. 34:9).

The chant of the angels that Isaiah heard subsequently becomes the Third Benediction in Jewish daily public worship, and has remained so to this day: "You are holy, your Name is holy, and the saints praise you every day. Praised are you, Holy God."[47] Following the *chazzan*'s recitation of this benediction, the congregation says: "Holy, holy, holy is the Lord of Hosts: the whole earth is full of his glory" (Isa. 6:3). This is not so much a citation of Isaiah as an appropriation of the angels' exclamations as he heard them.

Noting the performative aspect of praying the Psalms raises five issues: 1) the terms which are used in the performance; 2) the ways in which the terms are replaced by others or reinterpreted; 3) the re-appropriation of the prayers of others; 4) the *anamnesis* or remembrance of saving events (crossing of the Red Sea led by Moses; the giving of the commandments to Moses on Sinai, etc.); and 5) how *sung* poetry brings to life well-known prayers. Here, we focus on the more intimate dimension of prayer, its comparative anthropology, and less on the linguistic traits.

How God Shapes Man's Destiny through Prayer

Having noted the Psalms' belief that human prayer is only possible with the aid of God's initiative, what do the Psalms have to say about the relation of the human person to prayer in general? What is humanity's relationship to God? If we look closely, we find that the Psalms do indeed contain an anthropology of the human person and prayer. This vision of humanity continually develops, since, in the last books of the Hebrew Bible, the questions of man's resurrection and immortality are revealed. An early narrative of Genesis is paraphrased by Psalm 104:3–4, in which God "rides on the wings

46 M. Barker, in *On Earth as it is in Heaven* (1995) insists that, every time there is a description of a throne, it is a description of the Holy of Holies.

47 The *Amidah* is thus found in all *siddurim*, traditional Jewish prayer books. See M. Stern, ed., *Daily Prayers* (New York: Hebrew Publishing Company, 1928), 50–59.

of the wind" and "makes winds his messengers." But, if God is wind, he is also breath: "When you hide your face, they are terrified; when you take away their breath, they die and return to the dust" (Ps. 104:29). So what is the breath of life in man?

The similarity between spirit (*ruah*) and breath (*nechamah*) for Job comes from the fact that man is formed by the "Spirit of God" and given life by "the breath of the Almighty" (Job 33:4). But, in the book of Exodus, the spirit of God is related to His word, since the breath (*nechamah*) of God makes the waters of the Red Sea retreat at His verbal command (Exod. 14). Even earlier, in Genesis, mankind's composition is said to be dual: while man's flesh (*basar*) is doomed to death, his being, as a whole, is enlivened by the spirit of God (Gen. 6:30). This implies that man has his own soul, but his consciousness depends on being given his vital breath. If the *ruah* is centered in man's heart, for the Hebrews, the vegetative soul is located in the stomach. Basically, man's vital force is material; nevertheless, his breathing puts him in contact with the God who gave it to him. One does not hear in the Psalms that man's soul is immortal, but one often hears (23, 24) that contact with the Lord through prayer gives life to man's soul:

> Into your hands I commit my spirit;
> redeem me, O LORD, the God of truth. (Ps. 31:5)

> My life is consumed by anguish and my years by groaning;
> my strength fails because of my affliction, and my bones grow weak.
> (Ps. 31:10)

> But I trust in you, O LORD; I say, "You are my God."
> My times are in your hands....
> Let your face shine on your servant; save me in your unfailing love.
> (Ps. 31:14–16)

> In the shelter of your presence you hide them from the intrigues of men;
> in your dwelling you keep them safe from accusing tongues. (Ps. 31:20)

> In my alarm I said, "I am cut off from your sight!"
> Yet you heard my cry for mercy when I called to you for help.
> Love the LORD, all his saints! The LORD preserves the faithful....
> (Ps. 31:22–23)

Since we are discussing the Psalms as a perennial corpus of prayers, one cannot present here all the interpretations that they have undergone as part of prophetic revelation to later Judaism, let alone the interpretations found in Christianity. Yet, in the Eighteen Benedictions, the coming of an eternal and celestial Jerusalem is clearly invoked as the "kingdom" of God: "Return in compassion to your city, Jerusalem, and rest within it as you have said. Rebuild it speedily, and in our days, a structure forever" (Fourteenth Benediction). The prospect of God's kingdom being eternal links to the idea of man's relationship with God also being eternal. Although the Psalms date from a much earlier period, and were only completed as a collection around 300 BC, can we trace the beginnings of this concept of the eternity of individual human prayer? In Psalm 8, humankind is described as possessing glory and splendor a little lower than that of the angels; nothing is said concerning eternity.

The Wisdom of Solomon (ca. AD 100) reflects a much more recent period than that of the Psalms, and unambiguously claims that man is intended for immortality. Interestingly, it is in the same context that we read again of man's creation in the "image" of God:

> For God created man for immortality and made him an image of his own eternity.... But the souls of the righteous are in the hand of God and no torture will ever touch them.... Their hope is full of immortality. (Wisd. of Sol. 2:23, 3:1–4; KJV)

In the Wisdom literature, mankind's resemblance to God is by virtue of his immortality, and the formula "image of God" (*tselem 'Elohim*, Gen. 1:26–27; 9:6) is introduced as an expression of eternity. Whereas the word *tselem* usually refers to three-dimensional images, this is clearly not the sense in which it is used in this case (see Isa. 40:25); it refers to the divine image that is said to be reproduced in man.

While an impoverished interpretation of God's incorporeality is found in some of the inter-testamental Hellenistic Jewish literature, it is in later Jewish esoteric literature that the image of God moves on from mythical metaphorical image to mystical symbol. In the Psalter itself, however, man is understood not to have been created in the image of "a god" but in the image of the unique and transcendent God of whom no physical image can be made.

In the light of this understanding, the words that the *orans* of the Psalter exchanges with God merit closer description. For instance, in the confident opening proclamation of Psalm 89, "I will sing of the LORD's great love for ever," one senses that the words of prayer between God and man are guaranteed not to disappear, for the sincerity invested in them establishes a truth value that guarantees their permanence and stabilizes the relationship.

While the human words within the prayers of the Psalms are clearly identifiable, they also vary according to the specific genre of the invocation. The combination of personal lamentations, liturgical hymns, supplications versus thanksgiving hymns, royal psalms for court and temple ceremonies, messianic psalms, and didactic wisdom psalms adds to the comprehensive anthropology of the Psalms.[48] The genres represented are all variations on the theme of the renewal of God's relationship with Israel, whether collective or personal. Below, I list the various literary genres possible for cultic use to rejuvenate the covenant.[49]

Literary genres for cultic situations:
- The ascent and the sojourn: pilgrimage psalms and graduals
- Praises: hymns celebrating aspects of the covenant
- Hymns celebrating the royalty of Yahweh (psalms of his dominion) and the election of Zion (the canticles of Zion)
- Formulas of benediction
- Oracle-centered liturgies
- Sacrifices: supplication for sins and psalms of thanksgiving
- Celebrations of the covenant, including prophecies
- Psalms of the guest reflecting on one's election
- Royal psalms recalling the messianic promises
- Prophetic psalms against sinners: maledictions and diatribes

One senses that, with the writing, collection, and collective use in the temple of these prayers, they developed their own understanding of man's identity when he stands before God in worship and supplication. This happens when the psalmist sings the prayers with faith, repeating the revealed names of God day by day until they imprint themselves on his memory. At this point, turning toward God implies that the person knows that it is the Lord who is standing before him. This explains why, both individually and collectively, the anthropology of the Psalms constitutes a progressive experience for each generation that prays them. Psalm 89 contains several examples of this building up of spiritual transmission:

48 See A. Robert and A. Feuillet, *Introduction à la Bible* (Paris: Desclée de Brouwer, 1959), vol. I, 596–610; Odelin and Séguineau, *Les Psaumes* (Paris: Desclée de Brouwer, 1980), x–xx.

49 Adapted from M. Manati, *Les Psaumes* (Paris: Desclée de Brouwer, 1966), vol. I.

I will declare that your love stands firm for ever,
that you established your faithfulness in heaven itself.
You said, "I have made a covenant with my chosen one,
I have sworn to David my servant,
I will establish your line for ever
and make your throne firm through all generations." (Ps. 89:2–4)

In the council of the holy ones God is greatly feared. (v. 7)

Righteousness and justice are the foundation of your throne;
love and faithfulness go before you.
Blessed are those who have learned to acclaim you.... (vv. 14–15)

In the Psalter, truth (*èmèt*) and faith are paired to characterize the relationship between God and man.[50] Truth expresses confidence, which is then displayed by faithfulness. To believe (*hiphil*), to have faith in someone, is to rely on someone who is dependable. Truth possesses this quality of proven stability; the opposite of truth is not error, but lying. False gods are idols, whereas the "God of truth" (Ps. 31:5) is dependable, just as in Psalm 132: "The Lord swore an oath to David, a sure oath that he will not revoke" (Ps. 132:11).

A just man is one whom God has justified. The alliance, the testament uniting God and man, creates a community characterized by goodness (*hèsèd*). God's goodness is the value that is displayed in His faithful promises, as characterized by the eternal nature of His decision to bless His faithful: "This was credited to him as righteousness for endless generations to come" (Ps. 106:31).

In the Psalms, goodness is a genuine duty and takes the nature of a bond, rather than something one is moved to by feeling. What one receives is God's favor (*hén* in Hebrew); this goodness can also be distinguished from tenderness, the source of compassion (*raham*) that is felt in one's mother's womb.[51] It is not a question of the pity that is evoked by suffering, but of intimacy and warmth:

Have mercy on me, O God, according to your unfailing love; according
to your great compassion blot out my transgressions. (Ps. 51:1)

The God of the Psalms is the same as the God of the prophets Amos, Micah, Hosea, Isaiah, and Jeremiah, whose vocabulary influenced that of

---

50 From the verb to believe, *niphal* or *hiphil*, Hebrew forms of the Qal root *'mn*.
51 *Rahamim*, the plural of uterus or womb (Gen. 49:25).

the Psalms. Thus it is not surprising to find that Isaiah also draws a parallel between justice (*sèdèq*) and salvation (*yècha'*):

> My righteousness draws near speedily, my salvation is on the way, and
> my arm will bring justice to the nations. (Isa. 51:5)

In the light of the importance of God's grace, prayers and cries of distress in the first person singular (e.g., "hear the voice of my supplication") occupy an important place in the Psalms as a whole. They are called *tehinnah* (or *tahanun*) (Pss. 6:3–44; 28:2, 6; 119:170, etc.) and request the "favor" (*hén*) or grace of God.[52]

In the Psalms, an individual Israelite, so often broken by despair, requests God's justice, truth, salvation, goodness, and mercy. This is in sharp contrast to the prophetic writings, in which individual voices and themes are muted in favor of a collective Israelite voice, since liturgical hymns from the temple have been worked over by conventions to merge the otherwise distinct attributes of God into one. Here are five examples of these attributes in the same Psalm:

> Your love (*hèsèd*), O LORD, reaches to the heavens,
> your faithfulness (*èmunah*) to the skies.
> Your righteousness (*sèdèq*) is like the mighty mountains,
> Your justice (*michpat*) like the great deep.
> O LORD, you preserve (*yacha`*) both man and beast.
> How priceless is your unfailing love (*hèsèd*)!
> Continue your love (*hèsèd*) to those who know you.... (Ps. 36:5–7a, 10)

Yet, of all these attributes, the highest expression of God's faithfulness and love for mankind is His goodness in forgiving man's sins—His compassion. An elegant expression of this sentiment is found in Psalm 103:

> The Lord is compassionate and gracious,
> slow to anger, abounding in love.
>
>   . . .
>
> For as high as the heavens are above the earth,
> so great is his love for those who fear him;
> as far as the east is from the west,
> so far has he removed our transgressions from us. (Ps. 103:8, 11–12)

---

52 While the word itself appears only twice in the Psalter, the idea is common.

Forgiveness of this kind is a form of justice that only God is capable of. Such is the hope of the poor and persecuted. God's faithfulness exists forever, and it is just this manifestation of His faithfulness and mercy that the prayers of the Psalms implore. Here, what is described is not only a personal individual destiny, for, if justice and peace go together, they concern all of Israel in its eschatological perspective.

> I have seen you in the sanctuary
> and beheld your power and your glory.
> Because you love is better than life,
> my lips will glorify you. (Ps. 63:2–3)

The anthropology of the man who prays the Psalms is gradually "restored" into that of an *orans*—that is to say, man's heart opens up toward God as he traverses all the obscurities of life. But, laying aside moments of great distress when this happens spontaneously, men need to fast and to keep vigils to assure that their heart remains open toward God. Such ascetics is present in the vocabulary of the Psalms.

A Lexicon of Repentance

If the essence of heartfelt compunction, as in Psalm 51, is "a broken spirit, a broken and contrite heart" which God "will not despise," the psalm suggests that such prayer must be repeated. This reiterative dimension of repentance can be archaic; David relates this verbal prayer to physical expressions of penitence: the rebuilding of the walls of Jerusalem and the sacrificing of whole burnt offerings. Yet the permanence and prominence of Psalm 51 is indicative of its centrality. Nearly 3,000 years of repetition have not altered or diminished the vigor of this psalm, which, given all the changes in our mentalities, is, in itself, remarkable.

Another psalm that combines a reiterative approach with the theme of repentance is Psalm 119, and this leads us to propose the Psalms in general, and certain psalms in particular, as a "lexicon of repentance."

The ritual of reciting Psalm 119, "Blessed are they whose ways are blameless," provided an occasion for invocatory innovation using a restrained lexicon taken from a single psalm by varying its main theme. While Psalm 51 is the canonical Psalm par excellence, Psalm 119 is no less important. Analyzing its lexical terminology, we find that it creates a meditative vortex through the contemplative repetition of the same theme in different terms. Strictly speaking, the psalm is almost unreadable, simply too repetitive to maintain one's attention, unless it is recited with the sobriety that comes from the deep grief of separation from God.

Through its endless reiteration, Psalm 119 represents a distinct genre: its words are linked into a single semantic field and evoke chains of values. These chains are taken up in different ways, but all lead back to the same theme of the centrality of the law. Certain phrases take on the character of a refrain, such as, "Praise be to you, o LORD; teach me your decrees" (v. 12).

Psalm 119 develops its great theme by multiplying the names used for the law: it is variously referred to as the Lord's precepts, demands, will, and path. The law has a house, not only in man's heart (v. 161) but also in his soul (v. 175), in his mouth (v. 131), in his name, in his faithfulness, and in his promises. Thus the law is a covenant (*berith*) between God and man, evoked by repeating the name and the words (*dabar*, v. 118) of God. To speak of this eternal justice (v. 169) is already praise (*hallel*). To praise God is to feel his presence as peace (v. 165), as love (vv. 64, 76), as tenderness (v. 77). And, given man's distress, especially when he weeps (v. 136) for the humiliated, the abandoned, the exhausted and the anxious (v. 143), he returns to meditate on his word, for "Your word is a lamp to my feet" (v. 105).

While the liturgical order of the Psalms' arrangement is complex, one cannot help noticing that Psalm 119—the longest, with 176 verses—is immediately followed by a group of much shorter and more concise Psalms (120–134), whose initial verses express the same desperation in vibrant confidence:

> I call on the LORD in my distress, and he answers me. (Ps. 120:1)

> I lift my eyes to the hills—where does my help come from? My help comes from the LORD, the Maker of heaven and earth. (Ps. 121:1–2)

> I rejoiced with those who said to me, "Let us go to the house of the LORD." (Ps. 122:1)

> Those who trust in the LORD are like Mount Zion... (Ps. 125:1)

It is almost as though, through the repetition of Psalm 119, we have learned to condense and summarize its key movement, and express it in the shorter outbursts represented by Psalms 120–134. This gradual movement from long prayers to concise, monologic (*monologistoi* in Greek) prayers parallels the argument of a later Christian ascetic, Abba Makarios, who, when asked how one should pray, answered, "There is no need for long speeches. It suffices to raise one's hands and say, 'Lord, as you wish and as you understand, have mercy!' And, if the combat continues, 'Lord, help!'"[53]

Conclusion: The Psalms as Oral Asceticism

What explains the impressive permanence of the Psalms in both Jewish and Christian prayer? For over 3,000 years, the Psalms have extended their influence throughout the Abrahamic faiths, penetrating even into Islamic daily prayer, the *salāt*. Chouraqui insists that the spiritual landscape of the three Abrahamic religions is firmly rooted in the Psalter.[54] While this dependence may be more discreet in Muslim daily prayers (see Chapter 3), it is certainly true of Christianity, where monastic spirituality has always prioritized the praying of the Psalter, and where, even from the Church's earliest days, the Psalms occupied a key role: in the text of the four gospels, for example, half of biblical references are to the Psalms.[55]

The Psalms are characterized by the depth of the psalmists' need for contact with the Lord, their profound faith that their God will "deal" with them again, and their courageous refusal to relinquish hope in the face of adversity. What the Eastern Orthodox scholar John Breck has described as the Psalms' "rhetorical helix" would be overwhelming were it not for the fact that the consolation of the individual Israelite at prayer came from a wisdom derived from real experience.[56] This we can call the Psalms' sincerity, their authenticity. Supported by a prophet's vision of the word of God, Israel's experience of time and eschatology meant that one psalmist's experience of separation from God, of sin, was not an endpoint. The psalmist was not just another temple singer. As Sigmund Mowinckel has shown, these inspired psalmists provided models of hope for generations to come.[57] Other prayer collections, such as Ben Sira (Ecclesiasticus, 200–175 BC), the so-called "Psalms of Solomon" (second and first centuries BC), and the Qumran Psalter (*Hodhayoth*) also influenced the genre of early Christian liturgical hymns. As the literary genre of hymns evolved, the anthropology of the Psalter was integrated by every generation of Jews and Christians through regular weekly recitation.

53 *Apophthegmes des Pères du Désert, série alphabétique* (no author); Textes de Spiritualité Orientale, no. 1, Abbaye de Bellefontaine; Abba Makarios, no. 19.
54 Chouraqui, *Les Psaumes*, 17–45.
55 Ibid., 18.
56 John Breck, *The Shape of Biblical Language: Chiasmus in the Scriptures and Beyond* (Crestwood, NY: St Vladimir's Seminary Press, 1994), 38–58.
57 Mowinckel, *Israel's Worship*, 109–25.

And this was, above all, an oral asceticism, recitation as a struggle for concentration and deep sincerity. This oral status is key to understanding the Psalter's enduring status within the great monotheistic faiths.

Since St Augustine's general distinction between sacred and secular history, the relation of inner consciousness to the external history of the cosmos has become the dominant concern of Western intellectual civilization. But, as Walter Ong has shown, the word of God is to be understood primarily as image, as knowledge by vision—to use Ong's terms, as continuing shared consciousness of another's personal presence, as an inter-subjectivity.

> A theology of the Word of God as word will not, of course, explicate everything, if only because the history of the word of God among men is not identical with the history of the human word. For the history of the human word is not the history of salvation, as the history of God's word is.[58]

The one history does not explain the other, even if the two are related. Yet, because "the human word is uttered at the juncture where interior awareness and external event meet," the place where "encounter between person and person occurs at its most human depths," this history of man's word does have a particular relevance for studies of religious history. Thus Ong can claim, "Study of man in terms of changes in verbal media establishes new grounds for the relation of sacred and secular history."[59]

In Psalm 33, it is said that God "spoke, and it came to be; he commanded, and it stood firm" (Ps. 33:9). And, in Isaiah, ". . . so is my word that goes out from my mouth: It will not return to me empty, but will accomplish what I desire and achieve the purpose for which I sent it" (Isa. 55:11). So the word of God communicates not only by creating the entire universe but also with the still center of the human soul, which, together with this world, proclaims his glory: "The heavens declare the glory of God" (Ps. 19:1). But, as we have seen above, God's words are also sent as a message to be proclaimed by the prophets, who are sometimes inspired in spite of themselves. As Christians, we believe the oral status of the word of God is redefined as the primary "utterance" of the Father.[60] St Paul goes as far as to say, "no-one can say, 'Jesus is Lord,' except by the Holy Spirit" (1 Cor 12:3).

---

58 Walter J. Ong, SJ, *The Presence of the Word* (Minneapolis: University of Minnesota Press, 1967), 181.

59 Ibid.

60 Ibid., 185.

This vital difference changes the very nature of prayer as interlocution. Ong wrote:

> The Word, the Son, himself God, is, in classic Trinitarian theology, the one who takes to his person a human nature so that thenceforward the "Thou" which is addressed to the man Jesus Christ is addressed necessarily to God himself, in the Second Person, for there is only one "Thou" here . . . a divine and human actuality and "resonance". . . . [61]

Jesus Christ, who was once visible as the manifest Word of God, again becomes purely oral. The *verba infans* (non-speaking word) in the manger in Bethlehem is T.S. Eliot's "word within a word, unable to speak a word, / Swaddled with darkness."[62] Ong stressed St Paul's emphasis on *fides ex auditu*: the idea, as in Romans 10:17, that faith comes through hearing. The prophet Isaiah says, "the word of our God stands for ever" (Isa. 40:8). But this word, essential to faith, stands within a silence that deepens it. The psalmist sang at a time when little was written down. The great epics of the Middle East were orally developed over generations before they were first alphabetized with the emergence of chirographic cultures. Likewise, the Psalms, and even more so the Vedic hymns studied in Chapter 4, were sung prayers long before they found written expression. This communication between God and man was therefore undertaken in a way that assured its fertile impression on the human heart and religious imagination.

The scribes of the first courts of Jerusalem may have copied Canaanite hymnography to learn their profession, but the singers on the steps of the temple—like the Persian singers of the Zoroastrian *Avesta*, and those who, farther east, chanted the Rig-Vedic hymns of northwestern India in the same period—dominated the cultic background of the Psalms as prayers, and determined their place in Israel's worship. That the Psalms have remained an oral performance for over 3,000 years is an incredible tribute to the force of their poetry.

In Chapter 1, we accepted that it is God who puts the word of prayer on our lips. In this chapter, we see how painful and demanding prayer can be that would overcome our denial of suffering and implore the compassionate Lord for His presence. We will find these two features of Judeo-Christian prayer muted in the next chapter, as the Qur'an, used in the formulation of

---

61 Ibid., 185–86.

62 T.S. Eliot, "Gerontion," in *The Waste Land and Other Poems* (London: Faber and Faber, 1972), 15.

the five daily Muslim prayers, gives precedence to praise and the celebration of the unity of the Godhead. Not that praise is absent from the Psalms—far from it—but praise in the Qur'an seems to be addressed to Allah at a greater distance, perhaps due to fear or respect, than that wherein we find the Hebrew pleading for God's presence. For the *orans* of the Psalms, the Lord is next to him, by his side.

CHAPTER 3

Muslim Daily Prayer (Salāt): Four Readings

AFTER HIS EXPULSION FROM BOLSHEVIK RUSSIA IN 1922, and on arriving the next year in Istanbul or "*Tsargrad*" at the then-great mosque of Hagia Sophia, Bulgakov wrote:

> Now that it is Allah that one prays to here, this holy place has been taken away from Christ and given to a false prophet.... Nonetheless, also today, they pray to God in this place and they pray with dignity.... God has taken away the torch and given it to a foreign people as he did in the past to the sanctuary of the first temple [destroyed in 587 BC].... How beautiful in its own way is this [Muslim] manner of praying, how it inspires respect.[1]

The nature of Muslim prayer is a topic too broad to be covered in a whole book, let alone in a single chapter. For this reason, we focus on one aspect of Muslim prayer—their daily prayer, *salāt*—and limit our study to four distinct perspectives. While none of these can give a complete picture of Muslim prayer, together, they form a diverse approach that illuminates the depth and complexity of the topic.

We begin with an overview of Islam, and then turn to our four "readings" or approaches. Our first "reading" is *salāt* according to the Qur'an. From there, we will turn to look at the relationship between *salāt* and contemplation as understood by the Sufi tradition. Next, we turn to consider popular peasant Muslim understandings of *salāt*. And, finally, we will step back and consider Muslim prayer from an external perspective: the "reading" of the social sciences.

---

1 Sergei Bulgakov, *Ma Vie dans l'Orthodoxie* (Paris: Éditions de Syrtes, 2014), 144–45 (my translation).

The Nature of Islam

While Christian values in European culture gave rise to a religious morphology that may help describe Christianity, and may not be wholly inadequate to describe Judaism, it is certainly not sufficient for understanding Islam. Islam falls beyond traditional Judeo-Christian categories. In the past, European writing about Islam has always been a perilous enterprise because we do not share, or even know, one another's core beliefs. Even if we were more familiar with Islam, would it follow that we granted it any greater respect? As we will discover later in this chapter, the social sciences have recently attempted to sideline the issue by explaining Islam with an epistemology articulated around the axiom of purported neutrality. Yet events in the Middle East since 2003 have shown that secularism's concept of the separation of church and state is never neutral; indeed, it is hotly contested by both sides. Thus, instead of following the social sciences' approach, I accept that an outsider's perspective is inescapable; so I select an Arab, a Lebanese, whose essay on the nature of Islam was published for other Lebanese.[2] If one reflects on the ample commentaries on the Qur'an, one realizes that one does not possess their perspective no matter how penetrating and interesting they may be.[3] Comparisons between Christianity and Islam should be better than a simple regression to "objective" statements about what Muslims do or do not believe. What represents, for Europeans, already unlikely doctrine cannot be approached in this way. A better approach is to come to an understanding of the Muslim faith through its parallels with Christian or Jewish faith.

Just as Muslims' ignorance of the Hebrew Bible has impoverished their understanding of Judaism, few are the non-Muslims who find they can read the Qur'an with profit; its form of poetry and prayer is usually quite foreign to Westerners. Many Christians are scandalized by Islam's portrayal of Jesus as nothing more than a venerated prophet, and this complicates their efforts to truly understand Islam. Nonetheless, Christ is mentioned, directly and indirectly, over one hundred and eighty-seven times in the Qu'ran, making him the most mentioned person in the Qur'an as a whole.[4] The positions by which Islam is set apart from the other two great monotheistic faiths

2 Georges Khodr, "La Nature de l'Islam," *Courrier Oecuménique du Moyen Orient* 54 (2007), 30–54.

3 Such commentaries can be found throughout Seyyed Hossein Nasr's recent translation, *The Study Qur'an* (New York: Harper One, 2015).

4 He is mentioned twenty-five times by the name Isa, in the third person forty-eight times, in the first person thirty-five times, and elsewhere through titles and attributes.

have helped forge its reactive *sui generis* identity, which derives not only from Islam's very nature but also from its recent history.[5] Centuries after the establishment of Islam, all the Balkan Orthodox Christian countries except Romania were conquered by Muslims. The Ottoman Domination (1453–1923) created more negative attitudes toward Islam among the conquered peoples, just as later domination of the Middle East by European powers resulted in subsequent Arab nationalism. Mixed with secularization, this meant that Muslims' perspective on Western Christianity deteriorated even further.

Nevertheless, in the nineteenth and twentieth centuries, sympathetic students of Islam like the Hungarian Ignaz Goldziher (1850–1921) and the French scholar Louis Massignon (1883–1962) began advancing a more creative approach to Islam. Goldziher, who remained a faithful Jew all his life but occasionally prayed as a Muslim, wrote, in his diary, of a personal experience in a mosque in Cairo:

> In those weeks, I truly entered into the spirit of Islam to such an extent that ultimately I became inwardly convinced that I myself was a Muslim, and judiciously discovered that this was the only religion which, even in its doctrinal and official formulation, can satisfy philosophic minds. My ideal was to elevate Judaism to a similar rational level. Islam, as my experience taught me, is the only religion, in which superstitious and heathen ingredients are frowned upon not by rationalism, but by orthodox doctrine.[6]

One is hard put to understand how Goldziher's empathy for Islam elevated it above his Jewish convictions unless he only knew very popular expressions of such convictions. In any case, although Goldziher's view of the influence of heathen superstition on Muslim doctrine is unacceptable to some present-day students, it nevertheless reveals how a good knowledge of Muslim texts does not exclude a deep personal prejudice in their interpretation. Massignon, a Catholic with a deep theological understanding of the inter-religious convergences between Christians and Muslims, viewed Islam as a religion based on Muhammad's genuine inspiration, his awareness of the

5 John of Damascus (died AD 749) treated Islam as a deviant Christian sect. He was the earliest Christian monk and theologian to write about Islam, a century after Muhammad's death (632). Even if he was a friend of the Umayyad caliph Yazid II (687–724), his knowledge of Arabic was insufficient to read the Qur'an, so his early witness is of limited value. For more, see Andrew Louth, *St. John Damascene* (Oxford: Oxford University Press, 2002), 76–83.

6 Ignac Goldziher, *Tagebuch*, ed. Alexander Scheiber (Leiden: Brill, 1978), 59.

oneness (*tawhīd*) of Allah.[7] Muhammad had sought a monotheistic origin for all Arabs and received a "mysterious answer of (divine) grace to (Abraham's) prayer for Ishmael and the Arab race." For Massignon, the revelation (*tanzīl*) in Islam may be summarized as follows:[8]

1. God is free to reveal himself when and how he wants.
2. The action of God is also exercised in a world of grace outside Christianity; it can be found in Islam, in its mystical vocations.
3. Religious conversion and encounters have an existential character; a religious theme has significance for its seeker.
4. Religious science is a *religious* study in the proper sense of the word: it is a discovery of grace (i.e., the work of the Holy Spirit or the Rūh Allāh).[9]

Massignon's claims allow us to ask whether we can describe what is so unique about the prayers of Arabic monotheism. Why has Muslim *salāt,* its five daily prayers, been considered so foreign, so different, when no sacred scripture is so completely devoted to prayer as the Qur'an? The Qur'an reflects the deepest religious experience of the Prophet Muhammed's heart, repeated over the centuries as God's own message to him while he prayed.[10] If one refuses at the outset to recognize that God speaks to the human being through the Qur'an, through the canonical five daily *salāt* prayers, then the study of Muslim prayer becomes impossible. Yet surely there is one way, at least, in which we ought to be able to approach Islam: through invocations, which in one form or another are common to all Western faiths. Thus, perhaps our study will help those people who have hitherto found difficulty approaching Islam to find new ways of connecting. The inspiration (*tanzīl*) that led

7 See the remarks indexed under Massignon in Edward W. Said's *Orientalism* (New York; Vintage, 1978), 265–66, 280, 283, where Said admires Massignon's combination of erudition and intuition.

8 J.J. Waardenburg, *L'Islam dans le Miroir de l'Occident: comment quelques orientalistes occidentaux se sont penchés sur l'Islam et se sont formé une image de cette religion* (Paris: Mouton, 1969, 3rd ed.).

9 Maurice Borrmans, "Aspects Théologiques de la Pensée de Louis Massignon sur l'Islam," in *Louis Massignon et le dialogue des cultures*, ed. Daniel Massignon (Paris: Éditions du Cerf, 1996), 119ff.

10 In Henri Corbin's study, *Creative Imagination in the Sufism of Ibn 'Arabi* (Bollingen Series XCI, Princeton: Princeton University Press, 1969, 262–81), he elucidates the role of spiritual imagination in constructing the reciprocity of prayer (*munājāt*) between Lover and Beloved, between a unique individual and his unique God. This subject goes well beyond the scope of this modest sketch on *salāt*; the study of Sufism would merit a whole other chapter.

Muhammed to attribute so much importance to prayer has an historical, biographical context, and this context—its *Sitz im Leben*—may help to provide that personal respect for the prophet without which it is impossible for a non-Muslim to properly approach his "invocations."

Although the Qur'an mentions the patriarchs, it refers to few prophets (Arabic *nabī*, plural *anbiyā'*) in the narrow Hebrew sense of the word, other than Elijah, Jonah, Job, and John the Baptist. Muslim genealogies (*silsilah*) mix Biblical prophets with the non-Biblical *anbiyā'* of dubious origin from a Judeo-Christian point of view. Despite the references to earlier figures such as Abraham, Noah, and Jonah, and the fact that Muhammad is venerated as the seal of the prophets, this final prophet allows for no real pre-history of salvation, since he gives no role to any mediator between God and man like those mentioned in Genesis. Islam understands these earlier figures to have effected a personal reconciliation between God and man through their response to Allah's mercy (*rahmān*), but this is not redemption in the Christian understanding, where fallen man is re-fashioned into his original image and likeness of God. Thus, while Muhammad did not claim to bring anything new, he reiterated the message brought by Abraham, Moses, and Jesus. Still, as Georges Khodr tells us, by suppressing so much of the narrative of Judeo-Christian revelation, Islam concludes that humanity has known a single monotheism, of which it is a clear and pure representation.[11]

Mary's role in listening to God and in prayer is of utmost importance to traditional Christianity, yet she is not present in such a role within the Qur'an. She is, however, the only woman mentioned by name in the Qur'an (*sūrah* 19, vv. 16–36),[12] and, unlike in the Hebrew Bible, other mothers or sisters in the Qur'an play only minor roles, again demonstrating that Islam is not a Biblical religion. This is worth mentioning here because, for Christians, Mary's role in listening to God—in praying—is highly important. The Qur'an concentrates on proclaiming God's will to the pagan polytheists, its initial audience, and neither Jews nor Christians were targeted, even though they may have been present. The absolute transcendence of Allah refuses the reality of the Judeo-Christian progressive history of mankind's salvation where Mary plays such a crucial role. Furthermore, since the Qur'an as a book remains in heaven on a preserved tablet (*lawh al-mahfooz*), one cannot question its origins. This dogma has caused considerable consternation for those wishing to explore the relation of the language of the Qur'an to pre-Islamic

---

11 Khodr, "La Nature de l'Islam," 9.

12 The numeration of the verses of a given *sūrah* in the Qur'an may vary slightly. In quotations from the Qur'an, we will use Nasr's translation.

sixth-century Arabic poetry, which would have influenced the conditions surrounding the creation of the holy book.

So why did Muhammed ignore the Biblical traditions that, to some extent, inspired him? There is no mention in the Qur'an of churches or synagogues in Hejaz or al-Hijāz (the area stretching from Tabuk to Jeddah and Mecca/Makkah along the eastern coast of the Red Sea), even if they may well have been present. This is not surprising, since Muhammad knew neither Hebrew nor Greek nor Syriac, languages widely used elsewhere in the Arabian peninsula of his time. He seems never to have gone to Damascus, where he might have deepened his superficial familiarity with Jews and Christians. Paradoxically, given what we have just said, Muhammad, in the early Meccan chapters of the Qur'an, does not claim to provide any new message that one cannot already find in the Hebrew Bible or the Greek and Syriac apocryphal literature, which these *sūrah* resemble in different ways. The arrangement of the chapters of the Qur'an is by their length and not by their date of revelation, which complicates the study of the evolution of Muhammad's message. It is therefore habitual to break down the Qur'an's chapters according to the periods of their revelation/composition by Muhammad, since each period has dominant stylistic traits and themes corresponding to the progressive maturation of the Prophet's message. The establishment of the chapters' chronology was carried out by Muslim exegetes according to differences in vocabulary, prosody, and topic.

In Mecca (AD 610–622):

610–615: the first revelations concern eschatology, judgment by the one and only God, and his condemnation of the injustices committed toward the poor.

615–622: the role of the prophets and Muhammad are dealt with; and successively ensuing "pagan" Arab boycott of the nascent Muslim community (616–619); the omnipotence of Allah and human liberty (619–622); the two-part night journey (*isrā* and the *mi'rāj: sūrah* 17);[13]

13 Around the year 621, Muhammad mounted his Pegasus, Burāq, who, during the first part of the night (*isrā*), took him to the "farthest mosque" (*al-Aqsa* in Jerusalem; *al-Haram al-Sharīf* or "Noble Sanctuary," on the Dome of the Rock; *haram al-sharīf* is the Temple Mount itself; the other name for *al-āqsa* is *al-jama'a al-qiblī*) where he led the other prophets in prayer. In the second part of the same night (*mi'rāj*), Burāq took him to heaven, where Allah instructed him in the *ordo* of canonical prayer. *Sūrah* 17, "the night journey," speaks of this voyage. "Glory be to Him, who carried His servant by night from

Muhammad rides on a horse, the winged Burāq, to the "farthest mosque" (*al-Aqsa*) in Jerusalem to lead the prophets in prayer; after this, Muhammad ascends to heaven where Allah instructs him on the *salāt*; the pre-eternal covenant (*mīthāq*); the hegira (*hijrah*) from Mecca to Medina on September 20, 622 (dated the first of Muharram, year 1 of the *hegira*).

In Medina (622–639):

The main topic of the twenty-four chapters dating from the Medina period is Muslim community; their respective revelation is more difficult to determine than that of the Meccan chapters. The *umma*—the community or "nation" of Muslim believers—is a multi-ethnic community of faithful, as opposed to a territorial unity. The religious duty of struggle (*jihād*) is discussed.

In the Meccan chapters, the Prophet does not seek to distinguish himself from Judaism or Christianity, for, as a Muslim, he saw himself as the apostle of an orthodox renewal movement of the same God whose grace was given to Abraham, Moses, and Jesus. As Khodr puts it, Muhammed is a non-Hebrew practicing an Arab prophetism.[14] More pertinently, as a non-Jew, he belongs to a "nation" that, at that time, had no holy book—though this situation was quickly to be redressed, for Muhammad as an inspired poet would recite his revelations to his companions to be written down.[15]

In *surah* 112:3, the Qur'an says that Allah is one, the unique; he has not engendered women or djinns, nor has he been engendered. It is important to understand what kind of definition this is: it is a "negative" definition, explaining what Allah is not, rather than what he is. Massignon characterizes this *sūrah* as a negative definition of transcendence whereby the divine essence can only be considered *ad extra*.[16]

In the four famous verses of Qur'an 112, a chapter titled *al-Ikhlās*, one finds pure monotheism: "Say, 'He, God, is one, God, the Eternally Sufficient unto Himself. He begets not; nor was He begotten. And none is like unto Him'"

---

the Holy Mosque to the Further Mosque, the precincts of which we have blessed, that We might show him some of Our Signs. He is the All-Hearing, the All-Seeing. (2) And We gave Moses the Book, and made it guidance to the Children of Israel: 'Take not unto yourselves any Guardian apart from me.'"

14 Khodr, "La Nature de l'Islam," 9.

15 To recite (Arabic root *TLW*). See further in Régis Blachère, *Introduction au Coran*, (Paris: Besson and Chantemerle, 1959, 2nd edition), 18.

16 Louis Massignon, *Passion d'Al-Hallaj*, 2 vols. (Paris: Guethner, 1926), 76.

(Qur'an 112:1–4).[17] Nonetheless, some twenty-five times in the Qu'ran, Jesus is called "the son of Mary" ('Īsā ibn Maryam); elsewhere, as in Qur'an 4:171, he is presented as a threesome, namely, "the Messiah, Jesus an apostle of Allah his Word placed in Mary, [and] a Spirit emanating from Him." One can better understand this point of view if one realizes that Muhammad thought that Allah was understood by Christians to be the Messiah, the son of Mary. *Sūrah* 4:157 denies that Jesus was ever crucified, even if certain medieval Muslim exegetes, while discussing Christ's ascension, admitted that he died. If killing a man to whom Allah reveals himself is a grave crime, here non-Muslims want to ask why, elsewhere in the Qu'ran, it is also an obligation to kill those pagans called "associationists," who violate the strict monotheism Muhammad preached in the Arabian Desert.

Khodr is a Lebanese Orthodox Christian bishop widely known in the Middle East for his pride in being Arab. What is so difficult—and important—to understand here, Khodr argues, is the Muslims' refusal of the scandal of the cross.[18] The Last Judgment and the final retribution in Islam (see *sūrah* 80) reflect a Christian tradition; their vision of *gehenna* (*janna* in Arabic) has close links with fourth-century Syrian poetry, especially that of St Ephrem (AD 306–373).[19] The Qur'anic descriptions of paradise, on the other hand, reflect the pleasures of the senses and are not just symbolic. It is not surprising that no mention is found of any glorified body, for, in heaven, only Allah can abide. For the same reason, the incarnation is inconceivable, for it would mean that Allah could share his glory with mankind.

In the Qur'an, a multiplicity of religions is recognized, and, once having conquered and pacified the territory of their new caliphates, the norm was a certain tolerance: "let him who apostatizes apostatize and let him who believes believe" for "you have your religion and I have mine" (Qur'an 109:6). However, already under the first caliph, Abu Bakr (AD 632–634), no Muslim was allowed to leave Islam.

Thus the confusing distance that separates Islam and Christianity can only be understood by a better understanding of the Muslim faith as emerging from a nascent Arabic henotheism influenced by the political milieu of the

17 Trans. Nasr, 1579.

18 Khodr, "La Nature de l'Islam," 5.

19 *Gehenna/janna* is referred to by Christ as the place of final, everlasting punishment for the ungodly and the wicked after their death. This valley of Hinnom (Gehenna) lies south of Jerusalem (Joshua 15:8 and 18:16), where human sacrifices were reputedly offered to the Canaanite god Moloch. Josiah (2 Kings 23:10) destroys these altars in what Jeremiah (7:30–33) calls "the valley of slaughter." Although both *gehenna* and *shéol* were translated as "hell" in the King James Bible, *shéol* was more simply the place of the dead, not that of punishment.

early seventh century.[20] In and around the nation-state known today as "Jordan," this milieu was composed of the Ghassanides, Monophysite Christianized Arabs, and, in southern Iraq, the Lakhmids, Nestorian Christianized Arabs, who were vassal states of Byzantium. In the winter they went to the desert for pasture, and, in the summer, they fled the desert heat and went to the Fertile Crescent, with the result that they had no fixed territory. They played off allegiance to Byzantium and to the Persian Empire, forming confederations that were subsequently unraveled by these two powerful empires' diplomatic strategies.

Prior to the seventh century, beginning in the fifth, Nestorian Christianity began to spread among the Lakhmid Arabs on the lower Euphrates, and, after the 540s, in the western areas, the Ghassanid Arabs adopted Monophysitism. Both of these "conversions" signaled their desire for independence from Constantinople's Chalcedonian faith.

The Persian Sassanids in Ctesiphon near Baghdad were Zoroastrians and Manicheans. In 610, the Emperor Khosrow I of Persia defeated the Byzantine Emperor Heraclius and conquered Jerusalem, taking away the "true cross." Heraclius recaptured Jerusalem in 628 and Nineveh in 630, returning the Holy Cross to Jerusalem, as alluded to in the Qur'an (Qur'an 30:1–5). Farther south, there were large agrarian communities of Jewish refugees in the great oases of the coastal region of Hejaz, like Yahir, which became known as Medina after Muhammad's burial there. Christians were everywhere present, but were divided by sectarian disagreements, imbued with apocryphal teachings in addition to those of the New Testament. In this political context, the weakness of Byzantium and Sassanid Persia was an open invitation for the creation of a new kingdom between the two. Concomitantly, the entrance of the nomadic Bedouin Arabs into the commercial networks of their times encouraged sedentarization, which could not be continued without a stronger tribal confederation, and that, in turn, would have been favored by a new commonwealth of faith. From the point of view of political science, it was at this time that the Bedouin Arabs' nascent monotheism began to crystallize.

Now that we have reached the end of this introduction, it is easier to study *salāt* not as an unalterable way of prayer—which is what it has come to seem after so many centuries of practice—but as an integral part of Muhammad's personal faith as stated in the Qu'ran. He was determined to make such revealed prayer the center of his religious practice. Nonetheless, as we will see below, *salāt* has evolved both in its form and in Muslims' understanding

---

20 Garth Fowden, *Empire to Commonwealth: Consequences of Monotheism in Late Antiquity* (Princeton: Princeton University Press, 1994), 119–21.

of what it means to practice this prayer five times a day. In no sense should a history of *salāt*'s evolution be considered a denigration of its immutable form; rather it is to be understood from within the crucible of the unending Muslim reflection on what it means to be a monotheist.

Salāt According to the Qur'an

Even though *salāt* is not described in the Qur'an, there are passages suggesting that its basic characteristics were already in place in this period and that they did not change much with the passage of time. Like Jewish prayers, *salāt* was said standing, with bows (*rukū`*) and full prostrations (*sujūd* or *sajdah*), in the manner of Eastern Christians. Daily recitations from the Qur'an took place twice, as we see in references to the "morning Qur'an" (Qur'an 17:80; 84:20–21).

But in what historical context does *salāt* appear? In the Prophet's lifetime, several *ka'aba* (sacred houses or *al-Bayt al-harām*) were the focus of the Arabs' syncretic pantheon over which Allah was the greatest god. In the Qur'an's 22nd *sūrah* (chapter), verses 26–37, which deals with the pilgrimage to Mecca, we find the claim that the first *ka'aba* was built by Abraham (Ibrahim), the ancestor of the pure monotheists (*hanīf*) who, in the later "age of ignorance" before Muhammad's time, preserved something of this faith by refusing to associate any of the many lesser deities with Allah. Here begins a puzzle, for if Muhammad was determined to recover the unique God known to the Jews and the Christians, why is Arab monotheism neither Jewish nor Christian?[21] In this sense, Islam is not a Biblical religion, even if it is a prophetic one. While Islam uses a few aspects of the Hebrew Bible, the Christian Old Testament, it does not adopt its canon in its entirety.

Salāt does not simply mean "prayer."[22] It is distinct from both personal supplication (*du'ā*) and mystical recollection (*dhikr*, "invocation"), and describes, in a narrow sense, the canonical public prayer prescribed for all Muslims of age who are not excused by sickness or infirmity. All three terms referring to prayer (*salāt, du'ā,* and *dhikr*) that are found in the Qur'an reflect the cultural milieu of the gnostic, esoteric, magic, and mystical rituals of the Middle East of its time and are rooted in the effort to purify Arab tribal cults.[23]

21 Khodr, "La Nature de l'Islam," 30.
22 Throughout this section I refer to two articles: A.J. Wensinck, "*Salāt*," in *Encyclopédie de l'Islam* (Leiden and Paris: Brill & Klinckieck, 1934), vol. 4, 99–109; and Jane Dammen McAuliffe, "Prayer," in *Encyclopedia of the Qur'an* (Leiden: Brill, 2004), vol. 4. I have simplified the transcription of Arabic words. See also Wensinck, *Mohammed en de Joden te Medina*, (Leiden: Brill, 1908), 215–35.
23 Gerhard Bowering, "Prayer," *Encyclopedia of the Qur'an* (Leiden: Brill 2004), vol. 4,

Personal prayer in Arabic is *du'ā*, as opposed to canonical public prayer. This is a word not met with in pre-Qur'anic literature. Muhammad seems to have borrowed it from the Jewish and Christian communities of Arabia. The five canonical prayers that a Muslim should say each day are called *salāt*. This is also the pattern of the Zoroastrian practice, halfway between the three Jewish daily prayers and seven Christian daily prayers.[24] The word *salāt*, Arent Jan Wensinck has shown, is Aramaic in origin.[25] The Aramaic root *ṣ-l-'-* means to bend, as in bow but also twist or stretch. The noun *ṣelōṭā* indicates the action of bending, and here designates "prostration." This word refers to ritual or private prayer in various Aramaic dialects but not, surprisingly, in Syriac, although Wensinck claims that Muhammad borrowed from the Jews and the Christians not only the term but also a part of the form of what was to become daily Muslim ritual prayer. In Arabic, the term *salāt*, when derived from the trilateral root *ṣād bā ḥā* (ح ب ص), occurs forty-five times in the Qur'an. It can be a verbal noun, and, as a performative verb, came to mean to do *salāt*.

Canonical prayer alone and in community is distinguished from private personal prayer. In the Sufi current of both the Sunnite and Shia Islam, personal prayer (*du'ā*) came to occupy a considerable place. Muhammed's own personal prayer was to become the center of his experience of God. He had participated in the pagan rites at the *ka'aba* (see Qur'an 108:2) and believed the djinns and angels obeyed Allah's commands (Qur'an 72:1; 55:14). His earliest revelation consisted in nocturnal ecstatic inspirations and visions given by the angel Gabriel (Qur'an 17:1; 53:1–8; 81:19–25). "The utterances of his prayer were cast in rhymed prose marked by abrupt phrases, capturing cryptic meanings."[26] Muhammad felt that an angel was inspiring him (Qur'an 16:101–104), that God, or an angel, behind a veil was speaking to him just as he had spoken to Moses (Qur'an 20 *passim* and 42:50–51; Qur'an 2:97–98) and prophets such as Noah (Qur'an 23:27). These revelations were prefaced by the kinds of oaths Arabs had used earlier before their idols.[27] Despite his passing acquaintance with Jews and Christians, Muhammad imitated the oracular style (*saj'*) of pre-Muslim soothsayers: "I swear by the setting of the stars" (Qur'an 56:74) as well as by the planets and the stars (Qur'an 53:1), the sun (Qur'an 91:1), and the times of the day (Qur'an 84:16; 89:1; 92:1).

His prophetic call came during his reclusion on the Ghār Hirā' cave on the

---

215–30, esp. 215.

    24 Ibid., 227.

    25 Wensinck, "*Salāt.*"

    26 Bowering, "Prayer," 216.

    27 Ibid., 217.

Jabal al-Nūr hill outside Mecca. Allah commanded him to recite (*iqra'*; Qur'an 96). Shortly afterward, Muhammad began sharing these revelations with the inhabitants of Mecca, and thus began the practice of communal prayer within the nascent community. Only later, in 624 (Muslim year 2) in Medina, did he change the orientation, the direction (*qibla'*) of these invocations.

As interesting as the Jewish and Christian precedents for Muslim prayer are, the *salāt* obviously became *sui generis*. Why would Muhammad have taken any prayers over from his neighbors? The Qur'an *sūrah* 96:3–5, reputedly the first of the revelations received by Muhammad, implies that Muhammad had nothing to recite until (the Name of) the Lord inspired him:

> Recite: And thy Lord is the Most Generous, who taught by the Pen, taught Man what he knew not.

Already, in these early periods, there are other witnesses to Psalm-like prayers being integrated into the *salāt*; certain sections are even reminiscent of the creation Psalm 104, as is the case with the following passage:

> Hast thou not considered that God is glorified by whatsoever is in the heavens and on the earth, and by the birds spreading their wings? (Qur'an 24:41)[28]

The term for this ritual prayer, *salāt*, appears 78 times in the Qur'an. The word *salāt* in its verbal form appears among the earliest chapters of the Qur'an (75:31; 70:22; 107:4; 74:44; 108:2). There are suggestions elsewhere that the Prophet irritated the inhabitants of Mecca by his insistence on practicing this novel form of prayer:

> Say: "Call upon God, or call upon the compassionate. Whichever you call upon, to Him belong the Most Beautiful Names." And be not loud in thy prayer, nor quiet therein, but seek a way between. And say: "Praise be to God, who has no child! He has no partner in sovereignty nor has He any protector out of his lowliness." And proclaim His Greatness! (Qur'an 17:110)[29]

When Allah constantly exhorts Muhammad to imitate the patience of the earlier prophets, he implies that, in their times, they also encouraged

---

28 Trans. Nasr, 882.
29 Trans. Nasr, 726.

their entourage to practice the *salāt* (see Qur'an 19:32, 53–57; 14:40; 20:132). Gerhard Bowering finds traces of the use of the word Qur'an occurring before Muhammad's times.[30] Just as the term for blessing (*tasliya*), used as an epithet for the name of the Prophet, indicates that God's blessing, his prayer, is upon a person, likewise, in the Qur'an, Muhammad is told to bless those who have confessed their sins "as a comfort for them" (Qur'an 9:103). The whole of *sūrah* 21 is devoted to the prophets:

> And we bestowed upon him Isaac and Jacob as an added gift. And each of them we made righteous. And we made them imans; guiding according to Our Command. And we revealed unto them the doing of good deeds, the performance of prayer, and the giving of alms. And they were worshippers of us. (Qur'an 21:72ff)[31]

While the Qur'an often associates *salāt* with alms (*zakāt*), in *sūrah* 2:42 and 148, *salāt* is coupled with patience (*sabr*). The Qur'an does not otherwise mention the five columns of Islam. *Sūrah* 23:2–4 associates *salāt* with humility before God: "Prosperous are the believers who in their prayers are humble and from idle talk turn away and at almsgiving are active. . . ." Punctuality (*muhāfaza*) is also encouraged in the daily execution of the *salāt*. The term *kitāb mawkūt* is used to describe a service that follows strict rules:

> When you have completed the prayer, remember (and invoke) God standing and sitting and lying on your sides. Then, when you are secure, observe proper prayer; for prayer at fixed hours is prescribed for the believers. (Qur'an 4:103)[32]

Nonchalance in the execution of *salāt* is condemned (Qur'an 4:142) and sometimes attributed to the drinking of wine. Ablutions (*wudū*), or ritual purifications prior to prayer, are prescribed from the very beginning (Qur'an 5:6), and Friday prayer is also mandatory:

> O you who believe! When you are called to the congregational prayer, hasten to the remembrance of God and leave off trade. That is better for you, if you but knew. And when the prayer is completed, disperse

---

30 Bowering, "Prayer," 218.
31 Trans. Nasr, 822.
32 Trans. Nasr, 240.

throughout the land and seek the Bounty of God, and remember God much, that haply you may prosper. (Qur'an 62:9)[33]

Muhammad considered that those who adhered to Islam should immediately learn how to practice *salāt*. To this end, he sent As'ad b. Zurāra (or Mus'ab ibn 'Umair) to Medina to instruct neophytes in *salāt*, and sent letters to Arab tribes describing *salāt* as the duty of every Muslim.

The execution of a *salāt* fifty times a day is derived from the narrative of the night journey (*isrā'*) of Muhammad to Allah, where fifty daily *salāt* were prescribed to him. On Muhammad's way back to the earth, he met with Mūsa (Moses), who, on hearing what was required of the faithful, sent Muhammad back to Allah saying that it was simply not possible for Muslims to accomplish this. After several further trips between Allah and Moses, the number was finally negotiated down to five daily *salāt*.

Another well-known tradition explains how Muhammad learned to do the *salāt*. The archangel Gabriel in a single day taught Muhammad how to perform *salāt* and the correct manner of executing this prayer (al-Bukhārā, *Mawākāt*).[34]

And perform the prayer at the two ends of the day and in the early hours of the night. Truly the good deeds remove those that are evil. (Qur'an 11:114)[35]

This is confirmed by Qur'an 17:80, which prescribes a morning, a sunset, and a nocturnal *salāt*. In Qur'an 2:239, from the Medina period, an intermediary (*al-wusta*) *salāt* is mentioned, which may well imitate the threefold prayers (*tefillā*) executed by the Jews in that city.[36]

Thus, while there were only three *salāt* during Muhammad's lifetime, later two of them, the *salāt al-wusta* and the *ishāsalāt*, were reduplicated to make five a day. Whether this was a Persian influence or not, it seems to have occurred under the second Umayyad caliph Umar II (reigned A D 717 to 720), although it is still not completely clear when five *salāt* were prescribed; perhaps, in Muhammad's time, the five were condensed (by putting two together) into just three. In any case, since all the schools of Muslim law agree on five, one can imagine that this tradition was fixed by the end of the seventh century.

33 Trans. Nasr, 1372.
34 Wensinck, "*Salāt*," 101.
35 Trans. Nasr, 586.
36 From the root *hithpallel*, "to stand upright" and secondarily "to judge oneself."

With the exception of cemeteries, which are considered to be impure, the whole world—not just the mosque—is a suitable place for saying the *salāt*. In the mosque, attention is paid to the alignment of the rows (*al-saf*) of those who have come to pray. Just as the Jewish prayer begins with the *kawwānā*, the *salāt* begins with the declaration of one's intention (*nīya*). Again, as in the Jewish *tefillā* prayers, one begins by saying the *takbīr* "*Allāhu Akbār*," which delimits the sacred condition (*ihrām*) or purity necessary to accomplish *salāt*. After this, one says a prayer (*du'ā*), and the *salāt* continues with the *fātiha* said together and out loud with the *imām*.[37] Beginning with the second division (*kirā'a*), it suffices to listen to the voice of the *imām* reciting the subsequent prayers. Then follows:

- the first *rukū'* or bow (corresponding to the Jewish *kerī'a*)
- the standing position (*i'tidāl*): with one's hands in the air, obliging one to look heavenward to Allah, one says: "Allah listen to him who sings your praises."
- the prostration (*sujūd*), which is part of both Orthodox Christian and Jewish prayer. From the *fātiha* down to the second prostration forms one single *rak'a*. One says two *rak'a* for the morning *salāt*, four at the noon *salāt al-zuhr*, four for the afternoon *salāt al-'asr*, three for the sunset *salāt*, and four for the evening *salāt*.
- After the second prostration, while seated, one proclaims the profession of faith (*tashahhud*), then, still seated, says the hymns to the prophet with repetitions of the *salla Allāhu 'alayhiwasallam* ("May Allah honor him and grant him peace") and the final rite, the *salām*. During this concluding section, one turns to the right and to the left, repeating each time the complete formula (*al-salām 'alaykumwa-rahmatu Allāh*: "May the peace and mercy of Allah be with you") or an abbreviation thereof.

The drawing below, from T.W. Juynboll, lists these successive postures in numerical order.[38]

---

37 The Opening of the Book (*fātihat al-kitāb*) is apparently an addition, in that man addresses Allah, instead of Allah addressing man as in the other *sūrah*: "In the Name of God, the Compassionate, the Merciful. Praise be to God, Lord of the worlds, the Compassionate, the Merciful, Master of the Day of Judgment. Thee we worship and from Thee we seek help. Guide us upon the straight path, the path of those whom Thou hast blessed, not of those who incur wrath, nor of those who are astray." Qur'an 1:1–7, trans. Nasr, 5.

38 T.W. Juynboll, *Handleiding tot de kennis van de Mohammedaansche Wet* (Leiden: Brill, 1925), 60.

I   2   3   4   5
                           9   10   11

15   16   17

6   8   7
12   14   13

Basically, the initial sections (before the *kirā`a*) and the final parts (after the second *sujūd*) of each *rak`a* vary, while the central parts of each *rak`a* are identical.

In the prescriptions of the tradition (*sunna*), this simple and oft-repeated short prayer is augmented with many hymns and extracts from the Qur'an according to the occasion of its performance. Excessive additions were discouraged by Muhammad, who reminded these zealous *imāms* that there were elderly and young Muslims in their midst (*hadīth* of al-Bukhārā, *Kitab al-`Ilm*, b: 28). If, according to the *hadīth*, Muhammad tolerated greetings and the presence of children around him during the *salāt*, he eventually forbade these distractions. Muhammad had the reputation of being able to accomplish a *salāt* more rapidly and more completely than anyone else.

The nocturnal *salāt* is called *al-layl* or *tahajjud*. The latter designates the vigil, like the Syria *shahrā,* and, in fact, the composition of the *Ramadān* vigils, with readings from sacred scripture, meditation, and ritual prayer, formally resemble the Eastern Christian vigils that were practiced throughout the Middle East. Although not obligatory, these ascetic vigils were part of the earliest forms of communal prayer in Islam. Wensinck says that other *salāt,* for instance the feasts of `aīd al-Adha* (feast of Abraham's sacrifice) and the *salāt* for rain (*al-istisqā*), carried with them various older popular customs.[39]

Formally, the role of the *imām* resembles that of the leader (*shelīah has-sibbūr*) in the Jewish prayer service. Originally, Muhammad himself led the *salāt* until the day he became ill and Abu Bakr took over. The *imām* was initially the leader of the religious as well as the political community, and, even after the appearance of the first *khalīfa*, the leader of the formal (*fardh*) prayer services kept his title of *imām*, leader of the Sunni Muslim community in prayer.

Wensinck affirms that, wherever Islam took root in the Middle East, the *salāt* was the principal agent of the transformation of the pre-Muslim religious mentality. During the first two centuries of Islam, the *hadīth* confirms its importance by placing *salāt* as the second of the five pillars of Islam. Of the five pillars, four concern orthopraxis, and only one concerns matters of faith. The regular execution of the *salāt* is compared, in Islamic tradition, to a stream of good water flowing outside the door of each house. "If one enters these waters five times a day, do you think that impurity can remain?" (Mālik, *Kasr al-salāt fi'l-safar*, cited by Wensinck).[40] Al-Nasā'ī[41] says that the regular recitation of the *salāt* all by itself guarantees man's entrance into paradise. The *salāt* should be heartfelt, as any intimate conversation with Allah.

39 Wensinck, "*Salāt*," 105.
40 Ibid., 107.
41 Ibid., 197.

One says it *sotto voce* so as not to disturb the *salāt* of the person next to you. Thus reciprocity with a partner in prayer can be guaranteed: a famous *hadith kudsī* runs, "Allah said: I divided the *salāt* into two parts between myself and my servant; one part belongs to me and the other to my servant ... and he will obtain what he requested."[42] In some areas of the world, for instance in central Asia, the *salāt* is not observed with great stricture, but, in other countries—for example, Indonesia and Egypt—it is marked by a calm and modest piety, by sobriety, humility, and contrition.

For Bowering, the development of communal prayer took place in two phases: before and after the change in the direction of prayer, of the *qibla*.[43] From AD 610 to 623, Muhammad prayed in the direction of Jerusalem, but, on February 11, 624, during the *salāt* in Medina, he received a revelation to pray in the direction of Mecca, i.e., in the direction of the *qibla'* of the *ka'aba*. The earliest communal prayer of the first community thus evolved directly out of Muhammad's personal prayer: "command your people (or family) to observe the *salāt*" (Qur'an 20:132). Bowing in repentance recalls David's *sujūd*, his fear of the sentence of the Lord for his sins, but in the Middle East such bowing was also used before tribal chieftains, in royal courts, and in Christian worship. Still, Qur'an 22:27 implies that prostrations should only be used before Allah at the holy house created by Abraham, just as the angels do who have been brought near to God. The posture clearly depicts the meaning of the words of prayer, both the fear of God and hope in his mercy. The cosmos also bows before its Creator (Qur'an 22:18).

Exclamatory praise proclaiming Allah's transcendence appears some forty-four times in the Qur'an. The most famous is the *takbīr*: "*Allāhu Akbar*," which does not appear verbatim in the Qur'an but is mentioned therein (Qur'an 17:111; 74:3). Qur'an 17:1 is interpreted as the divine institution of the *salāt*, which occurred during Muhammad's night journey and ascension before God. Bowering shows that, in the Qur'an, one meets the Lord's face (*wajih*) wherever one turns (Qur'an 55:27), and those who "desire God's face" perform almsgiving (Qur'an 30:38–39).[44]

As stated above, recitation of the Qur'an was made an integral part of communal prayer early on (Qur'an 35:29), and the *fātiha* (opening *sūrah* of the Qur'an) seems to have been "composed" for an obligatory communal prayer. When the Qur'an is recited, those present "fall down on their faces in prostration," just as the patriarchs did (Qur'an 17:108–109; 19:59).

42 Ahmad b. Hanbal, II, 460; see Wensinck, "*Salāt*," 106–8.
43 Bowering, "Prayer," 219.
44 Ibid., 221.

The first communal prayers in Mecca were distinguished by prolonged night sessions (*tahajjada*), which would later be treated as non-obligatory (*nāfilatan* or *salāt al-nawāfil*). These nocturnal vigils may have been of Christian origin, for the Qur'an does mention a certain group of "People of the Book" standing to pray at night (Qur'an 3:113).[45]

Still, Muhammad claimed that the Qur'anic models of prayer were drawn from the precedents of Adam through Noah, and then from Abraham (Qur'an 14:38) and Israel (Qur'an 19:59), who "fell down prostrate (in prayer), weeping."

When the *salāt* performed at fixed times was consolidated along with almsgiving (or communal tax, *zakāt*) as an institutionalized obligation in the years before and after the *hijrah*, the Qur'an goes on to make it mandatory for women, too (Qur'an 33:33). In Mecca, the greeting "Peace be upon you" (*al-salām ʿalaykum*) is quoted as the salutation of the angels to the blessed in paradise (Qur'an 13:23–24; 39:73). In Medina, the greeting (*taslim*) of peace (*wa-sallimūtaslīman*) became the liturgical conclusion of the *salāt*, similar to the Jewish prayer or *tefillā*. It was also in Medina that the preparatory rituals (i.e., ablutions with water to purify from sexuality or intoxication) were instituted, as only those with pure hands could touch the Qur'an (Qur'an 56:76–9).

The *salāt* is inserted into a fixed *ordo* when performed in the mosque congregationally. The public call to prayer (*nādā*) following on from that of the muezzin from the minaret (*adhān*) appeared along with the *iqāma*, the second call to the mosque, for the day of assembly, the Friday market day. The initial sermon (*khutba*) pronounced from the pulpit (*member*) also took place in Medina, but the most revolutionary change there was the reorientation of the *qibla'*, reflecting the expulsion of the local Jewish tribes after the battle of Badr (Qur'an 2:142–150). This meant that the *kaʿaba* was becoming the holy mosque (*al-masjid al-harām*). From this point onward, says Bowering, "it visually symbolizes the shift from a religion confirming the scriptures of the 'People of the Book' (i.e., Jews and Christians) to an autonomous and newly directed religion reconfirming the natural monotheistic religion of Abraham. . . ."[46] The change in *qibla'* also coincided with the institution of the Ramadhan fast. That replaced the *asura* fast on the tenth day of the month of Muharram, the day that Allah saved the Children of Israel from Pharaoh, which paralleled the Jewish Day of Atonement.

The Qur'an claims that the Meccan sanctuary was laid out by Abraham and Ishmael (Qur'an 2:125–127); *duʿā* does reflect the invocation of

45 Ibid., 222.
46 Ibid., 226.

pre-Islamic deities (a dozen examples are found in the Qur'an) and is frequently mentioned in oaths. *Du`ā* can be an invocation for or against someone (Qur'an 17:11), but, in the Qur'an, *du`ā* becomes the invocation of Allah. In Qur'an 14:38–40, Abraham asks the Lord "to make me a performer of prayer" (*salāt*) and "accept my plea" (*du`ā*). So the two terms are elided despite the use of *du`ā* in earlier Arabic pagan prayer.[47] In the language of the Qur'an, the semantic fields of *du`ā, dhikr*, and *Qur'an* are related. Even the *al-Fātiha* is double-sided, i.e., it invokes God's name and demands that Allah not be angry. "For Allah is the true hearer of invocation" (Qur'an 14:40).

In Qur'an 20:13–14, *salāt* and *dhikr* (recollection of God) are paired when Moses is asked to "perform prayer of my remembrance" (*wa-aqāmi al-salātli-dhikrī*), for Satan would have Moses barred "from the remembrance of Allah" (*dhikr Allah*; Qur'an 3:58). *Dhikr* can mean: recalling Allah, reminding oneself of Allah, remembering Allah in one's mind and heart, mentioning Allah's name with one's tongue or one's heart (Qur'an 13:28).[48] The Qur'an itself and its recitation can be a way to remember Allah (Qur'an 7:63). An oath can be made "on" the Qur'an (38:1), as a serious reminder of what was said. Other sacred scriptures of the People of the Book are also ways of remembering Allah, for they are called "People of the Remembrance" (*ahl al-dhikr*, Qur'an 21:7). Remembrance is reciprocal (Qur'an 2:152), for, as we remember Allah, so he remembers us, and "the hearts of those that believe are at rest in God's remembrance" (Qur'an 13:28).

In this first "reading" of Muslim daily prayer, we have focused on an understanding of *salāt* drawn almost exclusively from the Qur'an itself. However, since—as in Christianity—it is artificial to separate scriptural texts from the authoritative tradition that interprets them, it is necessary to compare this perspective with several others, taken from the development of Muslim tradition. We turn first to consider a Sufi approach to *salāt*, which examines the relationship between the obligatory canonical prayer of the *salāt* and private contemplation, through the medium of "whispered prayer."

"Whispered Prayer" (Munājāt) as the Transition from *Salāt* to Private Contemplation according to the Sufi Tradition

The Sufi traditions penetrated both the strict Sunna (*Ahl al-Sunnah*, "People of the Tradition") and the Shia (*Shiat Ali*, the "Party of Ali"); their split occurred in 661 with the assassination of Ali. Massignon claimed that the widespread practice of *sotto voce* praying (from the root *num-jim-alif*, to communicate in

---

47 Ibid., 228–29.
48 Ibid., 230.

the ear of someone, from which is derived *nājiya* for confidential speech) after the *salāt*, called *munājāt* (a fervent whispered prayer), was the door through which "foreign" invocation and techniques of contemplation entered into Islam. It was only in Baghdad in the third century of the *hegira/hijrah* (AD 900s) that official Islam, the jurists and the doctors of dogmatics (*kalam*), began to combat these mystical practices. As the Sufi movement developed, it seemed to the jurists that *salāt* was taking second place to *dhikr* (meditation) and *wird* (esoteric knowledge). Any spiritual school of prayer that practiced "extra-*salāt*" invocation would be suspect. Two early Muslim mystics, al-Muhāsibi (died *hijrah* 243 or AD 867) and al-Tirmidhī (285 /AD 898), composed important reflections on the value of this post-*salāt* meditation.[49] Al-Tirmidhī, in turn, propounded a hierarchical scale of forty-two points for this mystical side of *salāt*. Later, it became common to call it *dhikr, remembrance* of God through recitation of His name. For some, the use of *wird*, formulaic invocations whose repetition favors meditating on Allah, became as important as (if not more so than) the daily recitation of the five *salāt*. Wensinck, in his article on *ka'aba* in the *Encyclopedia of Islam*, quotes an eleventh-century early Persian Sufi, Hudjwīrī:

> For ('Ali ibn 'Uthmān) Hudjwīrī the *salāt* is for novices an initiation onto the mystic path. Hudjwīrī however quotes some sayings of mystics, who no longer require the Ka'aba as an inducement to rise, and even despise it. Muhammad ben al-Fadl says: "I wonder at those who seek His temple in this world: why do they not seek contemplation of Him in their hearts? The temple they sometimes attain and sometimes miss, but contemplation they might always enjoy. If they are bound to visit a stone, which is looked at only once a year, surely they are more bound to visit the temple of the heart. . . . "[50]

Thus, for Hudjwīrī, ritual purity (*tahāra*) is the equivalent of conversion; the direction of Mecca (*qibla'*) that of the faithful's dependence on religious direction; the reciting during *salāt* that of the repetitions of formulae in *dhikr*. The prostrations (*rukū*') during the *salāt*, in turn, express humility; prostrations demonstrate self-knowledge. The final three sections said during the last portion of the *salāt*, when one repeats twice "*Assalamu 'alaykum warahmatu-Allah*"

---

49 Massignon *Passion d'Al-Hallaj*, 259, note 1.

50 See A.J. Wensinck and J. Jomier, "*Ka'aba*," in Encyclopedia of Islam Online, 2016. See also John Renard, trans., *Knowledge of God in Classical Sufism* (New York: Paulist Press, 2004), 38–40, 264–85. Ali Ibn Uthmān Hujwīrī (died c. 465/AD 1071) wrote the first major Sufi work in Persian and later lived and died in Lahore (now in Pakistan), where his tomb is still venerated.

("Peace and blessings of God be unto you"), facing once to the right, and once to the left, demonstrate renouncing of the world. The clearest example of the purification to be realized from such *salāt* is that of the "hidden Imām" (al-Mahdī, the eschatological redeemer of Islam), but this state of blessedness (*tashahhud*) is also the term for a Sufi stage on the way to *fanā'*, absent from self and present (*hadra*) only to God. Each Sufi emphasizes a different aspect of the presence (*hudūr*) of Allah and the absence (*ghayba*) of Allah. Hudjwīrī insists on devotion to *salāt*: "The state of one who has been withdrawn by God from visible appearance on earth, although he is still living invisibly on earth, is also called *ghayba*."[51] The disappearance (*fanā'*) or hiddenness (*ghayba*) of the person into Allah is in Sufi vocabulary used to describe the detaching of a person from his human attributes as he is engulfed into Allah.

For Avicenna (Ibn Sīnā), through *salāt*, one recognizes the existence of Allah and the necessity of His existence.[52] For each believer, this can be either an exterior or an interior recognition. The exterior aspect reflects the recognition by Muhammad that men need physical discipline to control their passions. Interiorly speaking, *salāt* represents the *mushāhadat al-haqq*, "surrender to the truth" of Allah with a pure heart, purified of all desires.

Among the numerous writings on *salāt*, al-Ghazālī (or Algazel), the great Persian Sufi (1058–1111), in his *Ihyā*, places *salāt* between ritual purity (*tahāra*) and almsgiving (*zakāt*), as do the schools of jurisprudence (*fikh*), and insists on its meticulous performance. As for the other devotions (*'ibāda*), al-Ghazālī distinguishes six interior states (*ma'ānī*) that give to the *salāt* the fullness of its meaning: the heartfelt presence (*hudūr al-kalb*), intelligence, esteem (*ta'zīm*), respect (*hayba*), hope and humility (*hayā*). Hātim al-Assam (d. 230/851) describes his ideal *salāt* as follows, and it is a useful reminder of how personal and interiorized *salāt* can become, especially since, from the outside, it can seem somewhat mechanical:

> When the hour for the *salāt* comes, I do a great ablution and head towards the place where I will do the *salāt*. There I sit down till my limbs are ready and I then rise facing precisely in the direction of the *ka'aba*, the *sirāt* (the narrow bridge which one must past on the day of judgment to get to paradise) at my feet, paradise (*jannah*) on my right and hell (*jahannam*) on my left, the angel of death behind me. And I reflect that this *salāt* is the last one I will perform during my life. Then it is that I vacillate between hope and despair, I recite the *takbīr* ("God is

51 Renard, *Knowledge of God*, 43.
52 Wensinck, "*Salāt*," 108.

great") with *tahkiki* (an incantation), I recite the *tartīl* (in an even slower incantatory mode), and I perform the *rukū'* with submission and the *sud-jūd* with humility, I sit on my left thigh, I stretch out the top of one of my feet, place my right leg on my big toe and I accomplish all this with *ikhlās* (serenity). I am unaware if my *salāt* has been accepted by Allah or not.[53]

Al-Ghazālī says that a *salāt* said with distractions only serves to distance oneself from God.[54] And in the chapter on the means to attain presence in the heart (*hudūr al-kalb*), Al-Ghazālī gives a list of the main thoughts, both exterior and interior, that provoke distractions or negligence (*ghafla*). The exterior ones arise from the senses; to avoid them, a small dark room is a good place to say the *salāt*. The interior distractions arise from the cares of this world and, above all, from desires. By preparing *salāt* with meditation on the world to come, our last destination (*akhira*) and The Day of Judgment, distractions diminish.

Concerning invocations, in general, it is difficult to exaggerate the contribution of the musical modes of recitation of sacred texts in the Semitic world. It seems that the ultimate source of the musical formulas for reciting prayers was the meaning of the words themselves, which gave rise to regular patterns of stress and pitch. Jewish modes, by which the eight tones of Byzantine chant were inspired, and the extraordinary elaboration and popularity of Arabic Qur'anic chant, cannot be ignored in any description of prayer.[55] But how to address the topic without introducing a full-blown ethno-musicology? In his book *The Mysticism of Sound and Music*,[56] the Indian Sufi Inayat Khan (1882–1927) attempted to specify the relationships between the sound of the words of prayer and music.[57] He connects the rhythm of musical chant to dance, while sound and voice have an effect for which the body is the intermediary. As the role of music in healing rituals demonstrates worldwide, vibrations and harmony affect the memory, the heart, and one's reason, even beyond the words of prayer themselves. While the Sufi movement was often a deeply ascetical one resembling the highest forms of monasticism in the West, we turn now to explore the fervor invested into prayer by the average Muslim.

53 Ibid.
54 Ibid.
55 Philippe Leroux, writing on the canons of liturgical music, remarks how difficult it has always been to define a particular musical tradition's marriage with a given language of prayer: Philippe Leroux, "Principes Liturgiques de Maxime Kovalevsky," Sagesse-Orthodoxe, last modified June 14, 2013, https://www.sagesse-orthodoxe.fr/wp-content/uploads/2013/06/Principes-liturgiques-de-Maxime-Kovalevsky.pdf.
56 Rockport, MA: Element Books, 1991.
57 Cf. also Inayat Khan, *The Sufi Message* (Delhi: Motilal Banarsidass, 1991).

Popular Muslim Understandings of *Salāt*

We come now to an overview of popular "market" Muslim understandings of *salāt*. How can we define "popular"? One option is to study the Muslim supplication manuals sold in markets and outside mosques, produced to aid common everyday prayer. Such manuals and booklets are available throughout the Muslim world and encourage the individual worshipper to deepen his or her prayer. Constance Padwick has made a study of these manuals in her book *Muslim Devotions*.[58] The advantage of using her anthology to elucidate the way everyday Muslims understand *salāt* is that her collection of manuals combines both orthodox and somewhat deviant understandings of Muslim prayer.

In the daily life of the Muslim worshipper, piety is composed of just such a compilation of cosmopolitan influences, stimulating devotion. Any attempt to separate out the prayer manuals by period and country of origin would be unscientific, that is to say, it would deny the medley of influences of this literature that circulates in the hands of modest Muslims worldwide today.[59] So Padwick structures devotional commentaries around the order of *salāt* drawn from the early saints (i.e., Uwais al-Qaranī or 'Al Zayn al-Abidīn), the medieval saints such as 'Abd al-Qādir al-Jīlānī (died A D 1166) or Abū'l-Hasan al-Shādhilī (died A D 1258) and the popular eighteenth-century Mustafā al-Badrī (1688–1749) and Ahmad al-Tījānī (1737–1815) as well as the nineteenth- and twentieth-century Sanūsī and rival al-Mirghanī, writers of devotion booklets.[60] Any quest for the *ipsissima ordo* of these devotional commentaries would also be artificial, ethnographically speaking, in the same way that one cannot separate out the use of the Qur'an as a psalter from its use as a lectionary.

Below, I have summarized some of the most interesting insights from Padwick's unusual collection of nineteenth- and twentieth-century "penny" pamphlets available in the bazaars. Only a person who had lived a long time in the Middle East—in her case over forty years—would have recognized the significance of these modest publications.

---

58   Constance E. Padwick, *Muslim Devotions: A Study of Prayer-Manuals in Common Use* (Oxford: One World, 1996 reprint).

59   John R. Bowen, *A New Anthropology of Islam* (Cambridge: Cambridge University Press, 2012), 11–41.

60   Padwick, *Muslim Devotions*, xviii–xx.

Reflections on "The Threshold" (or the Call to Prayer)

Anyone who has lived in a Muslim country has been awoken before dawn as the night comes to an end by the call (*takbīr*) to the first *salāt* worship: *Allāhu Akbār*. It is performed by an individual in the mosque of behalf of others to prepare their hearts to begin the day's cycle of prayers. The person who hears the *takbīr* should reply (*tarjī*): "God is most great (two times). I bear witness that there is no god save God. I bear witness that Muhammad is the apostle of God."[61] As an aside, let me mention that this call to prayer resembles the initial dialogues in the Eastern Christian liturgies between the priest and the deacon representing the congregation, as well as the introductory element to the *Shema* in the Jewish prayer.[62] In the Middle East, sometimes the shared spiritual Semitic roots are visible.

Today, in the Western media, one associates the phrase with the battle cries of urban riots. But, more seriously, more soberly, Muslims making the pilgrimage to Mecca kiss the sanctuary of the black stone with just this phrase. While men pray this invocation aloud, the rest of their prayers at the *ka'aba* are said *sotto voce*. This invocation, this *takbīr*, is so concise that Padwick finds almost no commentaries concerning it.

Magnifying the Lord has been ordered by the Qur'an (17:111): "And proclaim his greatness by magnifying." Some of the commentaries considered the *takbīr* a challenge to the dethroned demonic gods, who at the call to *salāt* return to challenge the faithful.[63] The proclamation of *Allāhu Akbār* is used on a multitude of occasions—sacrifices of animal flesh, epidemics, and for the protection of a newborn child.

Padwick's booklets take up the variation of *ordo* in the *salāt*, for instance saying that, in one *raka'āt,* or unit of a *salāt*, when there are two prostrations, eleven *takbīrāt* are appointed; however, when there are three prostrations, there are seventeen *takbīrāt*; during the devotions of the great feasts, twelve more are added; and so on. Thus these small tracts also give one a better command of the *salāt* in all its variations.

The first *takbīr* of the five *salāt*, called *takbīratu al-ihrām*, delimits the sacred zone of prayer. The *takbīr* is also used in funerals to declare the death of the deceased and to suggest that the deceased will next say the *takbīr* in the world

---

61 Ibid., 32.

62 "Hear, O Israel": the prayer composed from Deuteronomy 6:4–9 and 11:1–21 and Numbers 15:37–41.

63 Padwick, *Muslim Devotions*, 30–32.

to come.[64] In private devotions, the devotional booklets propose literally hundreds of ways to recite the *takbīrat*. The recognition of the greatness of Allah produces a quiet dignity, for, as they humbly proclaim, "Thy very greatness is a rest to weaklings as we are."[65]

The Prayer of Mediation

Both the person who makes the Call to Prayer and the second call (*iqāma*) from inside the mosque hall, as well as the one who hears it, go on to say what is called the prayer of mediation (*du'ā wu'l-wasīla*):

> O God, the Lord of this completed call and of the prayer-rite now inaugurated, give to our Lord Muhammad mediation and merit and a high rank, and that praiseworthy station which Thou hast promised him.[66]

Wasīla (mediation) as a noun is found twice in the Qur'an (5:34 and 17:54) and means a recommendation facilitating access. Despite restricting such mediation (*wasīla* or *shafā'a*) to Allah's intervention on our behalf, the desire to request intercession is very strong. In the Qur'an, one finds both forgiveness and sinful men unable to find forgiveness after their death (Qur'an 2:48, 123, 254; 7:53; 74:42–50). Mediation (*shafā'a*) is the strict prerogative of Allah (Qur'an 6:51, 70; 10:19; 32:3; 33:45). No one can intercede without the permission and approval of Allah: "And those on whom they call beside Him have not the authority for intercession" (Qur'an 43:86). Muslim journals are full of questions from their readers about the Divine permission for intercession, for some are tempted into "taking of helpers or mediators (*shafi'a*) other than God."[67] One answer to this issue: asking for intercession should be a matter of obedience. So we can ask Allah to appoint the Prophet as a mediator for ourselves. This is called a prayer of assurance (*du'ā 'l-wasīla*), for one has full confidence that one's petition is accepted through the *wasīla* of Muhammad. But who is included in the mediation of Muhammad: his own public (*umum*) or the whole Muslim community? With few exceptions, other prophets are dependent on the *wasīla* of Muhammad, who alone can intercede in both this world and the next. Any move from asking Allah for Muhammad's intercession to directly asking the Prophet to intercede is to

---

64 Ibid., 35
65 Ibid., 36.
66 Al-Bukhārī, quoted in Padwick, *Muslim Devotions*, 37.
67 Padwick, *Muslim Devotions*, 40.

turn mediation into the heresy of "associationism." Since the doctrine of the unity of Allah (*tawhīd*) is thus jeopardized, one should limit oneself to such prayers as that of 'Al Zayn al-Abidīn:

> If I remain silent no one will speak on my behalf and if I intercede for myself I am not worthy to be an intercessor. O God, call down blessing on Muhammad and his family and make Thy generosity the intercessor on behalf of my errors.[68]

In this way, one can see the unending battle in all Muslim countries between the strict Sunni and those who go to pray to Allah on the graves of local saints (*wali*) or friends of Allah.

The Intention (nīya)

For children as well as adults, acts of prayer are preceded by a declaration of intention. The benediction of the *nīya* can, in fact, be employed in any activity, and its extension beyond ritual use does not make it any less of a prayer.[69] One can use it as one walks toward the mosque. It can be used to describe the garment (*ihrām*) worn by Meccan pilgrims. Even when one proclaims one's intention, there remains an inner mental concentration of which writers like Al-Ghazālī, the Persian theologian who refuted Islamic Neo-Platonism, say the "recollectedness of heart is the spirit of set prayers.... Just so the prayer performance of one who is inattentive beyond the *takbīr* is like one alive but lacking movement" (*Ihyā'* 4:3).[70]

To describe the entering into the presence of Allah in spirit as well as in body, the manuals often cite phrases like "Deeds are only of value through the intention behind them," and "His rightness of intention makes a man's actions right." Al-Makkī takes Qur'an 2:151–152 to read that intention is more important than performance. So perfect observance of the ritual's form is secondary to spiritual purity of one's intention (see *Kash al-Mahjūb*).[71] To express the "presence of mind" (*hudūr al-kalb*), a superficial meaning can take a deeper signification, a heartfelt sense of the presence of the God one worships. On the other hand, the sincerity of intention (*ikhāsu al-nīya*)

---

68 Ibid., 45.

69 The *nīya* has its parallel in the Jewish *kawwānā*, meaning intention and devotion in the prayer, a meditative orientation of one's activity toward God.

70 Padwick, *Muslim Devotions*, 50.

71 Ibid., 51.

indicates a deep purification of intention that leaves space in one's heart for no other desire than for Allah. Thus one is united to the faithful intention of Muhammad. The ascetic's stripping off of all passions to arrive at singleness of heart is the result of the purification of intention that takes place in the heart, says al-Kūlīnī (a Shia jurist, d. 939), through purpose, determination, desire, and an act of will that leads to "full companionship" (see *Ahzabu wa awrādu Ahmad al-Tijānī*).[72]

The Prayer of Confrontation

Qibla', also called *mihrāb*, the niche in the wall of the mosque, physically indicates the direction of Mecca, of the *ka'aba*, in each and every mosque. Of course, when one is in front of the *ka'aba* in Mecca, one can pray before it from any of the four sides. Worldwide, the Muslim community of the faithful thus forms a ring around the *ka'aba*, albeit from afar. The Qur'an says (10:87) that Moses and Aaron in Egypt made their houses with a specific direction (*qibla'*) in which to pray, and one of the prayer manuals reports: "It is related that David said: O Lord, I find in the *Zabūr* [the Psalms] light streaming forth. Every time I recite it, my *mihrāb* is shaken, my heart rejoices and my mosque (or place of prostration) is lighted up."[73] This having been said, according to Padwick, the earliest devotional manuals show no sign that they knew that the earlier *qibla'* was Jerusalem.[74] For Muslims, Mecca and the direction toward it are a sort of spiritual reception address and the place which Muhammad described in the manuals as the heavenly *imam*—sometimes spiritualized, such as when heaven is described as the *qibla'* of petition.[75]

If the *qibla'* enshrines reception, the *mihrāb* originally was a throne, a niche where one was confronted (*tawajjuh*) with the royal presence. In Qur'an 3:38, it seems to mean a sanctuary of Allah's presence corresponding to a place in our hearts. Padwick cites glosses in devotional manuals identifying the spiritual and glorified Muhammad as the only one to fully have this "unique privilege of worship."[76]

The confrontation (*tawajjuh*) described in the Qur'an in a prayer attributed to Abraham gave rise to the prayer (*du'ā*), said in the *salāt* after the first *tasbīh*:

72 Ibid., 54.
73 Ibid., 55. The Book of Psalms (also called *Mazmur*) revealed to King David is mentioned three times in the Qur'an and, with the Torah (*Taurat*) and the Gospels (*al-injīl*), belongs to three "preceding" or earlier revelations of Allah.
74 Ibid., 55–56.
75 Ibid., 57.
76 Ibid., 58–59.

> Truly, as a *hanif*, I have turned my face towards Him who created the heavens and the earth, a sincere monotheist and I am not one of the idolaters. (Qur'an 6:79)

The *tawajjuh* is frequently employed to create a proper spiritual attitude before saying a *wird*,[77] as, for example: "Glory to Him who fills with the Light of His countenance the bases of His throne."[78] As an exclamatory prayer, such petitions requesting presence—also found in the Psalms, as we have seen above—are found throughout the Qur'an: "They desire the face of Allah"; "All things perish save the face of Allah" (Qur'an 28:88). These recall a Hebrew prayer, "The Lord turn his face toward you and give you peace" (Num. 6:26). The humility and concentration required to turn away from all things, for His sake only, is a great challenge. According to M.'Uthmān al-Mirghanī, "if a man in the *dhikr* (repetitive prayers) aims at becoming a saint, an idolater is better than he...."[79]

Padwick's sample collection of devotion manuals that explains *salāt* with two *raka'a* continues from the fifth constituent onward as thematically presented below:

5a. Worshipping with praise of transcendence
5b. Worshipping with praise of gratitude
6. Refuge-taking
7. the Name in worship
8. the Recitation
9. the worship of stillness
10a. Islamic witness (*shahāda*) to unity
10b. Islamic witness (*shahāda*) to the Prophet
11a. the calling down the blessing of the Prophet
11b. the calling down the blessing of Abraham and all the Prophets
12a. the worship of penance: the destitute sinner before his Lord
12b. the worship of penitence: the vocabulary of sinning in the manuals
12c. the worship of penitence: the forgiving Lord
13a. the worship of petition: traditional petition
13b. the worship of petition: the beggar at the door
14. the element of greeting

---

77 Related to recitation (*dhikr*), a *wird* is a verse taken from the Qur'an or elsewhere that one repeats.
78 Padwick, *Muslim Devotions*, 62.
79 Ibid.

It is their thematic vocabulary—of taking refuge, asking for pardon, and so on—and their semiology that show us that, behind the sobriety of their execution, *salāts* display a rich spectrum of deep human piety.

Muslim Prayer as Described by the Social Sciences

A number of academic ethnographies of Muslims communities have proposed other ways than the one used here to think of Islam.[80] These follow the basic methodological principles of modern sociology of religion. As with the works of social sciences more generally, these anthropologists take secularization's keystones of pluralism and tolerance for granted as the only way out of religious obscurantism. Yet their effort to structure values, where each religion is partially neutralized through co-habiting with others, presumes that pluralism is a social novelty. The situation on the ground is hardly that simple. Do non-practicing, "secularized" Muslims find such an approach comfortable? Islam is already a hybrid as one moves from one country to another, but normative Islam is hardly ignored by its "practitioners," no matter how embedded they are in their local culture. Does the social sciences' understanding of Islamic prayer make a home for those who can no longer pray? It is a hard question to answer. For the social scientist, a system of religious belief is fundamentally a set of interpretative resources and practices. How could they be otherwise, given the presumed contingent, contextual interpretative nature of religious endeavor? As has often been said since Nietzsche, there are no facts, only interpretations. Under such cognitive conditions, transcendence is a forbidden word to be avoided if prayer must be interpreted sociologically.

As Bowen claims, looking at the cutting edge of modern Islamic communications, Islam lies between the particular and the shared, between the creative and the imposed.[81] The basic interpretative practice of Islam is reciting (*qirā`a* has the same root as the word *Qur'an*, i.e., *q-r-'*), which provides contact with

---

80 See, for example, Bowen, *New Anthropology*; John Bowen, *Muslims Through Discourse: Religion and Ritual in Gayo Society* (Princeton: Princeton University Press, 1993); Janice Boddy, *Wombs and Alien Spirits: Women, Men and the Zār Cult in Northern Sudan* (Madison, WI: University of Wisconsin Press, 1989); Katherine Pratt Ewing, *Arguing Sainthood: Modernity, Psychoanalysis and Islam* (Durham, NC: Duke University Press, 1997); Joyce B. Flueckiger, *In Amma's Healing Room: Gender and Vernacular Islam in South India* (Bloomington: Indiana University Press, 2006); Saba Mahmood, *Politics of Piety: The Islamic Revival and the Feminist Subject* (Princeton: Princeton University Press, 2005); Magnus Marsden, *Living Islam: Muslim Religious Experience in Pakistan's North-West Frontier* (Cambridge: Cambridge University Press, 2005); Adeline Marie Masquelier, *Prayer Has Spoiled Everything: Possession, Power and Identity in an Islamic Town in Niger* (Durham, NC: Duke University Press, 2001).

81 Bowen, *New Anthropology*, 8.

the divine revelation (*tanzīl*). This is contextualized through the historical discipline of chains of transmission. However, into these chains of witnesses, the modern world introduced photocopy machines and, more recently, the Internet. Learning Islam in modern *madrasas* has become a system, capable of proposing roles for both scientific and religious praxis.

So how do social sciences present Muslim *salāt*, if at all? The social sciences are generally more at home asking other questions, especially those related to secularism, such as: if Islam is a religion of order and discipline, can a state co-opt this feature without being co-opted by Islam? We have said that social scientists propose several new ways of approaching Islam, so, among these various ways, is there anything "religious" about how they approach Muslim *salāt*? As prayer or worship of Allah is treated as separate from working for the welfare of other humans and participating in society as a whole, it is often difficult for social scientists to give studies of prayer the same importance as studies that concern broader aspects of life. Yet there are questions to be asked: how is the daily recitation of praise for Allah related to the social distinctions adopted for prayer? How does the pattern and shape of this daily prayer influence Muslims' relationship with Allah? Do prostrations of the body, as the Persian poet Rumi (Jalāl al-Dīn Muhammad Rūmī, 1207–1273) put it, exhibit the prostrations of the soul?

Despite the reluctance of anthropologists to address Muslim prayer in itself, steps have been taken to understand what happens in personal and communal prayer from the perspective of socio-linguistics, for instance in the anthology edited by Barbara Daly Metcalf, *Making Muslim Space in North America and Europe*.[82] Performative analysis attempts to explain that religious rituals are both socially and spiritually meaningful, for the congregation (*jama`a*) at prayer exemplifies both unity and equality, diagramming an orientation through belief. Charles Sanders Peirce (1839–1914), the "father of pragmatism," while not addressing Islam directly, developed an epistemology according to which certain acts "index" particular socio-religious statuses, which believers then take to be relations of co-presence.[83] Applied to Muslim *salāt*, this theory holds that *salāt*, as an obligation demanded by Allah, diagrams the *orans*'s submission to his will. An individual worshipper can index his or her status in the congregation even more clearly if he or she decides to stay afterward for mediation and contemplation through the repetition of further prayer formulas (*dhikr*).

82 Barbara Daly Metcalf, ed., *Making Muslim Space in North America and Europe* (Berkeley: University of California Press, 1998).

83 Charles S. Peirce, *Selected Writings: Values in a Universe of Change*, ed. Philip P. Wiener (New York: Dover, 1966).

Thus the supposed legitimacy of divine authority becomes a theater for social performance and a commentary on matters that concern the social relations of those present in the mosque. The power to decide on *ordo* is taken to found the discussions of the organization of the prayer rite. For instance, the selection of Qur'an texts for recitation during a *raka`a* may or may not be controversial; saying the prayer *bismillah* aloud (as modernists do) or silently (as did the Prophet, whose example is attested in a reliable *hadīth*) becomes an issue. When talking about the everyday attitudes of Muslims, the social sciences feel more at home dealing with popular Muslim understandings of *salāt*. As Bowen insists, these indexes of social affiliation provide endless possibilities above and beyond the main aim of worship.[84] By indexing worshippers' piety, one goes beyond the necessary sincerity of intention to opinions about one's disposition, internal states, and bodily habits.

When commonsense observations are made by many Muslims daily, these are the kind of observations social scientists are looking to find. For example, some people practice *salāt* seriously (with commitment, *iltizām*), then abandon it for a few years to engage in welfare work or even in political struggle. So an inevitable part of personal piety is that it may become public, with all sorts of different registers. It may make little sense anthropologically to ask what *salāt* means if we are already in the process of asking ourselves if we should choose other ways to approach God or neglect him altogether. Here the priority for social science is to see how, when Muslims are transforming their inner selves, they are providing a socialized performance of their inner sentiments.

Worship and sacrifice are interpreted locally in mosques by referring to commonly accepted "revealed" traditions. Personal prayer and healing rites may lead one away from the commands of the Qur'an, outside the Muslim framework of belief, as one tries to change the world with spells and invocation. Still, is all healing heretical? Might such practices draw down God's benevolence? These are questions also asked by Muslims. Spells in vernacular languages entreat spirits to leave the afflicted person by acting on unseen objects, spirits, and/or Allah. De Certeau pointed out that the ancient local praxis usually subsists inside the society by a complex articulation based on a separation between the beliefs that these practices may convey and their actual use, which no one is ready to give up entirely.[85] The fact that these societies have been, until recently, untouched by nihilism, atheism, and religious indifference creates conditions for a wholly different symbiosis.[86]

84 Bowen, *New Anthropology*, 54.
85 Michel de Certeau, *L'Ecriture de l'histoire* (Paris: Gallimard, 1978), 153–212.
86 See Stephen C. Headley, "Nier Allah, Réflexions javanaises sur la conversion à l'Islam,"

A diversity of rituals does not have to call Allah into question. One can, however, use these "marginal" rituals to attack the legalist Islam that would control any and all prayer as a cultural and religious "capital," both inside and outside the mosque.[87] More simply, ritual meals with Qur'an recitation are held worldwide on behalf of their hosts. A voluntary offering (*sadaqa*) of a cow for a feast puts the onus of moral responsibility for the sacrifice on Allah and the neighbors who participate. Prayers (*du'ā*) can simply ask that the malefactor receive the punishment he intended for his victim and avoid social disruption, because the prayer is private, not heard out loud. It is the *du'ā* that finds the person responsible for the illness. The notion that *du'ā* "sends" blessings to the dead and "benefits the living through reciprocal economy, and punishes misdeeds" can be justified by recalling that nothing should happen without God's consent, as Bowen reminds us.[88]

But do healing rites bring with them a theory of knowledge and become a theory of power, since humans individuate the light (*al-Nūr*) of Muhammad's energies captured in their own souls by *ma'arifa* (gnosis)? The main problem with such an explanation is that, when all is said and done, the only value that social sciences have no trouble recognizing is power, and they find it everywhere hiding under other guises, such as the traditional wisdom required by para-medical healing techniques.

For instance, social sciences have studied how the value of the Arabic letters in a patient's name can be used for creating amulets.[89] This is clearly a long way away from reading the Qur'an based on an eternal tablet protected in heaven. Why not simply stick with the notion that Allah alone creates primordial distinctions and let the polythetic categories of peasant Islam be what they are: relations of equivalence referring to different horizons of belief in the form of a syncretic transmission of authority? The point is that authority is a value and part of a larger hierarchy and not a uni-dimensional power. One is not dealing with administrations but healing through invocations in a complex cultural configuration. Healing techniques are a form of genuine prayer, but composed of notoriously hybrid notions and formulas.[90] A syncretic cult may cross cultural and religious boundaries in the interest of

---

in *Nier les Dieux, Nier Dieu*, ed. Gilles Dorival and Didier Pralon (Aix-en-Provence: Presses Universitaire de Provence, 2002), 393–404.

87 Stephen C. Headley, "Afterword: The Mirror in the Mosque..." in *Islamic Prayer across the Indian Ocean*, ed. Headley and Parkin, 213–38.

88 Bowen, *New Anthropology*, 106.

89 Flueckiger, *Amma's Healing Room*; Bowen, *New Anthropology*, 108–9.

90 See Stephen C. Headley, "Notes sur les types de soignants à Java," in *Soigner au Pluriel: Essais sur le pluralisme médical*, ed. Jean Benoist (Paris: Les Éditions Karthala, 1996), 218–40.

gender differences. For instance, women who are not allowed to direct the weekly *salāt* in the mosque may seek animate healing on sites outside the realm of conventional Islamic rituals.[91] Prayer as a locus of a community's concern exceeds the limits of *salāt*.

Inversely, Janet McIntosh describes how possession in Kenya rites reinforced the limits of the spirits' cultic boundaries, which had the effect of encouraging conversion to Islam. Here possession embodies ideas about their own *girama* impurity.[92] Bowen concludes that people employ such sacred and spiritual powers to create and transform other social boundaries.[93]

A final question: are these spiritual forces so accessible and easy to manipulate? Does Islam provide the repertoire of classifications and justification for such "social" therapies that have their origin outside of Islam, or does Islam more often resist being drawn into ambiguous practices in order to maintain its distinctive and all-inclusive prayer rite, the *salāt*? It is interesting to see how *salāt* appears in a non-monotheistic Indian context. *Salāt's* initial inspiration was to combat polytheism, and it never lost this orientation. But, by its desire to focus exclusively on praising the unity (*tawḥīd*) of Allah, as we have seen in the preceding "readings" of *salāt*, it creates a division between spaces "inside" and "outside" the mosque—and, inevitably, much of life will take place in the space "outside." Even if the compassion of Allah reaches out into the world, the territory of faith is strictly delimited and impossible to enforce.

In the next chapter on India and in the final chapter on Buddhism, we will address the profound cultural roots of South Asia, where Islam, while present, has little influence. Here, on Islam's periphery, the spread of ancient Indian cosmologies structures Asian religiosity down to the present day. In India, this gives Islam a clear identity, a purity, which is also the reason for its marginality. Below, I have diagrammed the tensions exercised in such a cultural context and the spectrum of theologies to be found on either side of Islam.

PANTHEISM AND ANCESTRAL CULTS	ORTHODOX ISLAM	RADICAL MONISM
The Creator is identified with the energies found in the cosmos by correspondence between macrocosm and microcosm.	Affirms a diminishing analogy of being as existence, emanates downward from Allah toward the cosmos.	Affirms that creation does not truly exist and is an illusion (as in the Saivite *māyā*), for all being is contained in the divine.

91 Masquelier, *Prayer Has Spoiled Everything*.
92 Janet McIntosh, "Spirits and Social Change," *Kenya Past and Present* 34 (2004), 68–72.
93 Bowen, *New Anthropology*, 118.

Conclusion

At the outset, we mentioned that, as Islam reacted to the ambient Jewish and Christian monotheism, it sought to free itself to define a "purer" monotheism. This it certainly accomplished, for such religious conversion or encounters have an existential character; a religious theme has a totally new significance for its seeker. In our first reading, *salāt* in the Qur'an appears as an inner prostration favoring the discovery of the grace of Allah's compassion through obedience to His commandments. In our second reading, we saw how the very intensity of *salāt* led to a prolonging of meditation on the words of these prayers and to the creation, both among the Sunni and the Shia, of the Sufi current, with its elite leaders and popular devotional following. In our third reading, we saw, in pamphlets distributed through the Muslim diaspora, a fervent popular meditation that allowed the *umma*, the Muslim community, to deepen its prayer life. Our fourth reading followed social scientists in their search for an adequate description of the network of religious authority and political power on the local level. We found that, in every instance, the social sciences' objectification of religious elements is motivated by the desire not to take belief on its own terms, as devotion to the author of the Qur'an and the revelation of *salāt*. Below is one prayer that may be said at the end of a reading from the Qur'an. For social scientists to engage with such deep respect is indeed a stumbling block; how can they describe what to any Muslim is self-evident—that Allah is speaking to them through the Qur'an?

> Author of the book of existence and of the Divine Word that is the Qur'an, we thank Thee for having given us the opportunity to live day and night all these years with Thy Word and to be transformed by this indescribable experience. Whatever we have been able to achieve is the result of Thy succor, and for whatever imperfection exists in our work we take full responsibility, asking for Thy Forgiveness before the Throne of Thy Mercy. Absolute Perfection belongs to Thee and to Thy revealed Word alone, no Translation or commentary on Thy Word by human beings can share in a Quality that is Thine alone.... [94]

So, for Muslims, since religious science is a *religious* study in the proper sense of the word, it is a discovery of grace (*Rūh Allāh*), an experience that is indeed, as proclaimed by the prayer above, "indescribable."

---

[94] Nasr, trans. *Study Qur'an*, xlix–l.

CHAPTER 4

Hindu Understandings of Prayer: Bhakti Poetry

THE RICH HISTORY AND TRADITION OF INVOCATION IN India leaves us with a dilemma: where to start if we are to discuss Hindu understandings of prayer? We will take as our focus Hindu *bhakti* devotional poetry, a distinct prayerful voice within the multitude of Hindu traditions. Yet, in order to understand the phenomenon of these early Tamil poetic devotions, which later spread to all of India, we must first trace their origins in India's formative texts. We begin, therefore, with an overview of prayer in the earliest hymns in the *Rig-Veda* (1500 and 900 BC) and trace how, over a thousand years later, these ancient forms recur and weave themselves into subsequent forms of devotional chanting, in both homes and temples. From there, we move to examine selections from the *Bhagavad-Gītā* (ca. 450–100 BC), which take us from the time of the *Rig-Veda* up to the dawn of Tamil forms of Bhakti poetry, that constitute the main focus of this chapter. Finally, I will turn to a case study of a long prayer-hymn to the goddess Durgā, and to a brief sketch of domestic prayer: how the average Hindu prays at home.

The prayers written by the *bhakti* devotional poets serve as a good focus for the study of so-called Hindu prayer, because their beauty and originality makes them appealing and accessible, and their style makes them almost modern. They also represent a distinct personal, individual form of prayer used by laymen and prayed in the vernacular, as opposed to the formal Sanskrit public rituals presided over by the Brahmin.

In the course of the chapter, I have also included brief excursuses to examine the parallels between Hindu understandings of prayer and those forms of prayer we have already considered so far—Christian, Jewish, and Muslim.

Prayer in India

Indians are implicated in prayer to an astounding degree. Morning and eve-ning, all over India, one can see them praying, sacrificing, fasting, and sharing alms. Yet, despite the ubiquity of religious observance, to study Hindus at prayer is no easy matter. It challenges many of the suppositions *we* have about invocations, for, while Hindu piety and devotion may seem superficially similar to monotheistic prayer, their cosmology and their understanding of personhood differ substantially from those of the monotheistic religions we looked at earlier in this study.[1] In addition to this, for our study of prayer, we have focused on oral, verbal prayer that is presented in written texts, and thus the many non-verbal aspects of Hindu worship—sacrificing, burning incense, fasting, and almsgiving—cannot, for our purposes, be explored as prayer in the same sense.

The diversity of Indian traditions makes it useful to focus not on the "objects" of beliefs—the termite hills, sacred rocks, and fashioned images—but on the formulations, the words of their invocations.[2] Just as partners are required in conversation, so prayer requires an "alterity" that escapes us as non-Hindus, but which is observable if we do not approach it as a kind of fetishism, superstition, or an exaltation of our own delusions. Empathy is not without its pitfalls, but, without empathy, we risk assuming that the poetry of this prayer, no matter how beautiful or trite, is basically nonsense. Reframing Hindu cults as communication and communion requires that we rein in our conceptual prejudices and try to feel, smell, and touch something of the *hic et nunc* of their experience.

In this chapter, we will follow the appearance of non-ritualized prayer in the landscape of Hindu religious praxis. However, it should be remembered that, even if our focus is on devotion poetry and prayer, rituals almost always find their way back in to create performances. Not only rituals but also myths, ancient and modern, influence the iconography and the narratives used in prayer.

1 For overviews of Hindu devotion, see Vasudha Narayanan, *The Vernacular Veda: Revelation, Recitation and Ritual* (Charleston: University of South Carolina, 1994); A.-M. Esnoul, "Le Courant Affectif à l'intérieur du Brahmanisme Ancien," *Bulletin de l'Ecole Française de l'Extrême-Orient* 48 (1956), 141–207; M. Biardeau, "L'activité et le principe spirituel humains dans la pensée Brahmanique de la période classique," in *Problèmes de la Personne*, ed. Ignace Meyerson (Paris: Ecole Pratique des Hautes Etudes/Mouton, 1972), 65–80, and ibid., "L'Absence de l'individu dans l'Inde," in *Problèmes de la Personne*, 99–109.

2 Christian theology distinguishes between "idols" and "images." See Jean-Luc Marion, *Dieu san l'être* (Paris: Presses Universitaires de France, 1991), 28–35. For a well-known effort to understand *darshan*, seeing and being seen in the temple, see Diana L. Eck, *Darśan: Seeing the Divine Image in India,* 3rd edition (New York: Columbia University Press, 1998).

It is necessary to note, for example, that Hindu mythology and cosmology itself has shifted to a much greater degree than in the monotheistic religions we have studied up to this point—and, with this shift in cosmology, there has been a shift in attitudes and approaches to prayer. Divinities of the earliest Vedic pantheon underwent radical change, becoming good or evil, better or worse; their status and rank within the pantheon displayed them as fiercer or more compassionate according to the evolution of their cults.[3] The ongoing elaboration of Indian mythology, beginning with the ancient (ca. 1500 BC) collection of the Veda ("knowledge"), consists of polymorphous texts that allow us to understand how some important divinities shifted within, and even disappeared from, this mythological landscape. These myths were subsequently developed in the genre of *Purâna* (literally "from ancient times," a vast range of texts dating from AD 200 onward), which contains prolonged and elaborate myths of divinities' exploits. Finally, these Puranic developments came to recompose Vedic hymnography in the form of devotional prayer poems called *bhakti*.[4] The earliest great songs to the paramount goddess, the *Devī-Māhātmya*, one of whose battles conquering evil is illustrated below, combines mythological narrative and four intense hymns of praise (*stotra, sukta,* or *stūti*).[5] These are still sung in rituals and available chanted in Sanskrit on cassettes in temple markets, as well as in translation into southern Indian languages like Tamil.[6]

The changing place of rituals in India, too, has an impact on the non-ritual forms of prayer we shall examine. Early studies of the origins of the Hindu

---

3 To a lesser extent, the same could be said of the classical Greek pantheon from 1500 to 500 BC. For similar examples from Ceylonese Buddhism, see Gananath Obeyesekere, *The Cult of the Goddess Pattini* (Chicago: Chicago University Press, 1984), and, for Bengal, see Rachel Fell McDermott, *Mother of My Heart, Daughter of My Dreams* (Oxford: Oxford University Press, 2000), 298–300.

4 Charlotte Vaudeville, *Myths, Saints, and Legends in Medieval India* (Delhi and Oxford: Oxford University Press, 1999).

5 Jean Varenne, *Célébration de la Grande Déesse (Devī-Māhātmya)* (Paris: Belles Lettres, 1975).

6 It is textually attested in Sanskrit ca. AD 500. The first translation into a European language was in Latin in 1831 by Ludovicus Poly; later, it was translated into European languages including Greek (1953). In Vindyācal, there has long been a pilgrimage center where the *Devī-Māhātmya* and the *Devī Bhāgavata Purāna* are recited as central to the worship of the goddess. Cynthia Ann Humes has conducted an ethnographic study of hundreds of pilgrims there to understand which texts they choose to recite and how. See Cynthia Ann Humes, "Glorifying the Great Goddess or Great Woman? Hindu Women's Experience in Ritual Recitation of the *Devi-Mahatmya*," in *Women and Goddess Traditions: In Antiquity and Today*, ed. Karen Torjesen and Karen King (Minneapolis, MN: Fortress Press, 1997), 39–63.

religion, conducted during colonial times, tried to measure the age and breadth of Vedic beliefs compared to contemporary religious customs.[7] Yet the interest in major philosophical currents should not have neglected ancient or recent rituals, considered as popular superstitions, even if these, based on deep religious sentiments, are not well understood by those who practice them. An individual's devotion to his gods is a psychosomatic whole, composed of actions, gestures, and concepts.

It was not because the Brahmanic rituals were abandoned 2,000 years ago that most philosophical schools denigrated the value of other kinds of ritual actions, as is often claimed.[8] The expensive and complex royal consecration, still appreciated by some kings in the first millennium, could not compensate for the disappearance of the naturalistic preoccupation of the Vedic and Brahmana rituals when the population no longer believed they were necessary.

The transitory vanities of this world became the object of disciplines searching to escape the here and now. Beyond the realm of forms lay reality itself, and, in the first centuries BC, both Buddhism and Jainism were anxious to demonstrate this in the face of Vedic ritualism. The *sannyāsin* ascetics—those who renounce this world to approach the eternal truth—needed no rites. However, the Mīmāmsā school of ritual affirmed, alongside its search for Brahman (*brahmajijñāsā*), the equal importance of action (*dharmajijñāsā*) in maintaining world order. In its analysis of the value of action, it retained, for the *sannyāsin*, a liturgical role as authorized by the *Bhagavad-Gītā* (V, 2, 6 and 7). If a *sannyāsin* does not officiate during rituals as a priest, he attends temple ceremonies and conducts his own private rituals.

While the great non-dualist philosopher Sankara (AD 788–820) taught that the world was an illusion masking Being, Rāmānuja (AD 1017–1137), a qualified non-dualist, taught that the world manifested Being. Even a Buddhist like Nāgārjuna (ca. AD 150–250), who taught that objects have no proper being, or the Vijnānavādin school, who treated objects as pure psychological projections, tolerated some rituals. For the latter, the highest level of the real (*paramārthasatya*) was empty, free of its own being (*svabhāvasūnya*), but there nevertheless existed an "enveloping real" (*samvrtisatya*) where it was possible to act. These Vijnānavādins were also practitioners of *yoga* (*Yogacara*), which enabled them to grasp the illusory quality of the physical and psychological world. Even Sankara allowed his disciples to continue to observe certain

7 See Jean Filliozat's preface to Rasik Vihari Joshi, *Le Rituel de la Dévotion Kṛṣṇaite* (Pondichéry: Institut Français d'Indologie, 1959), i–viii.

8 Louis Renou, *Le destin du Veda dans l'Inde* (Paris: Publication de l'Institut de Civilization Indiennes, 1960), 21–22.

rites favoring the well-being of the world. Rāmānuja considered that rites were necessary for a *sannyāsin*, calling ritual a disciplined activity favoring self-knowledge: this self-knowledge allows us to understand that we are not the agents of our actions, and so the great rituals (*mahāyajna*, proscribed by the laws of Manu) should be maintained. In Rāmānuja's *Nityagrantha* on daily rites, or purification, adoration and meditation are proscribed in detail, and he certainly used initiation rituals to initiate disciples into his congregation. The five "sacraments" that marked a newcomer's initiation into a disciple included *tāpa*, the mark of fire of the *cakra* and the *sankha* on the shoulders; the *ūrdhvapundra* or imposition of the emblem of the sect on the forehead; the *nāma* or giving of a new "slave" name expressing commitment to the religion; the revelation of the mantra; and the *yāga* or presentation of a sacrifice before the divine image. Ever since the Tamil poets, whom we will study below, a Vaishnava served Vishnu as a slave would his master.

In subsequent centuries, there were many disputes about which rituals to use, as seen, for example, in Rāmānuja's effort to impose a cult of Jagannātha according to the Pancarātra texts and traditions. The Vaishnava practices of South India had spread to Orissa, where they passed to Bengal via Caitanya (1486–1534), along with devotion to Vishnu using an eclectic ritual for Krishna.

Thus both rituals and mythology shifted, with an equal shift in approaches to and understandings of prayer. If innovation and development did take place, there is nothing to indicate that Indians are disturbed by this fact. In southern India, after A D 500, much of their cult and invocations came to focus on the hagiography of the saint-poets who renewed the celebration of their gods through vernacular devotional poetry.[9] The extent to which these poets' religious visions are responsible for the changes in the biographies of Hindu divinities cannot always be determined, but their high-quality poems, sung throughout India, are certainly responsible for the continuing popularity of Shivā and Krishna/Vishnu, and it is these prayer-poems that we shall study in this chapter.

Unlike the *Purânas*, which spread throughout India, the Dravidian hymnography of south India influences the "Sanskrit" north, with its dozen Tamil *ālvārs* (poet-saints) "immersed in God." These poets celebrated their longing and love for Lord Vishnu, incarnate as Krishna, from the sixth to the ninth centuries in Tamilnadu. The earliest Shaiva forms of devotion are found in the late theistic *Svetasvatara Upanisad*, designating the absolute as "Shivā" and

---

9 C. Mackensie Brown, *The Devī Gītā: the Song of the Goddess. A translation, annotation, and commentary* (Albany, NY: State University of New York Press, 1998); Tracy Pintchman, *The Rise of the Goddess in Hindu Tradition* (Albany, NY: State University of New York, 1994); and McDermott, *Mother of My Heart.*

employing the word *bhakti* for the devotion one pays in relation to him.[10] Later, Vaishnava *bhakti* (devotional) movements spread throughout the subcontinent. Distinct from the Sanskrit hymnography and Vedic cult, which were the exclusive privilege of the Brahmins, this new *bhakti* devotion was open to all Indians of whatever caste. Even the frontier between Hinduism and Islam was crossed through the fervor of these religious bards.[11]

Prayer in the Rig-Veda

The 1,028 hymns of the *Rig-Veda* have been sung daily throughout India since their "creation" in the second millennium BC. They have also resonated throughout the centuries in the subsequent hymnography of Hindu devotional poetry like the Tamil *Tiruvaymoli*.[12] Even if the pantheon and rituals of the Vedic age are now the preoccupation of a limited circle of Brahmins, they merit consideration here because of their prominence in the Indian religious landscape.

Vedic hymns were revealed as sound (audition, *śruti*), sacred syllables, words, and phrases exhaled by Brahman itself. Since Brahman is the infinite, eternal truth, the idea of these hymns as Brahman's own words bears some resemblance to the Christian and Jewish belief that prayer is always a gift from God to man, a case of God gifting his own words by which man might pray to him. Prayer is God's words on man's lips. The Vedic hymns had been conserved with their exact tonal accents and inflections in order to accompany ritually prescribed gestures used in Vedic sacrifices. Sound itself was a deity (*deva*), expressing the divine order (*rita*) in speech.

Before discussing the prayers of the *Rig-Veda* itself, it is necessary to say something about the collection's cosmogony, for the psalm-like hymns it contains situate prayer vis-à-vis creation and, thus, man's position as a created, praying being: a Hindu anthropology.[13] Within the theme of creation, three aspects are of particular importance: cosmogony, the (sacred) word, and sacrifice.

10 S. Radhakrishnan, *The Principal Upanisads* (London: George Allen & Unwin, 1953), 707–50. The even earlier *Shatarudriya Upanisad* lacks the term "*bhakti*," although it seems to acknowledge this form of devotion.

11 Jackie Assayag, *La colère de la déesse décapitée* (Paris: CNRS Editions, 1998).

12 Narayanan, *Vernacular Veda*, 19.

13 Stephanie Jamison and Joel Brereton, trans., *The Rigveda: The Earliest Religious Poetry of India* (Oxford and New York: Oxford University Press, 2014), 3 vols. The *Rig-Veda* is less well known to the average "Hindu" than are the *Yajur* and *Sāma Vedas*, which fulfill functional and meditative roles in rituals. These rituals serve earthly well-being (order/*dharma*, wealth/*artha*, and erotic love/*kāma*), whereas the *Rig-Veda* is more philosophical and provides a prelude to the great philosophical texts of the *Upanisads*. See Christine Mangala Frost, *The Human Icon: A Comparative Study of Hindu and Orthodox Christian Beliefs* (Cambridge: James Clark, 2017), 16–17.

Creation and Cosmogonies in the Rig-Veda

By the time the Aryans settled in the area of present-day Punjab, the chief Vedic divinity, Varuna, was already in decline and a formerly minor deity, Indra, was taking prominence.[14] Sacrifice was central to their ritual economy, and the fire deity, Agni, took on the role of patron and was displayed with brilliant invocations.[15]

At the same time, beyond the empirical world, the *rishi*, ascetics, learned to attend to their inner voices using techniques of concentration. It is from there that, in the late Vedic era, a higher reality was conceived, Brahman: not just another deity (*deva*) but a deep principle that allowed the cosmos to expand and inhere harmoniously. The Brahmin held verbal competitions to exchange formulae seeking to express this mystery, and the *Rig-Veda* collection consists of verses, prayers, and praises to be recited during sacrificial rituals.

Throughout the *Rig-Veda*, sacrifice and cosmogony are strongly linked. The preeminent cosmic deity, Prajāpati, wields as his weapons the *bandhu*, the ritual correspondences between heaven and earthly realities that permit a "yoking" of heaven and earth in a meso-cosmos. Prajāpati himself is the *bandhu* ("counterpart") of the year, since time emanated from his corpse on the day of creation. From his sacrificial body emanate the gods, whose limbs dismembered in sacrifice are also his *bandhu*.

In the *Brāhmanas*—commentaries on the sacrificial rituals for which the *Rig-Veda* provides hymnography—Prajāpati, their sacrificed creator, merges with another figure, Purusha.[16] Purusha is an archetypal man who, by allowing himself to be immolated, permits the world to come into being. Sacrifice is essential to this understanding of cosmogony and creation.

Themes of sacrifice and creation in the *Brāhmanas* also extend into the question of life after death, of freedom from mortality. In a charter myth found in *Jaiminīya Brāhmana* (2.60–70), Prajāpati swallows up Death "so that Death can become his *ātman* (inner self), becoming himself the sacrifice, (so) the sacrifice frees himself from death."

Further, in the *Satapatha Brāhmana* (II.2.2.5), both Purusha and Prajāpati

---

14 J.C. Heesterman, *The Broken World of Sacrifice: An Essay on Ancient India* (Chicago: University of Chicago Press, 1993), 123.

15 Roberto Calasso, *Ardor* (London: Allen Lane, 2013), traces the morphologies of this movement.

16 A *brāhmana* is a later (ca. 1000–800 BC) explanation in prose of one of the Vedic collections (*samhita*). By the time al-Biruni (eleventh century AD) wrote, the Veda had recently been committed to writing after having been transmitted orally for some 2,500 years.

are sacrificer and victim, for all sacrifices are this one sacrifice. Prajāpati, longing for offspring, practiced asceticism, and heat arose in his person that emanated divinities (*deva*), demons (*asura*), and all the Vedic hymnography, as well as human beings and the natural world. When he woke up, Agni put him back together again, making the world viable.

From there comes the idea that, with the knowledge of the correspondences or *bandhu*, sacrifice allows one to construct a stronger inner self, a godlike soul (*daiva ātman*) that continues to live after corporeal death. The art of the sacrifice taught that intuition into one's *ātman* emerges from the sound of his deepest speech like an "inner" fire. Later ritual texts even claimed that *solitary* meditation was just as effective as collective sacrifice for creating a divine *ātman*. Thus the sacrificer was no longer a divine celebrant, a *devayajnin,* but a self-sacrificer (*atmayajnin*). He was filled with the power of truth and reality, the energy of *brahman*.[17] Thus emerges in India, for the first time, the vision of an autonomous independent self, not to be confused with the modern Western individual, however.[18]

The *Brāhmanas* are interesting, and certainly reflect Vedic tradition, but it will help to study, briefly, the original hymns of the *Rig-Veda* itself, which touch most clearly upon the questions of creation and sacrifice.

The tenth book of the *Rig-Veda* presents us with hymns of individual reflections, speculations, and meditations that reflect the idiosyncratic explorations of a transcendent realm. There is no overall system to be discovered in these ruminations; each hymn is a separate poem. Yet the relations they discover between Purusha and Prajāpati are still relatively consistent. As Raimon Panikkar puts it, Purusha is "cosmo-theandric":

> God without man is . . . "no-thing." Man without God is exclusively a "thing,". . . while the world, the cosmos, without Man and God is "any-thing". . . sheer un-existing chaos. . . . The primordial man is . . . that total reality of which we are a reflection. . . . Purusha is . . . the personal aspect of the whole of reality.[19]

In *Rig-Veda* X.90, Purusha is sacrificed—like Prajāpati—and a feminine

17 The common word *brahmin*, as a masculine, is a priest, and *brahman* designates his caste; whereas the neuter word Brahman is a deity, one of the Hindu Trinity. This latter form, as a proper noun, can be capitalized, but, as a concept, as "the highest reality," is given in lower case.

18 Cf. Alexis Sanderson, "Power and Purity Amongst the Brahmans of Kashmir," in *The Category of the Person: Anthropology, Philosophy, History*, ed. Michael Carrithers, Steven Collins, and Steven Lukes (Cambridge: Cambridge University Press, 1985), 190–216.

19 R. Panikkar, *The Vedic Experience*, 3rd edition (Delhi: Motilal Banarsidass, 1994), 73.

element emerges from this sacrifice: *virāj* (v. 5). Through his dismemberment and self-immolation, all creation comes forth: man and animals (vv. 8 and 10); sacred hymns (v. 9); the four castes of humanity (v. 12); the moon, the sun, and the divinities Indra and Agni (v. 13); the sky and the air; the earth and its four directions (v. 14).[20] The metaphor here is still that of the Vedic sacrifice, but one in which the total man has been offered up. Again, as Panikkar puts it, "By sacrifice creation reverts to Man. The sacrifice of the cosmic Man signifies divine transcendence investing humanity."[21] The unity of the sacrifice is guaranteed by a descending movement of the All toward man and an ascendant movement of the world toward the All.

By the tenth century BC, the earlier Vedic pantheon began to be called into question, or at least to evolve.[22] Since, in most small villages in South Asia, one finds not one but several origin myths concerning the moon, the earth, rice, etc., it is not surprising that there are quite a few creation hymns in the *Rig-Veda*, each one proposing a different vision of that "moment" before any time or universe existed. In *Rig-Veda* X.121, the unnamed creative principle whom the hymn praises as a deity is referred to as *hiranyagarbhá*, "the golden embryo" or the yolk of an egg.[23] Only in the last verse is God given a name; until then, the hymn resounds with the questioning refrain, "What god shall we offer with our oblation?"[24] The unknown deity is also compared to the brilliance of a sun (vv. 1, 7–8). But, if God is not God until related to creatures, the poet still describes the "hatching" from within the womb or egg of an ultimate reality. So the golden embryo emerges as the Lord of all Being. Praised by the poet as God, who harmoniously unites the universe, he has no proper name, having as appellation only an interrogative *Ka*, "Who?" In the final verse of the hymn, this unknown ultimate creative principle is identified as an abstract deity, Prājapati.[25]

The creator god Prājapati came to provide a somewhat more personal-ized vision of Brahman as the "All." He was three-quarters immortal and one-quarter human, and, as his real name was *Ka*, the first Western translators

---

20 *Rig-Veda* X.90, trans. Jamison and Brereton, 1537–40.

21 Panikkar, *Vedic Experience*, 75.

22 See Stephanie Jamison, "The Rig-Veda Between Two Worlds," *Journal of the American Oriental Society* 127, no. 3 (2007), 354–58, for a discussion of the differences in the orientation and relationship to deity in the old Persian *Avesta*, and the *Rig-Veda* for another analysis of Vedic prayer.

23 *Rig-Veda* X.121: 1, trans. Jamison and Brereton, 1593.

24 See Panikkar, *Vedic Experience*, 71.

25 *Rig-Veda* X.121: 10, trans. Jamison and Brereton, 1594. Panikkar (*Vedic Experience*, 69, note 16) shows how Prājapati can convey personal intimacy, citing two texts from later Vedas, *Taittirīya Brāhmana* II,2, 10, 1–2 and *Aitereya Brāhmana* III, 21 (XII,10).

identified him with the statue on the Areopagus in Athens described by St Paul as "the unknown God" (Acts 17:23). When the later *Brāhmana* texts sought to eliminate violence from the sacrificial rites (for instance, Indra's decapitation of Vrita) and move toward non-violence, this creator god Prājapati "sponsored" the reinterpretation of these rites by himself becoming the object of sacrifice.

Rig-Veda X.129 provides a different vision of Creation, and reflects a more ambiguous perspective.[26] The final lines of the hymn lapse into uncertainty: "Who really knows? Who shall here proclaim it?.../This creation—from where it came to be, if it was produced or if not—he who is the overseer of this (world) in the furthest heaven, he surely knows. Or if he does not know...?"[27]

Creation: The Creative Word

The status of the word in these creation hymns is qualitatively different from the role played by the word in Hebrew thought, whether this is the Hebrew *dabar* of the Psalms or the Greek *logos* of Philo. In the Vedic creation hymns, a word can be sacrificed like a divinity out of whom creation can arise. Thus the sound of a word, as opposed to silence, that uncertain world that escapes the rituals (*Satapatha Brāhmana* 1.2.4.21), has, in the Veda, a relationship that takes on many forms.[28] Word (*vāc*) can be a deity (Brahman), a spell, or a sacrifice. As the "fruits of hearing" (*phalaśruti*), Vedic words were visual as well as auditive, since the "seers" (*rsis*) of the Veda received a beginning-less, eternally pre-existent sound (*vāc*) by intuition.[29] *Vāc* as prayer plays an important role in the *Rig-Veda,* as these words go to the gods if they are free of faults (*Brahmanaspati–sūkta*).[30] So we should begin here.

One of the issues with reading the Vedic creation hymns is that the role of the Word (*vāc*) in creation is sometimes present, sometimes absent, replaced by an interrogation, as in the hymn we just considered, *Rig-Veda* X:129. What are we to make of this fact? The Word (*vāc*) is only one of

26 *Rig-Veda* X.129, trans. Jamison and Brereton, 1607–9. See also Panikkar, *Vedic Experience.*
27 *Rig-Veda* X.129:6–7, trans. Jamison and Brereton, 1609.
28 Calasso, *Ardor,* 93.
29 On *Vāc* as prayer, see chapter 2 in Pratibha M. Pringle, *The Concept of Vāc in the Vedic Literature* (Delhi: Sri Satguru Publications, 2005); also Thomas Coburn, "Scripture in India: Towards a Typology of the Word in Hindu Life," *Journal of the American Academy of Religion* 42, no. 3 (September 1984), 435–60.
30 Pringle, *The Concept of Vāc in the Vedic Literature,* 80.

the names for the absolute.[31] In the later tantric schools, the Word is considered cosmogonic by definition, and, while the exact metaphors change from the Vedic hymns to the tantric mantra, their permanent intuition is similar: that an imperishable (*akshara*) phoneme is the basis not only of the discourse about creation, but of creation itself.[32] In *Rig-Veda* III.55 we read: "Then when the ancient dawns dawned forth, in the track of the cow a great imperishable (syllable) was born [/was discerned]."[33] This imperishable (*akshara*) syllable is the sacred, original and all-powerful Word (*vāc*). In *Rig-Veda* I.164, another metaphor for the Word is the cosmic cow with a multitude of feet, that is to say, a sacred imperishable Word with thousands of syllables.[34] And elsewhere in the same hymn, verse 39: "The syllable of the verse, upon which all the gods have settled, is in the highest heaven— / he who does not know that (syllable), what will he accomplish by his verse? Only those who know it sit here."[35]

Thus the sacrificial fire, the syllable, and the Word all maintain the cosmic order, even as they emerge from it.[36] The phonetic seed of their Word is this syllable, *Om*, that, by analogy, is considered the "metrics" for a "versification" of the cosmos. Later in the *Upanisads*, the principle syllable, *Om*, is identified with this imperishable, aural expression of Brahman as the fundamental sound and mantra.

The Liturgy as Cosmogony and Sacrifice

As seen in the preceding hymns, cosmogony is treated as a liturgy and not as narrative, whether philosophical or mythological.[37] Creation arising from a divine sacrifice can be prolonged in further sacrifices accomplished by men and symbolized by the weaving loom re-enacting the primordial

31   See also Guy L. Beck, *Sonic Liturgy: Ritual and Music in Hindu Tradition* (Delhi: Dev Publishers, 2012).

32   Padoux, *Vāc*.

33   *Rig-Veda* III.55:1, trans. Jamison and Brereton, 554.

34   *Rig-Veda* I.164:41–42, trans. Jamison and Brereton, 358. The same idea is developed in the *Jaiminīya-Upanisad Brāhmana* (I,10) where the immortal celestial cow is the syllable *Om*. In verse I,23, Prajāpati squeezes this Word to extract its essence, from which emerges Agni, Vāyu, and the sun, from which, in turn, emerges the three Vedas and finally the imperishable phoneme (*akshara*) *om*. See Padoux (*Vāc*, 27), who traces the identification of *om* with *brahman* in other *Upanisads*.

35   *Rig-Veda* I.164:39, trans. Jamison and Brereton, 358.

36   Padoux, *Vāc*, 25.

37   This is also known in Hebrew and Christian contexts in which creation is not complete on the sixth day but is perfected later on through prayer and liturgy.

weaving of existence. As Panikkar mentions, "There is nothing sociological here such as one finds in contemporary secular liturgies."[38]

Sacrifice features prominently in the *Rig-Veda*. One of the most striking passages is found in *Rig-Veda* X.130:

1. The sacrifice, which is extended in every direction by its warp threads and stretched out by a hundred and one acts of the gods— / these fathers who have traveled here weave that. They sit at the warp, saying, "Weave forth, weave back."
2. A man extends it [=the warp] and pulls it up (with the heddles); a man has extended it out upon the vault of heaven here. / Here are their pegs; they [=the gods?] sat down upon their seat and made the sāman-chants the shuttles for weaving.
3. What was its model, its image? What its connection? What was its melted butter? What was its frame? / What was the meter? What was the Praüga-recitation, what the hymn?—when all the gods offered the god [=the Sacrifice].[39]

Sacrifice is that which holds the universe together, and—strikingly—man himself participates in this work. The hymn goes on:

6. The seers, the sons of Manu, our fathers, arranged (the ritual) according to this, when the sacrifice was born in ancient times. / Seeing with my mind as my eye, I think of the ancient ones who offered this sacrifice.[40]

The poet ends by saying that the "insightful ones," the present-day priests, have now "taken hold of the reins (of the sacrifice) like charioteers" (v. 7).[41] Thus cosmogony, sacrifice, and the present-day cult are intricately linked.

In the early 1950s, the French Sanskritist Louis Renou began discussing the manner in which the hymns were recited ritually, what we now call their *pragmatics*.[42] To do so, he used the abundant ritual commentaries found in the *Brāhmana*. The *Brāhmana* explain how sacrifices should be performed and

38 Panikkar, *Vedic Experience*, 356.
39 *Rig-Veda* X.130:1–3, trans. Jamison and Brereton, 1610.
40 *Rig-Veda* X.130:6, trans. Jamison and Brereton, 1611.
41 *Rig-Veda* X.130:7, trans. Jamison and Brereton, 1611.
42 Louis Renou, "La valeur du silence dans le culte Védique," *Journal of the American Oriental Society* 69, no. 1 (1949), 11–18.

occasionally give interpretations on how to understand the rituals, such as those found in the *Rig-Veda*'s tenth and most recent book of hymns.

Renou found that, in the *Brāhmana*, "sacrifice is word." The short ritual phrases (*yajus*) of the sacrifices are either chanted or recited *sotto voce* (for those found in the *Yajursamhita*), while those in the *Rig Samhita* are to be said out loud (*uccaih*) by the priest (*hotr*). The *brahman* should say the prayers from the *Atharva samhita*, while the lay patron of the sacrifice makes his personal request to the divinity in murmured (*japa*) invocation, just as in domestic rituals. The *Grhyasutra* mentions three positions for the voice (abdominal, throat, and head), which parallel grave, middle, and sharp registers, greater speed accompanying the high tone.[43]

Below or underneath the *japa sotto voce* invocations there are silent (*tūsnīm*) prayers, said "in thought only" (*manasā*) or "with a restrained voice" (*vāgyatena*). Again, the silent acts are more numerous in the domestic rites than in the public sacrifices dealt with above. In the *Dharmasastra*, acts without words are attributed either to an attenuation in the ritual or to the need to proceed faster in its celebration.

This formulaic silence concerns *yajus* taken from the *Yajurveda* and never deals with the verses of the *Rig-Veda*. According to the *Brāhmana*, alongside those prayers that can be expressed (*nirukta*), there exists the domain of the inexpressible (*anirrukta*), the indefinable, the unlimited and uncertain (*anaddhā*). The inexpressible is required when "speaking" about the length of life, about breathing or breath and, above all, about thought as opposed to speech. Speech and silence are considered to be the two paths in sacrifice. *Anirrukta* occurs when "breath devours the word," and this occurs when addressing Prajāpati, for he is inexpressible and "silence belongs to him," and such inaudible invocations make him favorable. Formulaic silence is said to be the "eye of sacrifice." It makes sacrifice visible by going beyond that which one normally distinguishes, that which is perishable, entering into the world of the gods' totality, the unlimited, for "what one cannot attain by a word, one can attain by thought."

Silence and *sotto voce* invocations open out onto the domain of a global totality (*sarva*) or universe (*vishva*), beyond the additional enumeration provided by words. In the same way that silence brings an end to oral rites, so also silence terminates myths and philosophical speculations. In the *Aitereya Brāhmana* II.13, silent praise is said to be composed of syntactical elements (*bhūr agnir jyotih*) followed by a nasal resonance whose vocalization with

43 Hermann Oldenberg, *Sacred Books of the East*, vol. XXIX–XXX, *The Grihya-sūtras: Rules of Vedic Domestic Ceremonies,* trans. Max Müller (Oxford: Clarendon Press, 1886–1892).

an "o" is indeterminate (*anirrukta*) and is understood to say everything by saying nothing. Thus breath (breathing) may be said to be opposed to word.

If the deity Prajāpati is unnamable, and therefore dedicated to silence, it is because he concentrates in his person all that goes beyond the tangible. He represents Brahman as a neuter, an old Indian symbol of enigmatic equivalences. The priest, designated as *brahmin* (in the masculine), becomes this neuter Brahman during the sacrifice by his manner of praying. The masculine Brahmin does not act or sing or recite; his "actions" are defined by his thought. Every person officiating should not utter profane (*laukika*) speech. He should practice silence and "block" his voice (*vāgyamana*) from any "foreign" (*apavyāhr*) secular words. Thus silence, called *mauna*, means both silence and ascesis, and figures in the ten abstentions (*niyama*) of the hermit. As soon as one officiates in a sacrifice, one must restrain one's voice. To conclude, the *Satapatha Brāhmana* (III. 1, 3, 27) says that, by restraining one's voice (*vāgyamana*), the sacrificer seals the sacrifice in himself, thus preventing it from being dispersed. In this manner, the sacrificer ensures the continuation of the infinite form of Prājapati, which was created when he assembled his energies after the first sacrifice.[44]

The Micro- and Macro-Cosmological Co-ordinates of the Word

Having said all this, the hymns of the Veda are not exactly prayers, for the good reason that the value of their words is that of an interface between the cosmos and man instead of being an interface between God and man, as in the monotheistic religions that grew out of the Middle East. André Padoux, in the introduction to his book *Vāc*, explains how word (*vāc*) is a symbol for the godhead, how it reveals the divine presence in the cosmos as the force that maintains the universe. This qualification would again require differentiation from the *logos* of Christian belief.[45]

As we saw earlier, Hindus held that an active force was involved in creation, and that this force was sometimes identified as the Word. Unlike Christianity, in which the *Logos* is theo-linguistically related to the Father as a person, the Hindu Word, *vāc*, has *anthropo-cosmic* correlations. Every *sakti* is at once *vāc*, *cit* (thought), *samvid* (consciousness), breath, and vital "vibration" energy (*prāna*), for the creative act is an utterance but is also a

44 The role of the recitation of non-secular (*alaukika*) mantras as part of ritual praise is not dealt with here.

45 See Padoux, *Vāc*. This study of non-dualistic Kashmiri Saivism from the ninth century onward incorporates many texts originating from South India.

human act, since humans reproduce the archetypal divine act or process.

In later tantric thought, the universe emerges from within divine consciousness through four levels of speech. Explaining the "phonematic" emanation of Kashmiri Saivism, Padoux states that the categories (*tattva*) of cosmic manifestation are concomitant with the Sanskrit phonemes (*varna*). Thus Sanskrit grammar is the "gateway to salvation." Word as a means for liberation, writes Padoux, can be understood in four ways: (1) as an energy which brings the gods and the worlds into existence, (2) as the substance into which they are reabsorbed, (3) as that which allow humans to take hold of primal energy through mantra, to be free from becoming, and finally (4) as what achieves *svatantrya* (autonomy), which characterizes the supreme Word as spiritual energy.[46] Mantras are valued because they are free from the limitation of language. Otherwise, when the word loses this autonomy, it becomes subject to human conventions and is a source of bondage.

To summarize, while *vāc* relates to speaking, it also means voice, speech, word, utterance, and language. In the Vedas, *vāc* is an embodied divinized Word. A goddess is later identified as *vāc* (word), although this concept is not to be confused with the Greek philosophical term *logos* (rational intelligence or reasoning). While *vāc* is prior to language, the *bīja* mantra (the vowel or "seed" mantra) from which creation proceeds has no connection with language, so *vāc* can only be translated as speech in its verbal and aural character.

Why Mantras Are Not Prayers

I do not mean to suggest that, in the last two millennia, mantras have ceased being important in Hindu invocations. Harvey P. Alper proposes to distinguish mantra from propitiation, acquisition, and identification, and sets out the different types of mantras as in the diagram below. Alper distinguishes five kinds of mantra, which, while they are all mantras of one kind or another, can be distinguished by their proximity at the end of two axes: intentionality and linguistic properties. By comparing their use, he fits these mantras into a four-sided grid. Mantras are distinguished between those uttered for practical reasons (on the left) and those uttered to escape from *samsāra*, bad karma, etc. (on the right). On the vertical scale, mantras at the top are those that are perfectly clear, linguistically, as language, and those at the bottom are the *bīja* mantras that make little linguistic sense.

46 Padoux, *Vāc*, xii and chs. 4 and 5.

Grid for Comparing Mantras [47]

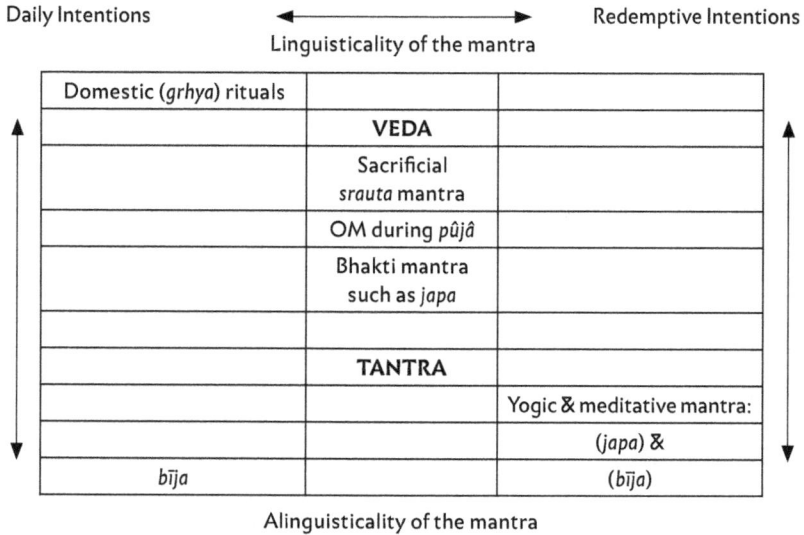

Daily Intentions ◄──────────────────► Redemptive Intentions

Linguisticality of the mantra

Domestic (*grhya*) rituals		
	VEDA	
	Sacrificial *srauta* mantra	
	OM during *pûjâ*	
	Bhakti mantra such as *japa*	
	TANTRA	
		Yogic & meditative mantra:
		(*japa*) &
bīja		(*bīja*)

Alinguisticality of the mantra

While a full discussion of mantra would require an in-depth overview of the tantric tradition as a whole, we will limit ourselves, here, to Dominic Goodall's summary of the practice of tantric prayer. [48] Tantric prayer, says Goodall, involves visualization of a divinity upon a throne, programmed daily. One also places this deity in one's heart as if on a throne. The form the divinity may take could be an icon, fire, a water pot, a colored diagram drawn on the ground. In the case of Shivā, this substrate is usually his symbolic linga. [49] In Hindu prayer, the essence of the divinity is in the mantra. The Mimamsaka exegetes of the Veda held that these ancient texts referred to neither persons nor events, and that the mantras themselves were the deities. In iconography, Shivā has five faces, each of which corresponds to a word (the *brahmamantra*). One installs a mantra in an object and then worships it by feeding it, bathing

47 Adapted from Harvey Alper, *Mantra* (Albany: SUNY Press, 1988), 7.

48 For a recent collection of articles on Saivitic tantra that provides an up-to-date bibliography, see Dominic Goodall and André Padoux, eds., *Mélanges tantriques à la mémoire d'Hélène Brunner* (Pondicherry and Paris: Institut Français de Pondichéry, École Française de l'Extrême-Orient, 2007). Especially important is Alexis Sanderson's long article that catalogues the *Saivasiddhānta* texts dedicated to the propitiation of Shivā, and the Śhākta texts dedicated to the propitiation of the goddess Bhairava.

49 See Dominic Goodall et al., "Introduction," in *The Pancavaranstava of Ahorasivacarya: A Twelfth-Century South Indian Prescription for the Visualisation of Sadasiva and his Retinue* (Pondicherry: Institut Français de Pondichéry, École Française de l'Extrême-Orient, 2005), 11–44.

it, burning incense before it, illuminating it with candles, or playing music in front of it. In the daily Saiddhantika, one does this imaginatively in one's heart, and then externally with the icon at hand.

All this allows one to identify oneself with the deity: "One who is not Siva may not worship Siva" (as in the formulaic tag: *nasivah sivam arcayet*). This relationship with the deity is held to be true in non-dualistic schools as well as in Saiva Siddhānta's "unreconcilable dualism," in which, while souls are distinct from Siva, they possess omniscience and omnipotence, although this is hampered by the impurity (*mala*) that envelopes them. So what is tantric worship that uses mantra? As Goodall writes: "The worshipper sees himself as God, but he also enacts his identification ritually by mentally burning away his physical body and replacing it with one made up with mantras that are held to be the 'body-parts' of Siva."[50]

Excursus 1:
Non-dual Relationships in Advaita Hinduism and Christianity

Given the centrality of the debates about personhood as a feature of one's relation to God, a comparison will help clarify the presentation of Indian prayer. The first comparison concerns non-dual relationships. In the Gospel of St John, Jesus says that he is fully one with his Father, and yet he is not the Father. Christians consider this to signify a *non-dual relationship*.[51] It involves not one but two who are united without confusion or separation. Indian religions also feature *advaita* (non-dualism), under many forms.[52] While most are inadequate to express the Christian faith, nonetheless the idea of *advaita*, "nonduality," itself, is also fundamental to a Christian understanding and always has been. "[T]hat all of them may be one, Father, just as you are in me and I am in you. May they also be in us so that the world may believe that you have sent me" (John 17:21). Bede Griffiths, an English Benedictine who lived in the ashram of Jules Montchanin near Bangalore in the early 1960s, wrote: "This is the Christian *advaita* . . . we are one in this mystery of the Godhead. . . . This would be an example of how to relate the cosmic relation to the Christian revelation."[53] For Fr Bede, clearly, there cannot be love in a monad without two—Creator and creature. "If God is a pure monad, as he is

---

50 Goodall et al., "Introduction," 13.

51 Bede Griffiths, *Essential Writings* (Maryknoll, NY: Orbis, 2004), 120–21.

52 Cf. the still ground-breaking study by Olivier Lacombe, *L'Absolu selon le Védânta: Les notions de Brahman et d'Atman dans les systèmes de Cankara et Râmânoudja* (Paris: Geuthner, 1937).

53 Griffiths, *Writings*, 121.

in Islam, and as he tends to be in Hinduism, he cannot be love in himself." Be that as it may, the devotional forms used in India all express intense love for and of God. Even if Hindu devotional literature is dualistic, the non-dualistic *bhakti* prayer subordinates this love to unity.

As we will see below, a theistic "Hinduism" moves the goal posts of invocation beyond mantra, making religious poetry the main vehicle of devotion in the period after the fourth and fifth centuries BC. Where does that leave those Christian theists when they study Indian *bhakti* poetic invocations? Francis Clooney, in his study of the Song of Songs and the Holy Word of Mouth (*Tiruvaymoli*), says:

> . . . a "delicate balance" between two religious truths, a most intense and particular truth—Jesus the beloved—and the unending aesthetic, dramatic, and truthful apprehension that draws us perilously near to other such loves—Krishna the beloved. The particularities of faith have been opened . . . even if there is no settled ending to love or true thinking . . . nothing matters more than Jesus, in the distinctiveness of his personhood, as the truth that is beautiful, right here; he is the beloved.[54]

Excursus 2: The First Muslim Description of Hindu Prayer

Our second excursus involves tracing an interesting facet of the relationship between Hinduism and Islam. As Michelle Voss Roberts has pointed out, the Indian traditions present "many facets of the Creator-creature union in differentiation" and "fine-tune a broad spectrum of positions."[55] Yet, for more than 2,000 years (1500 BC to AD 500), the classical Indian concept of yoga—of concentration and meditation—served to marginalize theism, and the kind of hymnography and prayer that would later accompany the rise of Indian devotional (*bhakti*) poetry. Even in the eleventh century, the characteristics of Indian religions caught the attention of the Persian pioneer of comparative religious studies, the Muslim polymath Al-Biruni (AD 973–1048).[56] Al-Biruni

---

54 Clooney, *His Hiding Place is Darkness*, 140.

55 Michelle Voss Roberts, *Dualities: A Theology of Difference* (Louisville, KY: John Knox Press, 2010), xix.

56 The Arabic text of *Kitab ta'rikh al-Hind* was finished around hajir 421/AD 1030 (English translation in 1910 by Edward C. Sachau in two volumes; recently reprinted under the title *Albiruni's India* (Dehli: M. Manoharlal, 2005). Al-Biruni seems to have spent some twelve years in India, gathering information about the country, studying Sanskrit and Hindu philosophy, and mathematics and astronomy.

observed that prayer in India is situated between two highly developed fields of religious knowledge and praxis: a "non-theistic" ascetic epistemology as proposed by the South Indian yogi Patañjali (ca. 450 BC) and the even older Vedic supranatural meso-cosmology that is preserved in collections of hymns and mantra used in the sacrificial rites of the Veda.[57] In Vedic mythology and mantra, a limited manifestation of eternal reality is preserved through "knowledge" (*veda*), "word-*brahman*," the creator principle, the original expression of divine speech that the Creator proffered, creating all phenomena. This was just one of many cosmologies put forth by the Veda. Yet none of this holds any implication of a "God" responsible for his creation *ex nihilo*, as found in the three monotheistic world religions of the Middle East. As an alternative to sacrificial Vedic cults, yoga proposed a freedom and immortality, and the *Yoga sutras* left only a limited role for the Lord (Isvara).

As a Muslim writing about India in the eleventh century, Al-Biruni provides a bridge to Indian "religion" from our study of *salāt* in Chapter 3. He looks at India through a remarkably open Muslim perspective and easily distinguishes between peasant village religious customs, about which he could know little, and the conceptual frameworks of those educated ascetics he read directly in the Sanskrit originals. What, since the British colonization of India, we have been accustomed to calling "Hinduism" is composed of highly diverse oral and written traditions practiced primarily in homes, on river banks (*ghat*), and, secondarily, in ashrams and temples, and, in any case, not always congregationally.[58] At the end of this chapter, we will look briefly at the everyday prayer practiced in contemporary India.

Three positions distinguish the three metaphysical outlooks that confronted Al-Biruni as he tried to understand what he calls, in the geography of his times, *al-hind* (India) and which he believed were to be found throughout south Asia:

57 Al-Biruni translated Pantañjali's 196 yogic aphorisms (*sutras*), which form one of the foundational texts of *rāja yoga*. The *Bhagavad-Gītā* developed an early Vaishnava Bhagavatas cult, but also borrowed from Samkhya cosmology and was more sectarian and theistic than the Yogasutras. While the Yoga school of philosophy's (*āstika*) ontology and its epistemology were often heavily influenced by the dualist (*purusha* and *prakṛti*) Samkhya, it later allows for a limited theistic devotion to the Lord (Isvara). See James Haughton Woods, *The Yoga-System of Patañjali: Or, the ancient Hindu doctrine of concentration of mind embracing the mnemonic rules, called Yoga-sūtras* (Delhi: Motilal Banarsidass, 1966); and Gerald Larson's "Yoga's 'A-Theistic' Theism," *Journal of Hindu-Christian Studies* 25 (2012), 17–24.

58 See David N. Lorenzen, "Who Invented Hinduism?" *Comparative Studies in Society and History* 41, no. 4 (October 1999), 630–59, and Brian K. Pennington, *Was Hinduism Invented? Britons, Indians, and the Colonial Construction of Religion* (New York: Oxford University Press, 2007).

1. Peasant pantheism, which identified the Creator with the energies found in the cosmos by tables of regular correspondences between the microcosm and the macrocosm.[59] The notion of creation *ex nihilo* is unknown, yet the cosmos is understood not as "nature" but cosmographically, as a world to read and to be discerned for its properties.
2. Radical monism, which takes creation as illusory, since all being is in the godhead; the issue of non-duality will be debated by Hindu philosophers and ascetics down until the twentieth century.[60]
3. Samkhya dualism of pure consciousness and primordial matter (*purusha* and *prakṛti*). Direct sense perception (*pratyakṣa* or *dṛṣṭam*), inference (*anumāna*), and the verbal testimony of the sages and *shāstras* are taken to be the only true sources of knowledge.

It is clarifying to begin by discussing the difference between the meditative prayers used at the end of *salāt*, especially by Sufi orders (see Chapter 3), and the Indian ascetical practice known as yoga. Yoga has often been integrated into the Samkhya dualistic philosophy, but here a little cultural history is needed. Recall Massignon's description of the rupture that would develop in Islam between ritual and moral asceticism on the one hand and mystical theology on the other.[61] This tension, which characterizes all of later Islamic spirituality, would be consummated with Ibn 'Arabi (1165–1240), whose influence postdates Al-Biruni's description by two centuries.

In Al-Biruni's time, the Sind, eastern Pakistan, was in direct contact with the *khalifs* via Basrah on the Persian Gulf. Only with the eighth-century expansion of Islam was north-eastern India incorporated into a proper Muslim kingdom.[62] For Al-Biruni, and for the next three centuries after him, the great teachers—al Hallaj, Tawhidī, Ghazāli, and Sohrawardi of Aleppo—still preserved the union between faith and practice.[63] It was during the decline of the political power of the Fatimids and the Ismailis that Ibn 'Arabi delivered Muslim mystical

---

59 In the Vedic sacrifices, the dismembered divinity Prajāpati's weapons are called the *bandhu*, that is to say, correspondences to the cosmic matrix permitting the orientation of rituals.

60 For an article comparing the Christian view of creation with that of a twentieth-century Hindu, Sri Aurobindo (1872–1950), on non-duality, see John M. Allison, "Of Bliss and Love: Methodological 'Play' in Hindu-Christian Comparative Theology," *Journal of Comparative Theology* 5 (January, 2015), 2–17. Allison compares Christian and Hindu understandings of creation.

61 Louis Massignon, *Essai sur les origines du lexique technique de la mystique musulmane* (Paris: Geuthner, 1922), ch. 2.

62 For the dates and details, cf. André Wink, *Al Hind: The Making of the Indo-Islamic World*, 3 vols. (Leiden: Brill 1990, 1997, 2004), vol. 2, ch. 4.

63 Massignon, *Essai sur les origines*, 61.

theology over into the hands of the Qarmates' syncretic monism. For Ibn 'Arabi, human souls and all creation are said to emanate from Allah in five stages and return to him through mystical union in five stages. To express this, Ibn 'Arabi used a syncretic Hellenistic vocabulary deploying arcane gnostic hierarchies. However, if Islam became so well implanted in northern India, it was due to another current, the Sufi brotherhoods.[64]

In the century following Al-Biruni's contacts with Hindus in northwestern India under Ghaznavid domination, many Muslim Sufis would immigrate to live in hermitages after having been driven from Persia by the Mongol invasion in the thirteenth century.

Al-Biruni knew of the ascetic epistemology proposed by the earlier *Upanisads*, which he translated. Massignon shows that the principal *Upanisads* strove for a unification of the soul through the purification of the heart, to be achieved by the progressive elimination of mental images.[65] No metaphysical or ritual outreach is to be permitted; no attributes are accorded to the personality or to divine grace; one is limited to a strictly psychological consciousness. The intermittent, partial, and external truths that facilitate consciousness are to be cut off. While the Vedanta schools all affirm an eternal Self (*ātman*), the Advaita Vedantins, as epitomized by Shankara, deny any ontological reality to personhood. They deny any permanent individual soul (*ātman*), while Samkhya allows only an instantaneous impersonal consciousness of the truth, to the eternal *purusha*. This purely intuitive realization (*sattvāpatti*) is called, by Al-Biruni, a "truth without content" and is the fruit of the strict control of *purusha*'s intellectual activity, representing final emancipation (*apavarga*).[66]

In Patañjali, Al-Biruni discovers four exercises that lead to pure contemplation (*samādhi*):

1. Abstinence (*yama*) accompanied by five ritual vows (*niyama*), one of which is dedicated to a divinity (Isvara; *Yogasutra* II.32), postures (*asana*), and breath control. Through abstraction (*pratyhara*) of the input of the five senses, breath control permits the mind to attain ecstatic concentration, a one-pointedness of mind. What follows is called, successively, synergy (*samyama; Yogasutra* III.4),

---

64 See Wink, *Al Hind*, vol. 2.

65 Massignon, *Essai sur les origines*, 70–80.

66 For studies that avoid Al-Biruni's circuitous routing (Sanskrit-Arabic-English), see Ian Whicher, *Integrity of Yoga Darsana* (Albany, NY: SUNY Press, 1998), Edwin F. Bryant, *The Yoga Sutras of Patañjali* (New York: North Point Press, 2009), and the translations of commentaries including Sankara's and Vijnanabhiksu's in T.S. Rukmani, trans., *Yogasutrabhasyavivarana of Sankara: Including Critical Notes* (Delhi: Munshiram Manoharlal Publishers, 2001), vol. 1.

a contemplation (*dhāranā*),[67] where the mind consists of only three things, the conscious subject (*purusha*), reality (*sattva*), and consciousness (*buddhi*), i.e., the intellect within which objects of cognition are perceived by the *Purusha*.

2. Patañjali's understanding of *dhyana* (*Yogasutra* III.2 and III.3) was taken up by the later commentaries, such as Vyasa's. The state of absorption (*dhyana*) is somewhat similar to the Muslim state of *dhikr* practiced at the end of *salāt*, where the mind only displays the conscious subject and the object of its consciousness. This corresponds *grosso modo* to the Muslim "extinction at the call of Allah" (*fanā 'an al dhikr;* see Qur'an 28:10).[68]

3. Finally, in the third state of this psychological ecstasy (*samādhi*), the mind is only conscious of itself.[69] For this, the Persian Sufi martyr al Hallaj (858–922) employs the term suspension thought (*tajrīd*), designating an unconscious ecstasy. In Islam, *fanā* designates the extinction of thought in its object or the extinction of the object in one's thought, whereas, in India, what is under consideration is the extinction of thought through its suspension and conjunction. As Massignon explains, this is because, for Islam, Allah is transcendentally real, not an object that one seeks to ignore, whereas, for Patañjali, introspection, not metaphysics, designates consciousness detached from all that is created.[70]

This last state occurs in three stages affecting the *vritti* or fluctuations of thought:

67 *Samyama* is not a form of *dhāranā* but rather the moment where *dhāranā, dhyana,* and *samādhi* meet.

68 The notion of "self-pronouncing" words is common to Islam, Eastern Christianity, Hinduism, and Buddhism. It appears among the Sufi brotherhoods around the twelfth century, in Christianity in the fourth century, and even earlier in Buddhism and Hinduism. It is the result of an intensive practice of inward recitation or meditation (*dhikr khafi*), and its relation to the rhythms of breathing are well studied. See Louis Massignon, "Le Souffle dans l'Islam," *Journal Asiatique* 134 (1943–45), 437–38; G.C. Anawati and Louis Gardet, *Mystique Musulmane: Aspects et Tendances, Expériences et Techniques* (Paris: Vrin, 1986), 187–212. The *Ihyā 'ulum al-dīn* of Al-Ghazālī gave *dhikr* a large place in official Islam, and his treatise "Revivification of the Sciences of Religion" is still widely read today. I found it in an Indonesian translation in a local mosque bookstore with its section on *dhikr: Bimbingan untuk mecapai Tingkat Mu'min* (Bandung: Diponegoro, 1989), 198–228.

69 Ben Williams, in a personal communication, says that, in *samādhi*, according to Patañjali and Vyasa, the object of meditation does not totally disappear but rather shines forth as a kind of raw datum, as if free of an essential substantive nature, i.e., devoid of the qualities and labels that the mind associates with it.

70 Louis Massignon, *Essai sur les origines*, 75.

1. Consciousness suspends its attachment to an object (*nirodhiparināma*), entering a void.
2. "Conscious psychological ecstasy" (*samādhi samprajnāta*) becomes increasingly insensitive, unconscious of this suspension, and returns to any identification with any object of its attention.
3. "Unconscious psychological ecstasy" (*samādhi asamprajnāta*) is simple, isolated from thought, having unified the three *guna* (primordial qualities emanating from the original nature of *prakṛti*) into one, *sattvā*, in which the conscious subject (*purusha*) is pure.

The status, nature, or genealogy of Isvara in the Yogasutras is a complicated issue, since Patañjali represents only one version of Indian Yoga along with Shaiva [Pasupata], Vaishnava, Hatha, and tantric yoga.[71] At first glance, it seems that Patañjali (*Yogasutra* 1:25 and 37; 2:45) separates himself from his Samkhya masters by admitting that a Lord (Isvara) as an imaginary divinity or historical hero can be useful to stimulate devotion and confirm one's vows. Nonetheless, this Isvara is inoperative once one attains the state of *enstasis* (*samādhi*), during which all idolatry vanishes through an "intuitive" destruction. Massignon calls this position an *ab intra* demonstration of the inanity of all polytheism. If, for Islam, only Allah himself can transfigure consciousness, Al-Biruni believes that here one finds partial agreement.[72] He writes:

> The Sufis use the same method as Patañjali concerning the unitive concentration in God. They say in effect, "As long as you elaborate expressions, you do not affirm the only God; until God takes over your expressions, making you forego them, you have not affirmed the one God, and so there will no longer subsist either the created *orans* or his human expression."[73]

Prayer in the Bhagavad-Gītā

We move from the *Rig-Veda* to the *Bhagavad-Gītā*. This collection was transmitted orally for centuries before achieving written form in the Gupta dynasty of the fourth century A D. It is here that we find, not the earliest, but perhaps the best-remembered watershed in the Indian ascetical understanding of

---

71 See Edwin F. Bryant, *The Yoga Sutras*; see also David Gordon White, *Sinister Yogis* (Chicago: University of Chicago Press, 2009).

72 See Sachau's translation in *Albiruni's India*, 68–69.

73 Louis Massignon, *Essai sur les origines*, 76.

prayer: the famous revelation of Krishna to Arjuna described in the 18th chapter of the *Bhagavad-Gītā*.[74] *Bhakti*, or "devotion," as it is portrayed in the *Bhagavad-Gītā*, is an alternative to the two major forms of religious practice at the time: the ascetical meditation of the recluse or *sannyāsin* and the rituals of devotion based on hymnography and offerings.

Any study of prayer in India needs to situate the *Bhagavad-Gītā*'s revolutionary theism in terms of the Rig-Vedic hymnography. The *Gītā* steps off from the *Purusha sūkta* hymn found in *Rig-Veda* X.90, where it is claimed that, following Purusha's sacrifice, a quarter of his body has been deployed as the universe and its human inhabitants, while the other three quarters are in the immortal heavens. The symbol used here is that of a paradoxical upside-down tree. As the *Chāndoya* (III.12.6) and *Maitrāyanī Upanisad* (VI.4) put it, using the simile of the *asvattha* (pipul) tree, three-quarters of Brahman "sits root upward." The *Katha Upanisad* (VI.1) says, more simply, that the universe is the eternal *asvattha* tree.

The *Gītā* paraphrases all this:

> The immutable *ashvattha* [tree], they say, [has its] roots above and [its] branches below, and its leaves are the [Vedic] hymns—he who knows this, he is a Veda-knower.[75]

By accepting this Rig-Vedic simile for God, the *Gītā* makes the point that the immanent cosmic universe is not illusion (*māyā*), but an emanation from God. The transcendent roots growing upward—from which the created world has "grown"—are the undifferentiated reality called Brahman, while God himself "in his super-personality transcends even Brahman … (who) is only a constitutive essence in the complex personality of God."[76] Where the *Gītā* really differs from the *Upanisad* is in its notion of incarnation (*avatar*).[77]

---

74 In some 700 verses, this poem figures in the *Bhishma Parva* of the Mahabharata epic. As only "remembered" tradition (*smriti*), the *Gītā* depends on the revealed texts (*śruti*) of the *Upanisads*, which it often paraphrases, leading to it being sometimes called "the Upanishad of the Upanishads." It is not possible here to describe how the monistic philosophy of the Vedas led to a doctrine of non-duality (*Advaita Vedanta*) gradually exposed in the *Upanishads*, the *Bhagavad-Gītā*, and *Brahma sutras*. For an overview of early Srī Vaishnava traditions in southern India starting with Alvār poetry, see Vasudha Narayanan, *The Way and the Goal* (Washington, DC: Institute for Vaishnava Studies, 1987).

75 *Bhagavad-Gītā* XV.1, trans. Georg and Brenda Feuerstein, *The Bhagavad-Gītā: A New Translation* (Boston and London: Shambhala, 2011), 273.

76 S. Dasgupta, *A History of Indian Philosophy* (Cambridge: Cambridge University Press, 1952), vol. 2, 524.

77 For a book-length comparison of Christian and "Indian" beliefs concerning

In *Bhagavad-Gītā* IV, Vishnu becomes incarnate as Krishna, the charioteer of Arjuna, and speaks through his mouth, saying:

> Although [I am] unborn, the immutable Self, [and] although being the Lord of [all] beings—[yet] by governing My own nature (*prakṛti*), I come-to-be through the creative-power (*māyā*) of Myself.[78]

As Surendranath Dasgupta puts it, it is the threefold nature of God that explains how God can exist in us and yet does not do so.[79] In *Gītā* IX.6–8, God is described as having three natures (*prakṛti*): cosmic matter, an illusory (*māyā*) matter, and a third, the *prakṛti* of God, from which spirit and life emanate. God's transcendence and matter are not distinguished. This third *prakṛti* is also called the eternal soul-principle (*jīva-bhūta*), active in living beings as "life force" (*prāna*). At several points, Dasgupta, as a clear-thinking philosopher, remarks that the *Gītā* is not aware that pantheism, deism, and theism mixed together do not constitute a coherent philosophic creed, for transcendentalism, immanentism, and pantheism lose their distinctive qualities when blended into the super-personality of God.[80] The *Gītā* proposes such relations of dependence and love for God as a third way outside the much older path of knowledge (*jñana-yoga*) and the path of duties (*karma-yoga*).[81] Of course, in order to dedicate one's actions to God and attain eternal life, one has to possess a personal commitment to meditating on and adoring God in what could only be a personal relationship. In short, the true wisdom of *bhakti* opens the way to communion with God, which becomes the keystone of the cult of Vishnu, the Vaishnava religious quest.

Beginning in chapter six, Arjuna raises the question concerning whether it is better to worship Vishnu as *saguna*, with form, or as *nirguna*, without form.[82] In *Bhagavad-Gītā* VI, Krishna discusses the discipline of meditation (*dhyanayoga*).

---

incarnation, see G. Parrinder, *Avatar and Incarnation* (New York: Oxford University Press, 1982), especially ch. 3 on Krishna in the *Bhagavad-Gītā*.

78 *Bhagavad-Gītā* IV.6, trans. Feuerstein, 137.

79 Dasgupta, *History of Indian Philosophy*, vol. 2, 526.

80 Ibid., 527; 533.

81 Bryant cites commentaries on Isvara as a personal but unnamed God (*The Yoga Sutras*, xxi–xxvi; 81ff.).

82 For a general survey of determinate and indeterminate forms of Siva, see Raghunath Giri, "Puranic Hinduism based on the Siva Purāna and other Siva Purānas," in *History of Science, Philosophy and Culture in Indian Civilization*, vol. VII, part 3, *Hindus I*, ed. N.S.S. Raman (New Delhi: ISPC, 2013), 77–98.

He should raise the self by the Self; he should not let the self sink; for, [as] the self is indeed the friend of the Self, [so also] is the self indeed Self's enemy.[83]

The man who wishes to be wise should practice "Yoga," discipline, "for [the purpose of] self-purification."[84] Meditation leads him to see "the Self (*ātmānaṃ*) abiding in all beings and all beings in the Self" and to see "Me everywhere" and "all in Me."[85]

In the next chapter, Krishna explains that he may be worshipped through a number of different forms:

> I am the flavor of water, O son-of-Kuntī. I am the radiance of sun and moon, the *pranava* [syllable Om] of all the Vedas, the sound in and of space, [and] the manhood of men.[86]

Whatever is good, luminous, and whatever is bad, obscuring, are equally "from Me," although Krishna emphasizes that "I am not in them; they are in Me."[87] Correspondingly, "Whatever form whichever devotee desires to worship with faith" may be used to legitimately offer praise. Krishna himself is "veiled," "not visible-light to all" by virtue of his "creative-power."[88]

In *Bhagavad-Gītā* VIII, he continues to discuss the discipline of the imperishable Brahman (*aksarabrahmayoga*). In verses 1–3, terms are used like higher-being (*adhibhūtam*), higher-divinity (*adhidaivam*), higher-worship (*adhiyajnāh*), and higher-soul (*adhyatman*) to define the innate nature.[89] This continues throughout the section, where Krishna says that whoever recites "OM, the monosyllable [signifying] Brahman," remembering him, will, when they leave the body, go "the supreme course," which is to escape the cycle of rebirth.[90] What is envisaged, ultimately, is the "unmanifest," that Supreme Person who is "everlasting" and "imperishable (*akshara*)," who does not perish when all beings perish, and the "Supreme Spirit (*Purushah*)," which

83 *Bhagavad-Gītā* VI.5, trans. Feuerstein, 157.
84 Ibid. VI.12, trans. Feuerstein, 159.
85 Ibid. VI.29–30, trans. Feuerstein, 163.
86 Ibid. VII.8, trans. Feuerstein, 173.
87 Ibid. VII.12, trans. Feuerstein, 173.
88 Ibid. VII.21, 25, trans. Feuerstein, 175, 177.
89 Compare with a parallel Greek term "hyper-" (ὑπέρ-) meaning "higher" used by Dionysius the Areopagite to affirm Christian apophatic declarations of transcendence. See discussion in Sarah Coakley and Charles Stang, eds., *Rethinking Dionysius the Areopagite* (Chichester: Wiley-Blackwell, 2009).
90 *Bhagavad-Gītā* VIII.13, 16, trans. Feuerstein, 185.

is won by "devotion [directed to] none other [than Me] (*bhaktyā labhyas*)."[91]

In *Bhagavad-Gītā* IX, the further discipline of royal knowledge is discussed. When theoretical knowledge (*jnānam*) is joined with practical (*vijnāna*), it is "a supreme purifier," "evident-to-one's-understanding, lawful, very easy to apply—[and yet] immutable."[92] It is in this mixture of theory and practice that Krishna is worshipped as "unity [in] diversity, manifold [and] facing everywhere."[93] Thus he may say:

> I am the rite. I am the sacrifice. I am the oblation. I am the herb. I am the mantra. I am the clarified-butter. I am the fire. I am the offering. I am the father of this universe, the mother, the supporter, the grandsire, [all that is] to-be-known, the purifier, the syllable OM, and the *Rig-*, *Sāma-*, and *Yajur-*[*Veda*].[94]

The multitude forms of ritual worship offered to Krishna do not simply end with this list, however—even those who are followers and worshippers of other deities, if they have faith, worship Krishna by what they do.[95]

It is only in *Bhagavad-Gītā* X that the language of prayer itself is brought up. Here, Krishna states, "Among speakers, I am [their] speech (*vādah*)," and likewise, "among chants, I am the great chant."[96]

In *Gītā* XI, Krishna tells Arjuna that he will give him "the divine eye" by which he will be able to see truly. Here begins the famous epiphany of Krishna, ending in ch. XI where Arjuna contemplates this terrifying apocalypse:

> O God, in Your body I behold the gods and all the [various] kinds of beings.... Everywhere, I behold You [who are] of endless form, [with] many arms, bellies, mouths, [and] eyes. I see in You no end, no middle, and also no beginning, O All-Lord, All-Form!... [You are] an immeasurable blazing radiance of sun-fire.[97]
>
> With flaming mouths, You lick up, devouring, all the worlds entirely. Filling the entire universe with [Your] brilliance, Your dreadful rays scorch [all], O Vishnu.[98]

---

91 Ibid. VIII.20–22, trans. Feuerstein, 187.
92 Ibid. IX.1–2, trans. Feuerstein, 191.
93 Ibid. IX.15, trans. Feuerstein, 195.
94 Ibid. IX.16–17, trans. Feuerstein, 195.
95 Ibid. IX.23, trans. Feuerstein, 197.
96 Ibid. X.31, 35, trans. Feuerstein, 215.
97 Ibid. XI.15–17, trans. Feuerstein, 225.
98 Ibid. XI.30, trans. Feuerstein, 233.

Krishna replies: "I am time, mighty wreaker of the world's destruction, engaged here in annihilating the worlds."[99] After expanding on this role, he finally ends with consoling words:

> You [need] not tremble. Do not [succumb to] a bewildered condition at seeing that horrifying form of Mine. Freed from [all] fear and glad minded, behold again this My [familiar physical] form, the very [form which you know so well].[100]

In the twelfth chapter of the *Bhagavad-Gītā*, Arjuna continues in other ways to ask Krishna to explain to him the two forms of worship of Vishnu: "Devotees who are thus ever yoked [and] worship You, or [those] who [worship] the Imperishable Unmanifest—which of these are the best knowers of Yoga?"[101] In other words, what kind of prayer is most pleasing to God? Krishna's response may build upon the themes already discussed in the previous chapters of the *Gītā*. Finally, in *Bhagavad-Gītā* XII, the discipline of devotion (*Bhaktiyoga*) is introduced, along with several key terms such as *samuddhartā* ("savior," v. 7), *abhyāsayoga* ("the discipline of practice," v. 9), and *matkarmaparam* ("dedicating one's actions to God," v. 10). This dedication, furthermore, can be considered as an ascension through several different levels of effort:

> For better than [ritual] practice is knowledge. Superior to knowledge is meditation. From meditation [comes] the relinquishment of actions' fruit. From relinquishment [results] immediate peace.[102]

The responses to Arjuna's initial questions are relatively understandable until *Gītā* XI on the discipline of the "vision of the universal form." Here, at his own request, Arjuna is presented with a vision of the gods in the Body of God, which displays the dissolution of all beings. It is an apocalyptic vision that terrifies Arjuna. For our purposes, it can be better understood when treated comparatively. Descriptively, this vision of dispassionate destruction completes the path of yoga, but how does the cessation of the perturbations of consciousness (*citta-vṛtti-nirodhah*) result in such a vision, for this disturbing epiphany seems as much catastrophe as dissolution?[103] In what sense is

---

99   Ibid. XI.32, trans. Feuerstein, 233.
100 Ibid. XI.49, trans. Feuerstein, 243.
101 Ibid. XII.1, trans. Feuerstein, 247.
102 Ibid. XII.12, trans. Feuerstein, 249.
103 In a personal communication, Ben Williams writes, "In the context of the Gītā,

this negative power liberating? How can the void, the abyss, darkness, and non-being be an experience of liberation?[104]

For the *Gītā*, Arjuna is liberated due to his vision and Krishna can continue to teach him to resolve his disturbing doubts. How so? In *Bhagavad-Gītā* VI–X, icons, hymnography, and liturgical rhythms are tolerated insofar as they advance one's concentration. What the Greeks call apophatism and the Latins call the *via negativa* is a style of theology and prayer where one's deepest intention, what one says, can conceptually grasp nothing. Search for God produces a purifying "de-consolation," a light that can be attained by going through the darkness of a long tunnel. Now in the Indian context, how one uses the prayers and mantra is primordial, for they permit one to render *unreal* the field of one's spiritual action. The common denominator here is that apophatic fact allows no bridge between discursive representation and this original, final experience. To reach the "ab-solu" (without restriction, therefore total), a set of oppositions is set in motion. The inadequacy of one concept indicates the nascent appearance of a transcendent concept that surpasses the preceding one.

When the *Gītā* uses the terms "higher-being" (*adhibhūtam*), "higher-divinity" (*adhidaivam*), "higher-worship" (*adhiyajnāh*), and "higher-soul" (*adhyatman*) to define the innate nature of the imperishable Brahman (*aksarabrahmayoga*), this recalls what the Greek language does to such terms by prefacing them with the prefix ὑπέρ in Greek (literally, "above, beyond"), as when Dionysius the Areopagite speaks of "beyond being" and "beyond divinity."[105] In India, more than anywhere else, the unremitting use of negation both logically and ontologically pushes aside all the limits of apparent being in quest for a pure, irreducible absolute that one approaches by knowledge or participation, but whose identity is known only to itself, i.e., in its void (*sūnyatā*). This experience of a positive perfection is flagged by the oppositions: single–multiple; personal–transpersonal; illusion–liberation, which nevertheless remain a cosmic absolute to be destroyed as in the apocalypse of *Bhagavad-Gītā* XI.

---

the restriction of mental fluctuations does not result in this vision, but rather it is Krishna bestowing a divine eye (*divyacaksu*) upon Arjuna which allows him to see it. This divine eye is a kind of yogic capacity of vision which also is described in the *Mahabharata* as being given to certain characters so that they can witness things non-locally."

104 In the distant past, this question was very often asked, and Indians admitted that there exists a plurality of answers. They even compiled lists of these answers with elaborate commentaries. Cf. Bhatta Rāmakantha, *Paramoksanirāsakārikāvritti: An Inquiry into the Nature of Liberation*, ed. and trans. by Alex Watson, Dominic Goodall, and S.L.P. Anjaneya Sarma (Paris and Pondicherry: École Française d'Extrême Orient, 2013).

105 *Pseudo-Dionysius, The Complete Works* (New York: Paulist Press, 1987), and the study of René Roques, *L'univers dionysien* (Paris: Cerf, 1983).

For André Scrima, the negative dialectic is necessary to go beyond the substantivism of any articulated epistemological or ontological manifestation and attain a full transfinite reality free of any predicates.[106] More than the void of what one has just denied, here one detects the opposition between being and doing. Doing is always cataphatic because it is linked to temporality and causality, far from the realm of eternal immobile being. The world was real for many Indians, including philosophers, but the issue here is that, for some, such "reality" might allow it to exist eternally. The illusion of its being would reside in the traces of all actions. Only this Indian *via negativa* allows one to enter their experience meta-empirically.

By contrast, Christian apophatic theology is riveted to the facts of revealed mystery: creation, incarnation, and deification.[107] For Christian theology, not all creation is cosmological, i.e., subject to causality. Thus Scrima writes:

> Conceptualized "sign" rather than being the end term of an intellectual process, it (creation) emerges at the surface of a movement without bottom (abyss) in order to situate the absolute limit (ἀρχή, "archē" in Greek, the founding origin) between the "side" of creation which is both being and void (creation implicating the *ex nihilo*) and the Uncreated (ἄναρχος, ἀκατάληπτος, "anarchos" and "akatalēptos" in Greek), the one whom one cannot pull downwards: God.[108]

One classic expression of the equivalence between the cataphatic and apophatic approaches to God in Christianity, which clarifies the relation between the two approaches, is that of St Maximus the Confessor (ca. 580–662) in his work *Mystagogy*:

> In what concerns God ... neither of the two denominations [i.e., being and non-being] can be properly contemplated.... Nothing of what is said or of what is not expressed can approach him.... For God is an ὕπαρξις ["hyparxis" in Greek, from ὑπάρχω, "hyparcho," "the originating existence-origin"] simple and unknowable and inaccessible to all, totally un-interpretable, being beyond all affirmation and negation.[109]

---

106 André Scrima, "L'Apophase et ses Connotations selon la tradition spirituelle de l'Orient chrétien," *Hermès: Recherches sur l'expérience spirituelle* 6 (1969), 157–69.

107 Parrinder, *Avatar and Incarnation*: chs. 2, 16.

108 Scrima, "L'Apophase," 160; my translation.

109 See Stephen C. Headley, "Liturgically Mediated Plurality," 401–22.

A second comparative "theology" posed in *Bhagavad-Gītā* (X:32) concerns the status of speech in prayer, for, if "I am speech (*vādah*) of them that speak," one is still addressing an illusory Lord. The influential interpretation of yoga imposed by Sankara, the eighth-century reformer, concerns this second aspect of nescience (*avidyā*) or illusion (*māyā*). To summarize: although it is not the world that is illusory, in Sankara's philosophy and ascetic practice, nescience is central for an "objective" principle of an awareness of non-dual Reality.[110] This occurs through the *sakti* of Brahman, his capacity for manifestation, of which there are two aspects: the capacity of concealment (*āvarana*) and that of projection (*viksepa*). Together, they account for the superimposition (*adhyāsa*) of Self and not-Self. In his commentary on the *Brahma Sutras* (II.i.14), Sankara uses illusion (*māyā*,) *sakti* (the capacity for manifestation), and *prakṛti* (nature) synonymously:

> Belonging to the Self, as it were, of the omniscient Lord, there are name and form, the figment of nescience, not to be defined either as being (Brahman) nor as different from it, the germs of the entire expanse of the phenomenal world, called in *śruti* (revealed texts) and in *smrti* (texts transmitted by tradition) the illusion (*māyā*), power (*sakti*) or nature (*prakṛti*) of the omniscient Lord . . .

While *māyā* is neither real nor unreal, since it is indeterminate (*anirvacaīya*), its effects are seen in the phenomenal world.[111] Nescience accounts for the concept of individuality of Self and the multitude of *jīvas*. Concerning the Lord, the *saguna* (or describable Brahman), Rangaswami says:

> As Brahman is *nirguna* [without attributes, hence indescribable], and the transcendental aspect difficult to grasp, for all practical purposes including the creation of the universe, Brahman is *saguna*, that is (Brahman + *māyā*), Isvara, God of religion.[112] Paradoxically for the post Sankara, Advaita (non-dualistic) tradition the identification of Brahman with Self permits the devotee to transcend duality.[113]

110 Sudhakshina Rangaswami, *The Roots of Vedanta* (Delhi: Penguin, 2012), 84.
111 Ibid., 85.
112 For a detailed discussion of the absolute (*Brahman*) relation to the soul (*ātman*) in Sankara and Rāmānuja, see Lacombe, *L'Absolu selon le Védānta*. The critical issue simplified down to the lowest common denominator can be formulated like this: in a vision of creation *ex nihilo* where man is formed in the image and resemblance of God, the vocative used in prayer, "Lord," is not subject to a philosophical analysis but remains a pragmatic act orienting the soul toward its immaterial maker.
113 Rangaswami, *Roots of Vedanta*, 117–18.

So, if *māyā* is that power of manifestation of Isvara that brings about the manifestation of the universe, the Hindu devotee has nowhere to begin his invocation other than accepting the provisional reality of his Lord.[114] This approach in the *Upanisads* is qualified as subjective and clearly corresponds to the devotional (*bhakti*) prayers to be studied below.[115]

In the primary *Upanisads* (ca. 400 BC), yoga had played a major role. Shankara would later force monistic interpretation on the *Upanisads*. For instance, in the *Katha Upanisad*, the monism of these early texts was integrated with an understanding of yoga resembling that of the later Samkhya dualism, juxtaposing consciousness (*Purusha*) and natural phenomena (*prakṛti*). For, after liberation (*moksa*), Isvara (the Lord) is no longer present, since such a final cause vanishes with the abolition of the distinction between individual and universal *Purusha.*[116] Dasgupta has speculated that the tantric image of a savage Kālī standing on a slumbering Shivā was inspired by the Samkhya conception of *prakṛti* as a dynamic agent and *Purusha* as a passive witness. Still, Samkhya and the later tantric schools differed clearly in their view on liberation. Tantra pursued the union of the male and female as ontological realities, while Samkhya continued its severe practice of ascesis for the withdrawal of consciousness from matter.

Certain beliefs, like those concerning the *avatara* (incarnations) of Vishnu, are better understood not separately but in the context of Hindu theologies with their complex and sometimes contradictory epistemologies and cosmologies. Depending on the school to which one adheres, categories move in one direction or another due to their place in a given overall morphology. Here is one example, but others will be given below. There are numerous Hindu liberation theories. Already in the first millennium AD, Sadyojyotih (675–725) and his commentator on the text *Paramoksanirāsakārikā*, Bhatta Rāmakantha (950–1000), enumerated twenty different conceptions of liberation.[117] What the diagram below illustrates is the fact that some theories of liberation are theistic and others are not. The non-theistic ones break

114 Ibid., 27.

115 In a personal communication, Ben Williams suggested that Advaita Vedanta does not create a framework for *bhakti* literature, nor is it a foundational view for all later traditions. It is just one stream of many, and, as such, should be distinguished from the *Upanisads* themselves, because it is one of many interpretations of the key themes of the *Upanisads*, one with which Rāmānuja, Madhva, and other Vedantins radically disagreed.

116 Samkhya is not one of the six Indian orthodox (*āstika*) philosophical schools (itself a late concept); it is extra Vedic for most Vedantins. Even the Nyaya school is unorthodox by its stress on inferential reasoning above the authority of scripture.

117 See Watson, Goodall, and Sarma, *Paramoksanirāsakārikāvritti*, 20.

down into those for which there is no self and those where the self exists in a liberated state. Whether individuality is preserved or not in liberation depends, again, on the school to which one belongs.

Indian Theologies of Liberation in Five Classifications[118]

Theories of Liberation		
Theistic	**Non-theistic**	
Liberation of the soul exists alongside, below, or, in one case, above God	There is no self	or that which exists in the liberated state is a self:
	Individuality is not preserved in liberation	Individuality is preserved in liberation

One could object and say that this is the domain of a certain scholasticism and has little to do with prayer. Still, these norms of knowledge (*pramāna*) and experience (*pratyaksa*) do structure aesthetic and yogic experience as well as how revelation (*sabda*), theology (*brahmavidyā*), and scriptures (*śruti*) are deployed in a given temple. José Pereira lists some 67 topics of Hindu theology.[119] Fortunately, they are structured by a hierarchy. Norms of knowledge are distinguished by experience, inference, and revelation. In turn, revelation proper is distinguished as unsystematized scriptures (i.e., an authoritative interpretation, tradition) or systematized as theology. Hindu theology, while separating objects of transcendent knowledge from those of phenomenal knowledge, is inclined to pursue elaborate distinctions of the categories of the phenomenon as they relate to the transcendent.[120] This is certainly the result of ascetical purification liberating the senses from the passions (*vairāgyam*) such that one's mental states change. This is especially clear in the Yogic teaching of Vijnāna Bhiksu (1550–1600), whose teaching heavily influenced Neo-Vedanta.[121] He shows how suppressible mental states are to be distinguished in terms of the stages of yogic attainment.

However, the major division in Hindu thought lies in the domain of monism, which contends that everything can be explained by a single reality. On this issue, there exist forty schools of thought, some much more influential than others. They can be divided up into schools of difference

---

118 Adapted from Watson, Goodall, and Sarma, *Paramoksanirāsakārikāvritti*, 20.

119 José Pereira, *Hindu Theology: Themes, Texts and Structures* (Delhi: Motilal Banarsidass, 1991 reprint); 411–12.

120 Pereira, *Hindu Theology*, 415.

121 Ibid., 457.

admitting a certain plurality. These are, *inter alia*, Sānkhya, Yoga, Ritualism (*Mimāmsā*), Logic (*Nyāya*), and the different schools of Saiva Siddhānta.[122] The other two groups of schools adopt a modified monism involving identity or non-difference. These include Vaishnava, mostly Vedantic, and Saiva theologies labeled difference in identity.[123] One of these is the influential school named Qualified Nondualism (*Visistādvaita*).

It is important to have mentioned this in our discussion of Hindu prayer, because these schools have very different views of the evolution (*sarga*) of the cosmos from the monad. Of course, in Vedanta, God can be spoken of in himself or as the goal of experience, as in Bādarāyana's commentary on the *Vedānta Sutras*.[124] More significant for the appearance of devotional practices (*bhakti*) is the impact of dualism or non-dualism on their understanding of the evolution of matter (*prakṛti*), for, say, in Sankhya, both the mind (*buddhi*) and the ego (*ahamkara*) actively evolve for better or for worse and are described carefully in each stage.[125]

Such evolution is viewed very differently in Yoga school's understanding of focused awareness (*samprajnātayoga*). Vedanta, on the other hand, allows for a host of intermediary beings called *cetana* (conscious dependent being) that create amongst themselves a whole spiritual sociology. This brings us back to the avatar of Vishnu.[126] For if, in non-dualism, the evolution of the universe leads one into reflections concerning the potency of knowledge (*jñānasakti*) that touch both the macrocosm and the microcosm, in the Vaishnava Sanskrit Agamic texts, one is presented with a variety of theophanies (*suddhasristi*)—thirty-nine in all—that are forms of pure creation, including incarnations or avatars of the ultimate reality (*paratattva*).[127]

With Rāmānuja (traditionally 1017–1137), another scheme allows us to understand the status of intrinsically conscious substances (*pratyak*) that includes not only Isvara, the Lord, but also theophanies (*vyūha*) and incarnations (*vibhava*), which explicitate the icons (*arcā*), objects of worship in Hindu temples.[128] They are differentiated as those that are self-manifested, those consecrated by gods, and those consecrated by men. The trinity of Vishnu (the embodiment of brightness), Brahmā (the *gunāvatāra* of Passions),

122 Ibid., 421–22
123 Ibid., 427–32; 435–36.
124 George Thibaut, trans., *The Vedānta Sutras of Bādarāyana* (New York: Dover reprint, 1962).
125 Pereira, *Hindu Theology*, 452–56.
126 Ibid., 473–74.
127 Ibid., 480–81.
128 Ibid., 484–85.

and Shivā (the embodiment of Darkness) may be relativized by qualifying that tripartite division as with their attributes, whereas Brahman is *nirguna*, attributeless.[129]

This "turbo" overview of Hindu philosophical systems in just a few pages has quickly brought us back to the Vaishnava temple where the average Hindu prays. In a Saivite cult, the so-called attribute incarnations (*gunā-vatāra*) maintain the famous distinctions between God creator, preserver, and destroyer. Still, in most schools, the omnipresence of the dimension of *sakti* (energy)—whether that of Krishna in Vrndāvana with Rādhā and the other cowherdesses, or Shivā's female manifestation (Sakti), which saves the world as Parvati, worshipped with a hundred names in all sorts of local mythologies—result in a multitude of "playful" incarnations (*līlāvatāra*) that baffle the visitor but not the Hindu who relates them in his own spiritual geography.

Bhakti: Devotional Prayer to the Lord

The first half of this chapter has helped us get a basic handle on the dense forest of Indian religious praxis from approximately 1500 BC to AD 500.[130] Such a brief overview is introductory at best, yet it prepares us to turn to a clearer understanding of the place occupied by prayer in India, both from an internal and an external perspective.

Bhakti prayer represents "invocation" in the more European sense of the word, as opposed to the traditional Indian realizations through mantras with mythological backgrounds. The *bhakti* tradition may be summarized as a separate strand of Hindu devotion that developed into non-Vedic, non-Sanskrit, vernacular Indian invocations, many of which are still in common use today.[131]

---

129 Ibid., 486, 492.

130 In order to understand what is scripture, as opposed to invocation, Barbara A. Holdrege, in *Veda and Torah* (Albany, NY: State University of New York Press, 1995), has compared these two systems of meaning, studying their uses and means of transmission. In Vedic literature, word or speech (*vāc*) is the source of many names (*nāmas*) and is hypnotized as the female aspect of the androgynous *Purusha*. Florina Dobre-Brat, "From Śabda-brahman to Śabad: The Way from a Transpersonal Concept to Personal Experience," in *Bhakti beyond the Forest: Current Research on Early Modern Literatures in North India 2003–2009*, ed. Imre Bangha (Delhi: Manohar, 2013), 191, explains that, as the mysterious first sacrificial substance, only one-quarter of her is spoken speech, while the other three-quarters remain unmoved (*Rigveda* X.125.3b).

131 If we move to the post-Vedic period, the research on Indian *bhakti* in English and French is already vast. For a survey of the origins South Indian *bhakti* in the Pallava period (fourth to sixth centuries), see Emmanuel Francis, "Royal and local Bhakti under the Pallavas" (2014). For a full overview of Tamil Vaishnava (Vishnuite) *bhakti* down until the twentieth century, see R. Varadadesikan, "Vaisnava Literature in Tamil," in *Mapping*

Since the seventh century, says A.K. Rāmanujan, "*bhakti* movements have arisen in different regions and languages, spanning the whole Indian sub-continent."[132] He insists that the *bhakti* defiance to tradition is not discontinuity and that *bhakti* is possessed of missionary zeal. The poet-saints of the movements are "drawn from every social class, caste and trade" and therefore represented a popularist approach to traditional religion, widening the access to ritual and prayer that had formerly been restricted to the priestly caste of the Brahmins.

Bhakti prayer and poetry emphasized the possibility of a closeness with the divine—the experience of *kṛpa* ("grace") that results from contact with God—and is not reliant upon set prayer formulas, rituals, and temple offerings. *Bhakti* also espoused the ideas of monotheism and the spiritual significance of personal belief, and thus, unlike classical Hinduism, *bhakti* religions came to proselytize.

The multitude of regions and languages spanned by the vernacular *bhakti* poets deserve separate study. We will simply begin in South India, in the Tamilnadu, the heartland of Indian theism, with the *ālvār* (or Ashwars, the "God-filled") devotional poets, who represent the earliest source of such vernacular *bhakti* devotion.

There are two main difficulties in approaching *bhakti* prayer: first, we are unfamiliar with the divinities addressed; second, *bhakti*'s entire hymnographic style is shot through with exotic and unusual metaphors. In this, *bhakti* religious love poems more closely resemble Sufi poetry than the Christian poetry known in the West, yet even this resemblance is of a limited nature.[133]

While Patañjali's *Yoga sutra* strove strictly after the cessation of consciousness (*citta-vrtti-nirodhah*), banishing theistic conceptualizations, the reader of the *Bhagavad Gītā* was led to achieve the experience of Brahman united to *ātman* through a yoga employing theistic devotions. In Vaishnavism, this allowed one to enter into the presence of Vishnu's avatar Krishna, while, in Shaivism's union with Shivā, his divine protection was obtained through yogic practices (*inter alia*, raising energies through the serpents, *kundalinis*, different *cakra*).

---

the Chronology of Bhakti: Milestones, Stepping Stones, and Stumbling Stones (Pondicherry and Paris: Institut Français de Pondichéry, École Française de l'Extrême-Orient, 2014), 287–303. On female royal patronage of *bhakti* temple worship (seventh to ninth centuries), cf. the conclusion to Charlotte Schmid, *La Bhakti d'une Reine: Siva à Tiruccennampunti* (Pondicherry and Paris: Institut Français de Pondichéry, École Française de l'Extrême-Orient, 2014).

132 A.K. Rāmanujan, ed. and trans., *Speaking of Śiva* (Harmondsworth: Penguin, 1973), 9, 15.

133 On Sufi religious poetry, see John Renard, *Knowledge of God in Classical Sufism* (New York: Paulist Press, 2004); Annemarie Schimmel, *The Mystical Dimensions of Islam* (Chapel Hill: North Carolina University Press, 1975).

The differences between these overlapping schools of *bhakti* over the centuries led to the distinction between five forms of devotion (*bhāva*) and four kinds of *bhakti*:

1. Devotion to the Supreme Self (*Atma-bhakti*);
2. Devotion to the Cosmic Lord as a formless being (*Ishvara-bhakti*);
3. Devotion to Lord in the form of various gods or goddesses (*Ishta Devata-bhakti*);
4. Devotion to God in the form of the guru (*Guru-bhakti*).

The "optional" qualities of God in these four forms may be explained philosophically, but this is not our priority here. More relevant to the study of Hindu prayer are the five "emotional" approaches to worship:

1. *śānta*, placid love for God;
2. *dāsya*, the attitude of a servant;
3. *sakhya*, the attitude of a friend;
4. *vātsalya*, the attitude of a mother toward her child;
5. *madhura*, the attitude of a woman toward her lover.

These will reappear below in the poetic metaphors expressing the four kinds of devotion to the Lord.

A Westerner reading *bhakti* poems for the first time might legitimately ask if the poems and hymns found in the anthologies of the great Indian *bhakti* poets are even prayers at all, and not simply scriptures presenting interpersonal dialogues. Yet they are clearly declarations of love for the Lord.[134] This is a delicate issue, for three poetic genres have succeeded one another. Classical *sangam* Tamil love poetry (first centuries AD) gave rise to devotional poems expressing inner (*akam*) emotions used in temple worship, where they displayed the pain of separation (*viraha*) of the devotee from his Lord. In its

---

134 My understanding of a Christian approach to non-Christian prayer is different from that of Clooney, *His Hiding Place is Darkness,* who compares the Hindu *Holy Word of Mouth* (*Tiruvaymoli*) with the Hebrew *Song of Songs* by reading the two poems conjointly, thereby increasing their mutual understanding. This is his fourth essay in comparative theology after *Seeing Through Texts: Doing Theology among the Śrīvaiṣṇava of South India* (Albany, NY: State University of New York Press, 1996); *Divine Mother, Blessed Mother: Hindu Goddesses and the Virgin Mary* (Oxford: Oxford University Press, 2005); and *Beyond Compare: St. Francis de Sales and Śrī Vedānta Deśika on Loving Surrender to God* (Washington, DC: Georgetown University Press, 2008). For other currents in comparative theology, see Clooney, ed., *The New Comparative Theology: Thinking Interreligiously in the 21st Century* (London and New York: T & T Clark International, 2010).

later Telugu forms, such poets as Ksetrayya even took the erotic metaphors found in temple *padam* poems back to their literal mercenary context, where the relationship with courtesans ends in the orgasm of sexual union.[135]

While devotion to Vishnu-Narayan, the Bhagavat, was spreading through Pancaratra theology, during the Pallavas (sixth to ninth centuries), the twelve Alvār poets were shunning philosophical speculations, yoga, and ritualism, uniting all social classes in the search for quasi-permanent contact with the *avatars* of Vishnu, Krishna, and Rāma. Their four thousand songs (*Divya Prabandha* or divine commentary) made up the first non-Sanskrit Hindu religious "text." In local sanctuaries, the Lord appeared to them in human form, in statues covered with jewels and clothing referencing the impersonal Brahman as a personal god on whom one is totally dependent, with whom one is certain to be united. Pre-occupations with *samsāra* have receded as they weep before Nārāyana in a nuptial mysticism stronger than anything seen in the *Bhagavad-Gītā*. In regretting one's sins, one admires the beauty of the Lord and abandons oneself to the eternal God with whom one becomes united, for the individual soul is only a manifestation of this grace (*prasâda*) that constitutes his substance and life.[136]

One often-overlooked dimension of this kind of hymnography arises from the fact that we read its words without hearing it sung.[137] To be understood, a prayer should be prayed, and not reduced to the printed page, which, while better than nothing, is but a pale reflection of the original. Most ancient Hindu prayers are also known to us in the contemporary (Carnatic) mode of recitation or singing;[138] still, some work has been done on earlier recitatives by recent ethnographic research.

Tamil Sangam Poetry: the Tēvāram Poems

The date of the oldest poems from the Tamil Sangam academy period is ca. 300 BC, although the songs existed orally before this date. *Sangam* poems

---

135 See A.K. Rāmanujan, Velcheru Narayana Rao, and David Shulman, eds. and trans., *When God is a Customer: Telugu Courtesan Songs by Ksetrayya and Others* (Oxford and Delhi: Oxford University Press, 1995).

136 Perhaps the closest Christian parallel to this devotional poetry is found in the Biblical Songs of Songs, which is interpreted in terms of a relationship between God and the believer, or group of believers, as bridegroom and bride.

137 For a perceptive description of how chant arises, not from music itself, but from the music inherent in the words of human speech, see ch. 12 in Madeleine Kovalevsky, *Maxime Kovalevsky: L'Homme qui chantait Dieu* (Paris: Éditions Osmondes, 1994).

138 For an overview, cf. T. M. Krishna, *A Southern Music. The Karnatik Story* (Harper Collins India, 2013).

fall into two types: those describing the "inner field" and the "outer field." "Inner field" topics refer to personal or human aspects, such as love and sexuality, and are dealt with in a metaphorical and abstract manner; "outer field" topics discuss all other aspects of human experience, such as heroism, ethics, benevolence, generosity, social life, and customs. Some of these poems are as old as the Hebrew Psalms. Generally speaking, the 2,381 poems by 473 poets, which have come down to us over the last 2,000 years, show no concern with devotion to a personal god, yet it is here that we find the earliest models for the *bhakti* prayer poems.

For instance, Tipputtolar wrote a praise of Murukan, "the Red One," a war god who was later identified with the god Shivā. Included in the anthology *Kuruntokai* (ca. 100 BC–AD 250), this evocation on the threshold of the nascent *bhakti* movement uses a violent style:

> Red is the battlefield; / as he crushes / the demons. /
> Red his arrow shafts, / Red the tusks / Of his elephants: /
>   This is the hill / Of the red One / With the whirling anklets, /
> The hill of red glory lilies / flowers of blood.[139]

From a later period comes the *Tévāram,* the first seven volumes of the *Tirumurai,* the twelve-volume collection of early Tamil Saivite devotional poetry.[140] Between the sixth and the eighth centuries, Tamil saints known as "masters" (*nāyanār*) wrote these song "offerings" later collected in the *Tévāram,* which came to constitute the primary scripture of Tamil Saiva sects. These *bhakti* prayers represented a revolutionary piety; down until the present day, almost every Tamil village has had a temple for Shivā where the lives of these saints, and the songs they composed, are sung. What is more, until the rise of *bhakti,* Sanskrit had been considered the language of the gods (*daiva-vānī*), and, just as Buddhism and Jainism broke that captivity by using Prakrits and Pali (vernacular forms of classical Sanskrit), so the rise of popular *bhakti* was accompanied by a more popular and accessible poetry implicating diverse sectors of Indian society: men, women, outcasts, and, later, even Muslims.

That this first occurred in Tamilnadu is not surprising, since Tamil alone

---

139 Andrew Schelling, *The Oxford Anthology of Bhakti Literature* (Oxford: Oxford University Press, 2011), 3; Rāmanujan, trans., *Speaking of Śiva.*

140 See the digital *Tévāram* prepared by Subramanya Alyar, Jean-Luc Chevillard, and S.A.S. Sarma, Collection Indologie no. 103, Institut Français de Pondichery & EFEO. The *Tévāram* is a collection of 800 Tamil hymns dating back to the seventh and eighth centuries, written by three poets collectively known as the "Three" and constituting the initial part (*Panniru Tirumurai*) of the Tamil Saiva scripture.

among the "non-Aryan" civilizations had such an ancient literary tradition. The role of poetry as sacred scripture plays a much larger role in Saiva and Vaishnava praxis than anything comparable in Europe, excepting the hymnography of the Eastern Orthodox from Greek and Syriac sources.[141] Peterson has written: "The *bhakti* lyrics of the *nāyanār* masters differ in many respects from the poetry of the saints of later *bhakti* cults in other regions in India. So it was that the *Tēvāram* over the centuries became a motivator and symbol for provincial Tamil sectarian and communal life."[142]

As early as the Pallava and Chōla kingdoms, *ōtuvār* (chanters) were asked to sing selections from the *Tirumurai* during public rituals, and this indeed continues up to today in important Shivā temples throughout Tamilnadu.[143] In some, the "song of place" is inscribed on the temple wall, from which people read before doing *darshana* in front of the statue of the deity. Indira Peterson provides a photo of some verses from the *Tēvāram* (Appar V, 196) inscribed on the wall of Truvânmiyûr temple, to which it is dedicated.[144]

Thus, inside the temple, words (both sung and written), statues, and music are used to evoke the *Tēvāram*. While South Indian philosophers could write in Sanskrit, the cult of Vishnu and Shivā spread instead in the vernacular *bhakti* poetry, overlaying the Brahmanic traditions. Sidhānta philosophers shared with the *nāyanārs* a common cosmology expressed in temple devotions, their writings on the nature of the soul, God, bondage, and release.[145] Their views of scripture evolved from the Vedas to the *agamas* (later sects with their own scriptures), whereas the *ācārya*, the spiritual guides, esteemed that the Alvār poems were the equals of the authors of the Vedas. A further difference was that, over time, the Saivas were mostly Vellala, while the Vaishnava were mainly Brahmins.[146] Today, when Tamil Saivas worship at secondary temples displaying a given aspect of Shivā, they sing selections from the *Tēvāram* and the *Tiruvācakam*, while Tamil Brahmins and members of others sects prefer recent Sanskrit *stotras* (devotional stanzas) and litanies

141 See Kamil V. Zvelelbil, "Tamil Literature," in *Handbuch der Orientalistik 2: Indien*, ed. Jan Gonda, Band 2; "Literatur und Bühne," Abschnitt 1 (Leiden/Cologne: E.J. Brill, 1975).

142 Indira Viswanathan Peterson, trans., *Poems to Siva: The Hymns of the Tamil Saints* (Delhi: Motilal Banarsidass, 1991), 5–6.

143 The Cholas dynasty flourished in the Kaveri river basin on India's southeast coast from the ninth until the thirteenth centuries. During the reign of Rajendra Chola ca. AD 1030, this dynasty extended to most of present-day western Indonesia.

144 Truvânmiyûr temple (Peterson [1991], figure no. 15).

145 Trans. Peterson, *Poems to Siva*, 53.

146 In the post-Chola history of Tamilnadu, these were rich non-Brahman peasant castes that arose out of the aristocracy of the ancient Tamil social order, categorized pejoratively as upper *shudra* (*sat-shudra*).

of the deity's names (*nāmāvalīs*). When the *ōtuvārs* sing Tamil hymns at the end of *pūjā* offerings, the Smārta Brahmins (Advaita Vedantins, regarding Adi Shankara as the definitive reformer of non-sectarian "orthodox Hinduism") consider this secondary, while the Saivites underline their belief that Shivā receives Tamil singing just as readily as he receives the mantras in Sanskrit. During festive processions of their temple icon (*utsavamūti*), the Brahmins lead the way, chanting Vedic hymns (especially the Saturudrīya hymn from the *Black Yajur Veda*), while a group of *ōtuvārs* follow behind the festival image singing the *Tēvāram*. The influence of the one on the other can also be seen in the techniques of memorization and repetition using Vedic methods (*adhyayana*). Paradoxically, while the Tamil Saivites only accept Vedic scripture as revelation, but without attaching special doctrinal significance to it, the Tamil Vaishnava have integrated the Vedas with the songs of the Alvār and its philosophy of qualified monism (*Vishishtadvaita Vedanta*) stemming from Rāmānuja.

Tamil Saiva are at pains to give their sect a proper primary scripture, that is to say, a hymnography.[147] Any Saiva's performance of the *Tirumurai*, composed from the sixth to the eleventh centuries—the four *nāyanārs'* song offerings for Shivā—has doctrinal value, because, as the experience of these four saints, the songs provide personal inspiration through devotional experience.[148] Contemporary editions of the *Tēvāram* further annotate certain hymns as being appropriate for those seeking marriage or children, for the demise of a family member, ill health, financial loss, etc.

On the other hand, the musical tradition of the hymns is an eleventh-century reconstruction. The ancient melodies composed of *pan* chants were attuned to different moods and times of day of the *Tēvāram*. These have been lost and were replaced early on (tenth century?) by Carnatic raga scales using musical concepts including *swara*, *raga*, and *tala*. The chanters or *ōtuvārs* are typically recruited in musical schools at the age of seven or eight, after which they begin to memorize the twelve divisions of the *Tirumurai* of these 63 *nāyanār* poets. Once fully trained, they will stand near the inner sanctum (*garbhagrha*) of a Tamil Shivā temple during the several daily *pūjā* (offerings), which are carried out by the Brahmin priests. If most of the regular visitors to the temples know the best-loved song offerings by heart, the *ōtuvārs* perform them using a free style (*viruttam* or *cuttānkam*) that improvises on the eight set tunes that coincide with the *pan*'s eight distinct beat patterns. This allows the *ōtuvārs* to repeat or skip over certain verses in

147   Trans. Peterson, *Poems to Siva*, 57.
148   Ibid., 59.

order to interpret the hymn's meaning. By these abbreviations, the chanter does not summarize, but "explores and expands the 'stanzaic' microcosm."[149] Since the tenth century, this *viruttam* style has also been used when the great Sanskrit epics and *Purānas* are recited in Tamil. Just as in Tamil street drama (*terukkūttu*) and the Carnatic dramatic musical traditions, both folk and classical, these fixed and free recitatives are present. Chanting or recitative (*virutham*: verses without rhythmic beats, only half-sung) is primarily used for narration, but, in the situation of reciting the *Tēvāram,* the *viruttam* style relates to the vocalization of religious verse, as does the Sanskrit *stotra.*

One *nāyanār,* Campatar, wrote seventy hymns dedicated to the Cattaināṭar Shivā temple in Cīrkāli. Here is an example of one of these hymns, sung there by an *ōtuvār* (recorded July 1978). Square brackets indicate emphasis through repetition and musical ornamentation.

> **The saint-poet Campatar (*Tēvāram* IV.83.1):**
> If you ask: / "What is the town / of him who holds the battle-axe / in his hand? The answer is: / "Kulumala, where the flag flutters / on the gateways of the great mansions, / this great town / here herons gather in the canals in the fields / and bees, drunk on honey from their beloved's lips, / cling to every flowering palm."

> **Campatar (*Tēvāram* IV.82.6):**
> [This Tōnipuram,] / beautiful with [enduring life, / and grandeur and justice,] / [once floated] / on the rising waves of the cosmic flood / The flower [feet of Kalumalam's Lord] / who burned the triple city with his arrow / rule us forever.
> [My Lord who is ambrosia to me,] / the Lord who is dear to all who seek him, / he who holds fire in his hand, / skull-bearer who flayed the huge killer elephant, / god with the poison-stained throat, / is the great god who lives / in Piramapuram / of fragrant groves.

> **Campatar (*Tēvāram* II.176.11):**
> He who gives blessing to his devotees, / the Lord who is the ultimate truth, / the king who dwells in the stone-walled Piramapuram / [Campatan] once attained him. / [Those who know these ten verses] of the poet / are blessed, / and [will have riches,] / and [enjoyment of every kind].[150]

---

149 Ibid., 66.
150 Ibid., 67–72.

Hymns to Shivā in Kannada

The "heroic Saivite hymns" (*vacana*), translated from the Kannada language spoken in the South Indian state of Mysore, were composed as prayers by four *bhakti* poet-saints from the tenth to twelfth centuries.[151] These poets' several thousand *vacanas* have set the standard for all subsequent poets—"in all the length and variety" of literature in Kannada, says their translator Rāmanujan, "there is no body of lyrics more strikingly original and impassioned."[152] They are considered to be philosophical epigrams, the Kannada *Upanisads*, and the psalms of Saivism.[153]

Vīrasaivism, followed by the "militant devotees of Siva," was a protest movement against the temples of the rich, which they despised as "standing" (*sthāvara*) because such temples, built in stone, were capable only of symbolism, while devotion to the Vīrasaiva Trinity (*guru, linga*, i.e., wandering mendicant monks, or *jangam*), on the other hand, opened all things to the possibility of sanctification. There exist permeable membranes between the public Hindu religion and the personal religion of these combative poets, indicated by dotted lines in the diagram proposed below.[154] Just as the division between the three major denominations of Christianity and the delineation between Shi'ite and Sunni Islam is not watertight, there exists interpenetration between the cults of Shivā and Vishnu.

HINDUISM[155]

	STRUCTURE		ANTI-STRUCTURE
	Establishment "Public" Religion		Protect "Personal" Religion
	GREAT TRADITION	LITTLE TRADITION	
TEXT	Vedas, etc.	Local Purānas, etc.	
PERFORMANCE	Vedic ritual	Local sacrifices, etc.	V. Bhakti
SOCIAL ORGANIZATION	Caste-hierarchy	Sects and cults	
MYTHOLOGY	Pan-Indian deities	Regional deities	

Vīrasaiva rejected both rituals and offerings in favor of grace (*kr.pa*), which these Vishnuites claimed cannot be called down on command. In the *vacana* poems, they proclaim the priority of experience (*anubhava*) of unpredictable,

---

151 These hymns are translated in Rāmanujan, *Speaking of Śiva*.
152 Rāmanujan, trans., *Speaking of Śiva*, translator's note.
153 Ibid.
154 Ibid., 16.
155 Adapted from Rāmanujan, *Speaking of Śiva*, 16.

unmediated vision. The received (*śruti*) and remembered (*smriti*) religious practices and texts expressing superstitions, image worship, and Vedic sacrifices (*yajna*) are ridiculed as too conventional (*phalaśruti*) to constitute a real relationship with God. It is not by doing "good" that one can ensure one's salvation; non-discursive being and knowing alone conveys grace. The Vīrasaiva have eight emblems (*astāvarana*), which do not constitute a betrayal of, or a detachment from, *bhakti,* but are simply pious symbols of observances.[156] For instance, a poem of Chowdayya, the ferryman, says that, just as the winnower must wait for the wind, so the grace of god cannot be provoked, but only received by the worshipper who needs nothing, neither the names of god, nor anything else, as he waits on his Lord.[157]

The ninth-century Tamil poet Manikkavacaker explores the personal experience of the god's power that, he says, renders organized religion useless:

> He grabbed me / lest I go astray / Wax before an unspent fire, / mind melted / body trampled.
> I bowed, I wept, / danced and cried aloud, / I sang, and I praised him; / Unyielding, as they say / as an elephant's jaw / Or a woman's grasp / Was love's unrelenting / seizure.
> Love pierced me, / like a nail / driven into a green tree. / Overflowing, I tossed / like a sea, / heart growing tender, / body shivering. / While the world called me Demon! / And laughed at me, / I left shame behind, / Took as an ornament / the mockery of local folk. / Unswerving, I lost my cleverness / in the bewilderment of ecstasy.

As said above, this revolution of piety that occurred in South India between the sixth and the ninth centuries split into two strands: the Saivite poets (*nāyanār* singers) and the *Vaishnava* or the twelve *ālvār* ("deep divers," i.e., drowned in Vishnu), both groups stressing surrender to a personal God. Their followers were almost as devoted to their guru poet-saints as to the divinity. The female Alvar poet was found by Periyalvar in the soil while he was hoeing the ground. As Antal grew up, her devotion to Vishnu's *avatar* was disturbing in such a young girl:

156 These emblems are: having a guru to lead one to Shivā; wearing a symbol of Shivā (*linga*) around one's neck; a wandering mendicant (*jangama*) who represents the community of Shaivite saints; receiving holy water (*pādōdaka*) at the feet of one's guru as a mark of devotion; receiving food (*prasâda*) blessed by the touch of the guru; receiving holy ascetical ash (*vibhūti*) from a virtuous man; having a prayer rope of *rudrāksa* (eyes of Shivā) seeds; using the five syllable (*pāncāskarā*) mantra.
157 Rāmanujan, trans., *Speaking of Śiva*, 13–14.

> Her concerned father (Periyalvar)—unclear what to make of his daughter's fixation on Krishna, and her stubborn refusal to wed a human husband—learnt from the later dream that Vishnu intended to marry her. A wedding was organized at great expense. And Antal was carried to Vishnu's temple at Rankanata in a bridal procession. When the retinue arrived, Antal climbed from the palanquin. She approached the image of Vishnu, embraced its feet, climbed on to the serpent couch, and vanished.[158]

This was the first example of such a "disappearance" of a female poetess, but later *bhakta* poets like Mirabai, Muktabai, and Lal Ded will also disappear when absorbed into their deity.

The poet Nammâlvâr ("our own ālvār," immersed deep in love for Vishnu), who lived ca. 880–930, is considered the greatest of these poet saints. He is known for his 1,102 verses, the "Sacred Utterance" (*Tiruvaymoli*), which poured from his mouth as a boy *yogin*, who, prior to that moment, was mute. Called the "ocean of Tamil *veda*," these verses, which the translator Rāmanujan describes as "an icon for endless, ever-changing forms of the Lord,"[159] are characterized by spontaneity. The originality of this poet is that his constant relationship with the god leads him to proclaim that everyone can become a singer of their Lord. In one poem, he describes this intimacy from several points of view, dividing the poem into sections:

> What she said; what he said; what her mother said; what his mother said; What she said; What he said; What she said; What she said to her girlfriend; What her foster mother said; What her girlfriend said.[160]

The poem ends in this way:

> . . . . what shall I say / to stop? / Being all three worlds / and nothing / being desire / being rage / being both the flower-born Laksmi / and the anti-Laksmi / black goddess of ill-luck / being both honor and shame / our Lord / lives in Vinnakar / city named sky / which the gods worship lovingly / and in my evil heart / he lives forever / flame of flames.[161]

---

158 Schelling, *Oxford Anthology of Bhakti Literature*, 10.

159 A.K. Rāmanujan, *Hymns for Drowning: Poems by Nammalvar for Vishnu* (London: Penguin, 2005); quoted in Schelling, *Oxford Anthology of Bhakti Literature*, 18.

160 Schelling, *Oxford Anthology of Bhakti Literature*, 19–27.

161 Ibid.

In the *Tiruvaymoli*, the Lord (Vishnu) speaks through the poet, the paradigmatic seeker for union. But Nammâlvâr is both human and divine, for the *Tiruvaymoli* is also an authorless creation of the Lord. Here revelation is not one-sided, not exclusively given by the Lord to a devotee, for the latter, by a process of apotheosis, becomes the one he adores.[162] As Vasudha Narayanan explains, when one recites this revelation one is always close to the Lord, for the poem itself is of trans-human (*apaurseya*) origin.[163] This makes ritual recitation possible for everyone, both in the temple and at home. But, over time, the Brahmin Vishnuites in the temples tended to take over recitation.[164]

A Vaishnava Poet: Basavanna (ca. AD 1106–1167)

The most prominent of these poet saints was Basavanna. As he and many other *bhakta* poets describe, the devotee's search for the kingdom of the Lord—for an experience of a face-to-face relationship—is symbolized by the intimacy of lover/beloved, father/son, mother/child, whore/customer, or master/man.

> I don't know anything like time beats and meter / Not the arithmetic of strings and drums / I don't know the count of iamb and dactyl. / My Lord of the meeting of the rivers (*Kūdalasangamadéva*), / As nothing will hurt you / I'll sing as I love. (Poem 949)[165]

Just as in North India in the poetry of Kabir (ca. 1368–?), we have, in South Indian Vīrasaiva, a form of *bhakti* prayer addressed to the *nirguna* (attributeless) god, who, even if he has the name of Shivā, has none of his mythology. While the cult of Krishna is the best example of *saguna* ("with attributes") of a god with attributes, most of the Vīrasaiva saint-poets practiced a *nirguna bhakti*.

In Poem 820 ("The Temple and the Body"), we see further treatment of

---

162 In the Hellenistic Roman world, beginning with Philip II of Macedonia and down to Julius Caesar, emperors began to accord themselves divine honor, but, in the earlier "hero temples" (ninth century BC onward), these rites were linked to the mythology of certain topologies. By the fifth century BC, these were basically civic rites. I mention this here because, in the case of *bhakti*, apotheosis is something totally different. Again, the deification as understood by Christianity is something else: "For this is why the Word became man, and the Son of God became the Son of man: so that man, by entering into communion with the Word and thus receiving divine sonship, might become a son of God." See Irenaeus of Lyon, *Adversus haereses*, 3.19.1, trans. Adelin Rousseau (Paris: Éditions du Cerf, 1984), my translation into English.

163 Narayanan, *Vernacular Veda*, 11.

164 Ibid., ch. 3.

165 Rāmanujan, trans., *Speaking of Śiva*, 43–47. "Lord of the meeting of the rivers" (Kūdalasangamadéva) is the name of Basavanna's guru and appears at the end of all his poems.

the theme of poverty and its role in worship:

> The rich / Will make temples for Siva. / What shall I / A poor man, do?
> / My legs are pillars / The body the shrine / The head a cupola / Of gold.
> / Listen, O Lord of the meeting rivers, / things standing shall fall, / but
> the moving ever shall stay.[166]

As Rāmanujan explains, the poor can become what they are—the Lord's temple—while the rich can only build them. Basavanna prefers the original to the symbol, the body to the temple, what is moving (*jangama*) to what is static (*sthāvara*). The wandering mendicant or *jangama*, by his poverty, is the type of monk who, by his ascesis, lives "forever." While this *bhakti* poetry may seem more secular and, in certain cases, certainly more erotic than the Vedic hymns, that poetry undeniably celebrates the glory of divinity through the prism of their own passion for their Lord. Some of the "God immersed" (Azhwar) poets stated boldly that their goal was not liberation (*moksa*), but Krishna or Vishnu themselves. This love for God is sometimes confusing to us, as God in an avatar may seem to be a human person. Thus, in the *Periyazhwar* collection, the famous Azhwar poet Vishnucittan (ninth century A D) wrote lullabies for Krishna and used metaphors such as a mother's anxiety for her absent son, or pain at watching her young daughter enamored of Krishna, or the fact that her runaway daughter has eloped with Krishna.[167]

Indeed, as a noun, *bhakta* means both a worshipper and a lover, for its verbal root (*bhaj*) means to share, partake, enjoy, participate, and to make love. In Sanskrit poetics, a "twilight" speech (*sandhya-bhasa*) poetically destroys and recreates language in order to better seize ineffable experience. In the vernacular languages of India, this oral speech, recited and chanted in temples, "does" prayer. It is obviously not the official speech of state ceremonies, even if Tamil oratory with its Dravidian aesthetics largely overlaps the sphere of *bhakti* overflowing into political rhetoric.[168]

What characterizes *bhakti* prayer poems is that they were often composed orally and spontaneously, which explains why some collections of *vacana* are so large. Each rendition is intoned or chanted differently. Reflecting through images brings out paradoxes and illogical formulae that capture the

---

166 Ibid., 1.

167 P.S. Sundaram, trans., *The Azhwars: For the Love of God* (London: Penguin, 1996), 6–8; 8–9; 10–12; 13–15.

168 See Bernard Bate, *Tamil Oratory and the Dravidian Aesthetic: Democratic Practice in South India* (New York: Columbia University Press, 2009).

intensity and honesty of the devotee. These poets often fix the attention of the surrounding public by using dance and sensuality, not to describe or teach, but to multiply the voice of the poem.[169] On the other hand, in the *nirguna* devotion of the North Indian Kabir, his deity Ram is an ineffable "true name" (*Sat Nam*), which his poetry tries to convey.

Hymns to Vishnu in Telugu

Annamayya was a Telugu poet who lived at the famous South Indian hilltop shrine of Tirupati. During the 1420s and 30s, he wrote thousands of devotional poems to Venkatesvara—Vishnu, as locally venerated.[170] Annamayya's poems comprise two primary genres, metaphysical and erotic, but both elevate the quest for intimacy with Vishnu into a form of worship using sung poems as prayers. When the poems are explicitly addressed to Vishnu, they "cajole, taunt, ridicule and toy with" the poet's relationship to his god.[171] Annamayya's innovative form of poetry spread throughout the Tamil- and Telugu-speaking areas and created a major musical heritage in Carnatic music.

Reading the extract from the beginning of the poem below, one senses that "modernity" began in India long ago in the form of introspection through poetry:

> Tell him this one thing. /
> Distant rivers always reach the sea.
>
> Being far is just like being near. / Would I think of him if I were far? /
> The sun in the sky is very far from the lotus. / From a distance, friend-
> ship is intense.
> Distant rivers reach the sea.
>
> The moment he looks at me, I look back at him. / My face is turned
> only toward him. / Clouds are in the sky, the peacock in the forest. /
> Longing is in the look that connects.
> Distant rivers reach the sea.

169 The word for shaman in the sense of those capable of possession in Tamil is *camiyati* and, in the Kallar country, *kodangi*, which, like *camiyati*, refers to those who go into a trance and speak the gods, "say oracles."

170 Spoken by some 75 million people, the Telugu language is found in many areas of South India in Andra Pradesh. See Annamayya, *God on the Hill. Temple Poems from Tirupati*, trans. Velcheru Narayana Rao and David Shulman (Oxford and New York: Oxford University Press, 2005), vii.

171 Annamayya, *God on the Hill*, 125.

Tirupati Venkata, temple Andra Pradesh

To speak of desire is as good as coming close. / Haven't I come close to him? / The god on the hill is on the hill / and where am I? Look, we made love. / Miracles do happen.
Distant rivers reach the sea.[172]

In this poem, we see Annamayya's characteristic use of refrains following each stanza. As with this example, such refrains frequently evoke Vishnu through a specific poetic image. Annamayya casts his relationship with his god in strikingly intimate terms: "What use is ecstasy," he asks, "without the agony of separation?" He describes his love as a "burning sun," asks whether there is any point to "patience without the fury of passion," and cries out, "Beauty is empty without desire." He attests to the thrill at the possibility—even if uncertain—of intimacy with his "god on the hill," undermining his own devotional endeavor ("Why speak tender words when there is no closeness?") while emphasizing his continued hope ("Intimacy is dull without doubt.... Bring in our god on the hill").[173]

172 Trans. Rao and Shulman, 2005, 4.
173 Ibid., 5.

We now turn to the immense hymnography in praise of the goddess Durgā. The hymns addressed to her represent a very different type of religious movement, which continued parallel to *bhakti*, but with quite a different emphasis.

Case Study: Hymns to the Goddess Durgā

The pan-Indian deity known by many names, pre-eminently Devī and Durgā, has an iconography both benign and dreadful. She may be represented in an irritated state of violence (*rajas*), distinguished from the two other cosmic qualities (*guna*): serenity (*sattva*) and torpor (*tamas*). The hymns dedicated to her discussed below are not addressed to a divine person. She is the form of an immobile and infinite "formless" absolute. She incarnates the energy of creation that emerged initially as vibration (*nādā*); concentrated on a white point (*bindu*), Shivā, and on a red point, Shivā's *sakti*, this vibration expresses creative desire (*kāma*). Shivā is without division (*nish-kalā*) but associated with a female *shakti*; he has attributes (*sa-kalā*). *Prakrti-shakti* is the essence of the goddess Devī, an aboriginal substance. The three *guna*, when they enter into differentiation, create the cosmic illusion that is *māyā*. A tantric analysis of desire (*kāma*) distinguishes each one of these energies as mantric phonemes. Devī is sometimes represented dancing on the prostrate body of Shivā, symbolizing the creative projection of Devī by the absolute, which nonetheless remains unperturbed, just as the dichotomies she encompasses—good and evil, ugliness and beauty—are all illusory. Durgā binds mankind to *samsāra*, yet the experience of suffering and death leads them on to an understanding of liberation. Less metaphysically, David Kinsley shows how Kālī (i.e., Devī or Durgā), like Krishna, is a non-Vedic deity, the "dark one," associated with the earth.[174] The devotee's life and death in the hands of the goddess and the quest for purity is realized and attained through blood sacrifices. The naked goddess of iconography is unsheathed power leading the devotee to symbolic death when he transgresses the sexuality of the goddess.[175] This is the death of ignorance, i.e., the loss of egoism, a salvation while still on earth, leading one to be reborn in the womb of the goddess, his "mother." In both these cases, if the goddess's polarities are embedded in her identity, prayer to her looks more like a psychological alchemy as practiced by the tantrics.[176]

---

174 David Kinsley, *Hindu Goddesses: Visions of the Divine Feminine in the Hindu Religious Tradition* (Berkeley and Los Angeles/London: University of California Press, 1986), ch. 8, 116–22.

175 D.K. Shulman, *Tamil Temple Myths* (Princeton: Princeton University Press, 1980), 140–41.

176 See David Gordon White, *The Alchemical Body: Siddha Tradition in Medieval India*

During the Sanggam period in South India (300 BC–AD 300), the goddess Korravai was a deity of war and victory who was later conceptualized, like Devī, as a consort goddess.[177] Korravai, as the patron of arid regions, was linked to an ideology of raid, heroism, and gift. Beginning in AD 300–600, Tamilnadu shifted from pastoralism to a plough-based economy. Accompanying stronger state integration, competition sprang up between Jain, Buddhist, and Brahmanic religions for patronage with the kingdoms of Pallava-Pandya (seventh to ninth centuries AD). On the one hand, there were *brahmadeya* or tax-free brahmin agrarian settlements and, on the other, the *bhakti* sectarian movements proposing the equality of all before God. During Chola (tenth to thirteenth centuries), *bhakti* spiritualties were integrated into the temple cults, with insistence on the analogy of cosmos, territory, and temple. When royal and sacred authority was so conceptualized coherently, royalty became the ideal patron for a temple. Thus, if, in the early medieval period, ruling classes adopted Brahmanic religion and its Puranic idiom to propagate their claims to kingship and power, the *bhakti* movement's quest for an egalitarian religion was all the more cogent.

In the Vedic period in India, goddesses also had different forms, myths, and epithets; the epithet of Vāc (the speech goddess) was Ambhrnī. The Veda knew female goddesses like Prthivī and Aditī (the undivided divine consciousness), and already the iconography of the late Vedic goddess Ambikā showed the influence of *bhakti*. Devī, in the famous Puranic song *Devī-Māhātmya*, discussed below, incorporates features of the earlier goddesses, such as Saumyā and Kālikā. Most importantly, once Brahman loses status in the *Purāna*, Devī rises as *saktī*, equal of Shiva.[178] It is obvious that some sort of syncretism is taking place, or at least a succession of pre-eminent figures.[179]

But are similar goddesses being identified with a paramount one, or are local cults, of which there were a multitude, being more loosely integrated into the figure of the Vindhya region's buffalo slayer goddess (Durgā), who in turn integrated into Saivism via the Purānic hymn of the *Devī-Māhātmya*? With so

---

(Chicago and London: University of Chicago Press, 1996), and his *Sinister Yogis* (Chicago: University of Chicago Press, 2009).

177 R. Mahalakshmi, *The Making of the Goddess: Kurravai Durga in Tamil Traditions* (London: Penguin, 2011), 2–4.

178 *Saktā* designates the doctrine (veneration of the goddess), while *saktī* is the dynamic feminine aspect of the Absolute.

179 Thomas B. Coburn, *Devī-Māhātmya: The Crystallization of the Goddess Tradition* (Delhi: Motilal Banarsidass, 1984), 89–208. Coburn studies epithets, myths, and hymns similarly found in previously distinct goddess motifs.

many common traits, all female divinities may be invoked as mother.[180] Kunal
Chakrabarti studied the major and minor traditions as they were integrated
in the secondary *Upapurāna* in the early medieval period in Bengal.[181] He
claims that, by comparison, Mahāyāna Buddhism was more structured than
the Brahmanical religion, which, by encouraging Sanskritization, nonetheless
leads to a "carefully constructed Śhākta theological tapestry... with local
goddesses in their unitary theistic form, *mūlaprakriti*." In a way, one could
say the historical evolution matches the metaphysical synthesis presented
above. The *Devī-Māhātmya* is the first comprehensive account of the goddess
to appear in Sanskrit, for originally she was a "non-Aryan" or southern Indian
vision of the divine.[182]

The Value of a Hymn

The *Devī-Māhātmya* is the name given to an extract from the *Markandeya
Purāna* (chapters 81–93), which contains a hymn to Durgā.[183] This hymn's
value as a prayer-text does not derive immediately from its addressee, the
goddess Durgā—still less so if she is considered to be more a "cosmic force"
than a person.

We may approach this hymn in a manner analogous to approaching the
Rig-Veda. Following F. Staal, what matters in Vedic ritual is not the words themselves, but rather *how* the words are recited. A reciter of the Veda (*srotriya*) is,
like a medieval monk, simply focused on copying the form of his manuscript;
form is placed before meaning.[184] This fact helps us understand how the eclipse
of Vedic rituals and the rise of devotional praxis led to "Vedic" orality becoming
a means, a technique of invocation, that made *bhakti* possible. Since the Veda
was never translated into the vernacular, we must ask in what sense it can really
be understood. Renou suggests that the boundary between the heard, *śruti*, as
in listening, and the remembered, *smriti*, is that between orality and editing.[185]

Coburn claims that it is in precisely this way, as the extract from a longer text, that the *Devī-Māhātmya* still resonates with the Vedas as "the
heard to the remembered (*śruti* to *smrti*)." What is more, the *Devī-Māhātmya*

180 Mahalakshmi, *The Making of the Goddess*, 13.
181 Kunal Chakrabarti, *Religious Process: The Purānas and the Making of a Regional
Tradition* (Delhi/Oxford: Oxford University Press, 2001).
182 Coburn, *Crystallization of the Goddess Tradition*, 84.
183 F.E. Pargiter and Jośi Kanhaiyālāla, trans. and eds., *The* Mārkandeya-purānam: *Sanskrit text, English translation with notes, and index of verses* (Delhi: Parimal Publications, 2004).
184 Renou, "La valeur du silence," 11–18.
185 Ibid.

subsequently itself was treated itself as "heard" (*śruti*). Whenever and wherever the *Devī-Māhātmya* was finally written down, this "text" incarnated just one moment in its development in the historical Indian religion.[186] Because *Devī-Māhātmya* was memorized and transmitted orally (and verbatim, like the *Purāṇa* and the epics) for use in recitation in a religious context, the simple act of copying it constituted an act of devotion. Since the hymn's function changed over time, Coburn believes that it is not essential to discover its exact scriptural origin.

For Coburn, the hymns of the *Devī-Māhātmya* (found in parts 1, 5, and 11) are counterpoint to the accounts of the goddess's salvific activity in the world.[187] A commentator, Jagadīsvarānanda, considers these songs so sweet that they must *always* be chanted, so the value of the hymns lies in their transcendent ahistorical quality.[188]

The *Devī-Māhātmya*'s recitation comes out of a much older tradition. Louis Renou states that since the *Rig-Veda* mantras are viewed as eternal (*apauruseya*), there exists a distinctive self-consciousness about the fact of utterance—the power of the spoken word, *vāc*, functions as the precursor of the substratum of reality, *ātman-brahman*. The Veda refer to themselves as feminine, i.e., fertilized by a male deity, a reflection of the higher neuter abstraction (*brahman akshara*). For Thomas Coburn, the Veda do not tell a story, but their expression is part of a ritual formula praising God in a liturgical context.[189] Thus their diction is characterized by intentionality, which means that the way they are said is as important as what they say.

G. van der Leeuw remarked that hymns, prayers, exorcisms, etc., share the trait of names that do not designate personalities but are essential to specify, through the name, the actuality of the god in a word.[190] Thus individual gods can represent an idea, fire, word, etc.[191] This is the case in the goddess Durgā,

---

186 Coburn, *Crystallization of the Goddess Tradition*, 67.

187 Ibid., 72.

188 This is clearly true of any oral tradition of sung prayer; the beauty of the words enhances the chant, and the chant enhances the meaning of the poetry. The illustration closest to European culture would be the Romano-Frankish monadic chant of the Middle Ages (eighth to the tenth centuries). Cf. François Cassingen-Trevedy, OSB, "Speciousus forma (Psalm 44:3) l'enluminure sonore des mots qui dissent la beauté dans le répertoire du chant romano-franc," in *Colloque Le Beau et la beauté au Moyen âge* (Paris: Institut Catholique de Paris, 2011), 18–19, 14. See also Sivaprasad Bhattacarya, "Indian Hymnology," *Cultural Heritage of India* 4, 464–78.

189 Coburn, *Crystallization of the Goddess Tradition*, 76.

190 G. van der Leeuw, *Religion in Essence and Manifestation: A Study in Phenomenology* (New York: Harper and Row, 1963 reprint).

191 On the names of gods, see van der Leeuw, *Religion in Essence and Manifestation*, 148–49.

whose name translates as "difficult to approach." In this context, Coburn points out that the popularity of the recitation of names (*namastotras*), which "capture" power through such recitation, derives from the earlier Vedic intuition of the eternity of sound forms, which leads on to intentionality in diction and devotional fervor of the hymnography.[192] While there may be *mythological* antecedents for the *Devī-Māhātmya*, it is the frequency of the well-known epithets of Durgā ("hard to approach") or of Chandikā ("the Terrible")—who defeats Mahisa, the buffalo king of the *asura* demons—that emerges out of this Vedic background.[193] This is how the *Devī-Māhātmya* makes the Vedic Sanskrit tradition contemporary, at the same time keeping the worship of the goddess traditional. J.A.B. van Buitenen even shows how the *Bhagavata Purāna* sounds like the Veda, since its liturgical and devotional repertory resembles that of the *Rig-Veda*. In this sense, the *Purāna* are a harmonious revision of the Veda, a confirming elaboration of those much earlier hymns. *Devī Māhātmya* is both a culmination and a threshold.

We turn now to a brief summary of the hymn itself, following Jean Varenne's analysis.[194]

The Devī Māhātmya

The *geste* of the great goddess contains three successive narratives (*carita*), each of which describes one of her battles with evil. The first episode is brief. At the end of the preceding cosmic cycle, while the universe was still only water, Vishnu was resting on the serpent Shésha in a yogic sleep (*yoga-nidrā*) proper to the inter-cosmic cycles. Brahmā-Prajāpati is about to create the universe when he realizes that two demons (*asura*) are planning to kill him to prevent this creation. To escape this fate, he concentrates his thought on the yogic sleep to awaken God, in whose eye the goddess resides. With the singing (*tustāva*) of a hymn, this incantation makes the obscure goddess come out of God's body and stand before Brahmā. In a hymn (*stuti* or *stotra*), the goddess of great illusion (*mahā-māyā*) is celebrated by Brahmā (I, vv. 73–87) so that she will next emerge from Vishnu, who can then go on to slay these two demons Madhu and Kaiṭabha.[195]

---

192 Coburn, *Crystallization of the Goddess Tradition*, 7.
193 See the birth of Mahisa in G.P. Bhatt, ed. and trans., *Vamana Purāna* (Delhi: Motilal Banarsidass, 2013), chs. 17 and 18.
194 Varenne, *Grande Déesse*, xix–xxviii.
195 Or, in *Markandeya Purāna*'s continuous numbering, 81.54–67.

The *Brahma-stuti* (song I.54–67):

[Brahmā said:]

54. You are Svāhā, you are Svadhā, you are the exclamation *vaṣaṭ*, having speech as your very soul. / You are the nectar of the gods, O imperishable, eternal one; you abide with the threefold syllabic moment (*mātrā*) as your very being.

55. (You are) the half-*mātrā*, steadfast, eternal, which cannot be uttered distinctly. / You are she; you are Sāvitrī (the Gāyatrī *mantra*); you are the Goddess, the supreme mother.

56. By you is everything supported, by you is the world created; / By you is it protected, O Goddess, and you always consume (it) at the end (of time).

57. At (its) emanation, you have the form of creation; in (its) protection (you have) the form of steadiness; / Likewise at the end of this world (you have) the form of destruction, O you who consist of the world!

58. You are the great knowledge (*mahāvidyā*), the great illusion (*mahāmāyā*), the great insight (*mahāmedhā*), the great memory, / And the great delusion, the great Goddess (*mahādevī*), the great demoness (*mahāsurī*).

59. You are the primordial material (*prakṛti*) of everything, manifesting the triad of constituent strands, / The night of destruction, the great night, and the terrible night of delusion.

60. You are *śrī*, you are the queen, you modesty, you intelligence, characterized by knowing; / Modesty, well-being, contentment, too, tranquility and forbearance are you.

61. Terrible with your sword and spear, likewise with cudgel and discus, / With conch and bow, having arrows, sling, and iron mace as your weapons,

62. Gentle, more gentle than other gentle ones, exceedingly beautiful, / You are superior to the high and low, the supreme queen.

63. Whatever and wherever anything exists, whether it be real or unreal, O you who have everything as your very soul, / Of all that, you are the power (*śakti*); how then can you be adequately praised?

64. By you the creator of the world, the protector of the world, who (also) consumes the world (i.e., lord Viṣṇu) / Is (here) brought under the influence of sleep (*nidrā*); who here is capable of praising you?

65. Since Viṣṇu, Śiva, and I [Brahma] have been made to assume bodily form / By you, who could have the capacity of (adequately) praising you?

66. May you, praised in this fashion, O Goddess, with your superior powers / Confuse these two unassailable Asuras, Madhu and Kaiṭabha,

67. And may the imperishable lord of the world be quickly awakened, / And may his alertness be used to slay these two great Asuras.[196]

Vishnu, awakened to the gravity of the attack, and thanks to an illusion created by the goddess who encourages the two *asura* to charge, promptly cuts off both of their heads with his discus.

The second episode of this myth (songs 2–4) describes the goddess's victory over the demon buffalo (*mahisa-asura*). This famous victory is celebrated in sculptures all over India, throughout Java, and in much of Southeast Asia.

Statue of Durgā slaying Mahiṣāsura, Dulmi, Manbhum District, West Bengal[197]

196 Translation by Thomas B. Coburn, *Encountering the Goddess: A Translation of the* Devī-Māhātmya *and a Study of its Interpretation* (Albany, NY: State University of New York Press, 1991), 36–38. Verse numbering follows Coburn.

197 http://www.oldindianphotos.in/2010/10/statue-of-durga-slaying-mahisasura.html

The setting of the Goddess's battle with the demon is firmly Vedic: the universe is already in place and is governed by Indra. After a century-long battle, the demon buffalo and the *asura* conquer Indra and take over the heavens (*svarga*). The gods wander on earth like simple mortals and pray to Vishnu and Shivā for deliverance; from the faces of these two emerges a great anger, a giant light that illumines the universe, and which mingles with light from the other gods and coalesces into the female (*narī*) form of a goddess (*amarā*). This female champion is given the weapons of each of the gods: the trident of Shivā, the thunderbolt of Indra, the club of Yama, etc., and is decked out with female jewelry; the gods acclaim her with shouting. As the demons approach, struggling to understand, the goddess is given the name Chandikā ("the terrible one"), and proceeds to cut to pieces the first demon troops and their lieutenants.

Finally, Chandikā comes face-to-face with Mahiṣāsura, a demon who switches form between buffalo, lion, man, and elephant, before returning to his original buffalo form. Chandikā pierces his back with her trident. A man then emerges from the mouth of the buffalo, but, before he can attack the goddess, she decapitates him and grasps his severed head in one of her hands (3:20–39).

The fourth song describes the hymns that pleased her; she promises to always come to the gods' aid. Next, in the fifth song, the twin demons Shumbha and Nishumbha usurp the gods' sovereignty. The deities return to the Himalayas to sing to the goddess (song 5:11), addressing her successively with both Saivite names—Shivā, Gauri, Rudra, Durgā—and Vaishnava names—Vishnumāya, Yoga-nidrā, and Laksmī. Thus alerted, the goddess of the Mountains, Pārvatī, asks who is singing this hymn. Ambikā comes out of her body, causing her to lose her luster such that henceforth she is called the Black One (Kālilā). At this point, Shumbha asks Durgā to marry him, to which she replies, "Only if you defeat me in battle." In the sixth song, she defeats his army, and, in the seventh song, he sends into battle his lieutenants Chanda and Munda. Retaliating in a black fury, the goddess, here called Kālī (the Dark One), defeats this army, but, later, Ambikā, Kālī, and the lion are surrounded by Shumbha's third wave of troops. The gods (Brahmā, Shivā, Kumara, Vishnu, Vahāra, the boar avatar of Vishnu) and Indra come to their aid by emanating seven goddesses (or energies, *sakti*) called the seven Mothers (*mātr-gana*) (7:17–23). In the eighth song, Durgā sends Shivā to mediate with Shumbha, but this is of no avail. In the subsequent battle, the *asura* are scattered until the demon Ratabīja appears. The blood flowing from his wounds is transformed into as many troops. To save the day, Chandikā tells Kālī that she should drink his blood until he dies.

In the ninth song, the final battle with the twin demons begins. First Nishumbha is killed, but from the mouth of his corpse appears a person (*Purusha*) whom Chandikā immediately beheads. In the tenth song, Chandikā breaks Shumbha's weapons one by one. When Shumbha is floored, the contact with the earth restores all his power. He charges her and grabs Chandikā, after which the battle becomes aerial. Finally the evil one (*dur-ātman*) is killed by Chandikā's lance and the universe shines while, moving into the eleventh song, the gods begin a long litany to celebrate Nārāyanī—i.e., Durgā, Kālī, Chandī, and Ambikā, all of whom are forms of Devī (the goddess).

Chandī promises to protect the gods each time the *asura* attack, and, in a series of prophecies, we learn that Shumbha and Nishumbha will return but that the goddess will incarnate herself in a man (Krishna) or a woman called Kitchen Garden (*sākambharī*), from whose body vegetables will appear after she confronts the Drought demon. One senses here the dawning of the mythological landscape of the Indian middle ages.[198]

In the twelfth song, Chandī tells the gods how to worship her by listening to the tales of her prowess, building temples for her for the recitation of these hymns, and offering her *pūjā* in the autumn (12:12). The most important devotion of all, however, is that of listening to the *Devī-Māhātmya*. Thus the devotee who hears this hymn will be saved from a long list (12:13–29) of calamities.

This resumé of the main episodes for the Western reader is tedious, but, in contemporary Bengal, the celebration of the Durgāpuja, a mammoth festival (*ustav*), has become an all-night celebration of togetherness, a return of the collective village life in an urban setting. Disenchantment has been deferred! The spectacle, by taking on Bollywood glamour and techno qualities, presents a real theater of dreams that Durgā's mythic victory had never known before.[199] Nonetheless, it remains an epiphany of the goddess; it was in the *Devī-Māhātmya* of the *Mārkandeya Purāna* that, for the first time, the articulation of energies as it appears in Saktism was proposed. For example, Chakrabarti summarizes how, in medieval Bengal, once the *brāhmana* migration began in the Gupta period (third to sixth centuries AD), "the newcomers, who had to adjust with the prevailing tradition, adopted these goddesses with suitable modification and transformed them into brahmanic divinities by means of a carefully constructed *Śhākta* theology—precisely that phenomenon which I have called the Puranic process."[200]

198 Vaudeville, *Myths, Saints, and Legends*, part 1.

199 Cf. Sudipta Kaviraj, "Disenchantment deferred," Akeel Bilgrami, *Beyond the Secular West* (New York: Columbia University Press, 2016), 135–87.

200 Chakrabarti, *Religious Process*, 171–72.

Durgā killing Mahesa, the leader of the demon armies. A domestic icon for celebrating the annual autumnal Durgā Puja, sold at Kalighat, Calcutta (photo S.C. Headley).[201]

Hindu Domestic Prayer

We turn now to consider briefly how all of this impacts Hindu domestic prayer. As we have seen, among the goddess's epithets are the Vedic ritual words *svadhā* and *svāhā*, even if she is never explicitly called the Word (*vāc*). As an ultimate reality, the goddess is understood as an interior phenomenon or *nitya* (the inwardly eternal one), while *sraddhā* (the movement of the heart

201 The Bengali *Devīpurāna* sold in the temple market at Kalighat in Calcutta (2016) contains the poems; it is also readily available in cassette recordings.

in faith) is our reaction to her, "... as [a] *sakti*, the universal manifestation of capability, regardless of who or what is the external form of its manifestation."[202]

In Indo-European languages, "to believe," *credo*, is cognate with the Sanskrit *sraddhā*; their common root is **krid-do* (the giving of credit). But, in Europe, prayer is always associated with faith in a person, while Hindu cosmology so enlarges the concept of living beings that it expands to include all creation, which thus potentially becomes the object of worship. So faith is an epithet of the supreme goddess of sacred energies, since the goddess abides in all creatures that are good and true.[203] This was already the topic of *Rig-Veda* X.151:

1. With trust is the fire kindled; with trust is the oblation poured. / We at the head of good fortune make known our trust with speech.
2. O Trust, this (speech) spoken by me: make it dear to him who gives, dear to him who intends to give, / and dear among the benefactors who offer sacrifice, o Trust.
3. Just as the gods created trust in themselves among the powerful lords, so among the benefactors who offer sacrifice make what has been spoken by us trust(ed).
4. Trust do the gods revere, sacrificing for themselves with Vāyu as their herdsman— / trust, with a purpose that comes from their heart. By trust one gains possession of good.
5. Trust do we call early in the morning, trust at midday, / trust at the setting of the sun. O Trust, place a trusting heart here in us.[204]

While there is nothing exotic about the importance of faith in the daily life of Hindus, for the European, this expression of faith may seem unfamiliar because it does not fit with the idea that faith always means faith in a person. But is this really so, and if it is, how does it differ between the two religious cultures?

Stephen Huyler, in his photographic essay "Meeting God: Elements of Hindu Devotion," describes the devotions of a certain Rāmachandra who lives in southern India, where Mariamman (the goddess Shakti) is commemorated every Tuesday morning.[205] Having bathed, Rāmachandra leaves his house, where, in front of the front door, his younger sister has just finished

---

202 Coburn, "Scripture in India," 304.
203 Ibid., 169–74.
204 *Rig-Veda* X.151:1–5, trans. Jamison and Brereton, 1636.
205 Stephen Huyler, *Meeting God: Elements of Hindu Devotion* (New Haven: Yale University Press, 2002), 4–50.

drawing with colored rice powder a *kolam* on the ground in the form of a lotus. Every Tuesday, to fulfill his vow to Mariamman, Rāmachandra fasts the whole day, keeping his mind and body pure so as to provide a conduit for the goddess's guidance. While he worships the goddess daily in his household shrine during his morning *pūjā*, Tuesdays are special: he goes to the local temple for *darshan*, "to see with piety" his deity.

Before entering the temple, Rāmachandra buys a package of white camphor and a coconut, which he adds to the basket of bananas and the red hibiscus flowers that he picked from his garden before leaving home. Leaving his sandals (and hence the dirt of impurities) at the entrance to the temple, he walks around the central sanctuary, leaving it on his right. Rāmachandra then stands in line with other men to enter the sanctum sanctorum (or "chamber of the womb," *garbhagrha*). As he goes up the steps, he rings a temple bell hanging from the ceiling whose tone clears his mind from distractions. In other temples, one would give one's name, community of origin, and astrological birth date to be uttered by the priest, holding one's gifts on an offering tray (*ârâti*) to be presented inside before the divinity. There, in the rear, stands the decorated statue of Mariamman, barely visible under her layers of clothes and garlands.

The priest moves along the line of worshippers and collects their offerings before returning to the icon in the interior of the temple. He may pull the curtain shut for several minutes. When the bells ring, he opens the curtain, while he waves a tray of seven camphor flames before the goddess, who now appears with a fresh garland of flowers, illuminated in all her brilliance. Rāmachandra gazes into her eyes, thus meeting (*darshan*) her, and feels his world being restored with centeredness and well-being. The priest comes back out with the tray of lighted camphor, and those in attendance, eyes closed, wipe their faces with its smoke. On the same tray are ash (*vibhūti*), symbolizing purification, and vermillion powder (*kumkum*), representing Shakti. Placing the fourth finger of their right hand in these two powders, the persons present, or the *pujari*, "dot" their foreheads. Their offering baskets are returned, minus an offering to the temple, and each person brings his basket of *prashad* (offerings to a divinity) home to be shared with his family. The process of reciprocity has been completed.

In some temples, icons that are *svayambhu* (not carved by the hands of men), i.e., formed naturally by God, are specially venerated. This is often the case, as in the photo below, with aniconic Shivā *linga*. The bronzes of Dancing Shivā are considered iconic, whereas the brute stone "sculptures" like these three *linga* are considered non-iconic. As abstract sculptures of *phalluses*, they display his energy.

A village shrine to the great nâga deity that here takes on modest
proportions. They are designated by yellow and red powder markings,
bracelets attached to the tree trunk, and flower offerings.

Even if the priests chant Sanskrit verses (*sloka*) or other prayers, it is important to note that, outwardly, the devotees commune with their eyes as much
as their voice. When a new statue of a divinity is created, it is the eyes that
are carved, or painted in, last, just before the life force is "breathed into" the
icon (*prana pratishtha*).

Srisa Chandra Vasu, in his *Daily Practice of the Hindu*, gives the Vedic mantra
according to the strict order of worship of the divinities: first the Pancha
Devata (Aditya/the Sun), Ganesha, Devī, Rudra, Shivā, and Nārāyana, before
one's family deity and one's personal deity (*ishta-devatā*).[206] The sixteen verses,
used as mantra, are taken successively from the hymn in *Rig-Veda* X.90, cited
above; they have meaning, but it is their enunciation at the appropriate
moment that counts. Once these mantras have been uttered, the "holy basil"
(*tulasi*) leaf offering begins, followed by the benediction of water, etc.[207]

206 Srisa Chandra Vasu, *The Daily Practice of the Hindus: Containing the Morning and
Midday Duties* (Delhi: Munshiram Manoharlal, 1991), 128–34.
207 Vasu, *Daily Practice*, 134–38; 139–51.

Huyler describes the *ordo* of daily worship, *pūjā,* of a Hindu extended family, as if it resembled the different gears of a watch, each in a separate place, but all functioning together.[208] While the wife rises early to paint designs on the outer courtyard wall, representing her family's deities of protection as a visual form of invocation and thus expressing the family's piety, her husband begins his day attending to the holy basil bush (*tulasi*) kept in front of their house. The *tulasi* plant is an incarnation of Laksmī. As he walks around the plant carrying a brass pot of water, a new strip of red cloth, and a marigold garland, he calmly chants his prayers to the goddess. Removing the dusty red cloth placed on the plant the day before, he pours water on it while chanting a litany of Laksmī's names and attributes. Having placed the garland around the upper branches, he shakes the basil bush to make several leaves fall. These he gathers up and takes inside.

In the meantime, the grandmother prepares the day's offerings in the kitchen, and, once they are ready, she brings them out in front of the *pūjā* platform. There, this senior female of the family sits down on the left of the platform and conducts the rituals, beginning with a prayer before removing from the statues the garlands of the preceding day. In this particular household, the hereditary family deity is Krishna, who is depicted in the statue playing his flute with his consort Rādhā at his side. On the right is a stone statue of Surya, the sun god, and on the left is Hanuman, the monkey god. Below are two black fossils, ammonite shells (*salagramas*) representing Vishnu. On the wall above are framed photographs of the deceased father and framed polychromes (*samipadam*) of gods and goddess, some having advertisements on their borders for local businesses. At this point, the master of the house takes the basil leaves, places one under his tongue, and give the others to his wife and mother to do the same. The leaves of the Lakshmi plant confer well-being. His wife now pours holy water from a brass pot over the statues and rubs them clean with her fingers. Next, her mother-in-law passes to her the fresh clothes with which she dresses the statues while chanting prayers. Having placed a fresh vermillion dot on their foreheads, she decorates the statues with marigold and hibiscus. The framed photograph is also garlanded.

Now the main *pūjā* can begin. The plates of food prepared by the grandmother are held up before the *pūjā* platform. The wife takes burning cubes of camphor from on the *ārāti* tray and waves them in a circular manner before each image. She also rings a brass bell with her left hand, attuning the family's spirits to that of the deities. Each person should then open his heart

208 Huyler, *Meeting God,* 66–89.

in *darshan* to his chosen god. The *ârâti* tray is passed around so everyone can place their hands in the "cooling" flames of the camphor. Thus the home and the family's divinities and spirits have been honored and "seen."

Just as the household rituals of each family differ, so also the temples of India represent and reflect an immense network of individual, family, and regional affinities. The *kuladevata* is the protector of home and family, and, traditionally, it embodied the energies of all the other members of the house, past and present. The rituals that ensure the purity of the *kuladevata* remove from the house negativity created by death or violence. Preserving the harmony of the extended family is thus attributable to the *kuladevata* of the family clan. But the *kuladevata* cannot easily be made to change houses, even if, in some areas, rituals exist to request the *kuladevata* to enter an earthenware pot of water during the time it takes to install it in its new house.

On the other hand—while each individual is free to change sects and so personalize the form of a pan-Indian divinity with which he associates specifically—whenever a bride leaves her parents' house and its *kuladevata*, she adopts the household god of her husband's family. When she brings her own personal private devotions to her chosen god into the new house, this will include his icon. One's personal divinity (*ishta-devatā*) presents directly the un-manifest Brahman, guiding one like a guardian angel through life. While one venerates one's *ishta-devatā* at home daily, one may decide to undertake a long pilgrimage to a certain mountain like Tirumalai (Andra Pradesh), or temple like that of Menakshi in Madurai (southern Tamilnadu) to experience more ascetically—and hence intensely—the *darshan* of one's *ishta-devatā* there where he or she is particularly present. Famous poet-saints have composed song offerings in these places, which pilgrims recite en route or listen to once they have arrived in the temple. While all consecrated images, however modest, are receptacles of divine energy, the annual celebration of the main divinity in an important regional temple will be attended by hundreds of thousands of devotees. In certain temples, the main icon is revealed only briefly, but, prior to that, many prayers have been said and sung.

Conclusion

At the beginning of this chapter, we claimed that the character of prayer in India was different from that in Europe, since the Hindu notion of personhood requires deconstruction in order to obtain union with the absolute. As Panikkar puts it, in Vedic Hinduism, "[by] sacrifice creation reverts to Man. The sacrifice of the cosmic Man signifies divine transcendence investing humanity."[209] In Europe today, the understanding of personhood is also changing rapidly, but nihilistically so.[210] The doctrine of the Hebrew Bible concerning the creation of man "in the image and the likeness of God" (Gen. 1:26–27) is fading from the European consciousness, allowing little room for a Christian "animism" that celebrates how all creation praises God (Pss. 148–150).

A second factor that makes Hindu prayer different arises from its understanding of creation. Hinduism is an anthropo-cosmic religion. Despite the strength of the *bhakti* devotional movement, addressing one's prayers to a Lord, *Isvara*, remains optional. The attribute-less (*nirguna*) Brahman, whether conceived of as a monad or as partially dualistic, leaves little room for any relationship between God and man that we in the West would call personal, which seems to follow from the idea that personhood is a de-constructible obstacle to enlightenment. The main Hindu preoccupation, perhaps due to a pervasive "horizontal" animism (all matter contains life-bearing energies), is to reorient the vision vertically to a fully transcendent horizon, an absolute beyond all absolutes. As we will see in the prayers described in the short Chapter 5 on Buddhism, it is less the form and words of prayer that can be changed than their orientation and purpose. Prayer is an eminently flexible expression of man's hunger for life through purification and communion.

209 Panikkar, *Vedic Experience*, 75.
210 See the monthly review *Esprit* (no. 403, March–April 2014).

CHAPTER 5
Prayers Versus Chanting in Buddhism

FROM OUR STUDY OF PRAYER IN HINDUISM, WE NOW TURN, however briefly, to another of the great Asian religions: Buddhism. What can one say about prayer here? First of all, we should note that Buddhism, still more than Hinduism, is not easy to classify in terms of Western religious categories. While Buddhism is considered wisdom—spiritual hygiene with a deep and well-articulated doctrine—it should not be called a religion unless we are speaking institutionally and sociologically. It is the oldest monastic institution in India after the Jains, dating from some five centuries BC. These meditative traditions disparage the flow of the inconsequential thought that characterizes much of life, and instead focus on the renouncement of all passions, and emphasize that all human beings should be treated with compassion equally, despite their differences. What space might there be in such a belief system for prayer, as we understand it? One could argue that, just as, when one chants the Hebrew psalms, one is proclaiming the qualities of God, when chanting Buddhist sutras, it is more a question of proclaiming than any prayer "to" a god.

In the Theravadin or *Shâvakayâna* (Listeners') monasteries of Sri Lanka and Southeast Asia, Pali scripture studies concern general morality and contemplation; but it is only the "basket" of scriptures concerning wisdom that are specific to Buddhism, the rest being basically morality common to all Indian spirituality. The psychological dialectics and pragmatism characteristic of Buddhism are definitely a method. By overthrowing conceptual mindsets and freeing oneself from epistemological contradictions, "the vastness of the unlimited space of truth opens up."[1] Buddha, the Tathāgata ("the one who comes and goes in the same way"), taught a doctrine of "no-beings" or of not-self (*anâtman*). Here we will not enter into the details about what Gautama Buddha himself actually taught—for an analysis of the collection of his sermons, while fascinating, is a lengthy undertaking—but will briefly mention

---

1 Edward Conze, *Buddhism: Its Essence and Development* (New York: Harper Torchbook, 1959), 19.

the major changes in the formulations of his initial doctrine:

- The path toward salvation becomes accessible to all mankind, thanks to
  the intervention of the *bodhisattva* (compassionate enlightened beings).
- Impermanence and the suffering that life brings with it are now
  viewed more positively; the void (*sūnyatā*) constitutes the universe.
  The cosmic Buddha's nature is shared by nature and all mankind.
- Salvation by renouncing the world is focused on the possibility of
  illumination, liberation, *nirvana* in *samsāra*.

After these major changes in the paradigm of Buddhism, the basic tension
between the monastic practice of early *arhats* (worthy, perfected ascetics)
and popular piety, in the Mahāyāna school, were resolved by the role of the
bodhisattva, who, in the "Great Vehicle," postpone their own enlightenment
in order to help others attain it.

In the Pali-language canon, the Buddha taught that suffering only arises
because of our belief in self.[2] So *self-extinction* is the prelude to *nirvana*, and
provides the ultimate meaning of life. Self is not a fact, because it corresponds
to no reality, but only to day-to-day illusions. The goal of Buddhist wisdom is
to learn how to live without the illusion of an ego. We are, of course, naturally
reluctant to engage in what seems initially to be such a pessimistic path, yet,
once we agree that paradise is not found on earth, the joy of such a monastic
renunciation can be profound. While we may be concerned that such an
understanding of non-self will encourage nihilism, it is, in fact, possible to
view it as spiritually healthy.

The belief in, or rather the illusion of, self arises from the five *skandha,* the
aggregates of Body, Feelings, Perceptions, Impulsive Emotions, and Consciousness. The oldest Buddhist sermons, the *Dharma* (or *sutra* doctrine), the *Vinaya*
(monastic rules), and a fourth section of advanced doctrine (the *Abhidharma*), are
those works retained by the first Buddhist council held after Buddha's death.[3]

The total production of Buddhist writings in all the languages where
Buddhism developed is gigantic. The canon of Buddhist scriptures, *Tripitaka,*
which contains sermons and discussions of these sermons, varies with the
different schools of Buddhism. While not enough works survive in Sanskrit
to form a canon, many were translated into Tibetan and included in their

---

2 Pali is a simplified (*prakit*) later form of Sanskrit, the "perfect language"; from the
fifth century BC, it was used in Sri Lanka and Southeast Asia for the Buddhist scriptures.

3 The first Buddhist council was held c. 400 BC at Sattapanni caves, Rajgrih, presided
over by the monk Mahakasyapa.

Kanjur and *Tanjur*—these total some one hundred volumes. All *sutras* begin by describing what the author claims Buddha once said in a certain place and at a certain time. The great *sastras* of later authors like Nāgārjuna and Vasubandhu of the Yogācāra (yogic practice) school are, by contrast, veritable philosophical/epistemological ascetic treatises. While many documents were transmitted orally and are now lost, what has survived in Sanskrit, Pali, Tibetan, Chinese, and Japanese is a tribute to the seriousness with which Buddhist monks preserved and completed their tradition, often undertaking pilgrimages from China to India to study at the Buddhist university at Nalanda, in Bihar south of Nepal. This *mahāvihāra*, or great monastery, had up to ten thousand monks at its apogee and survived for a thousand years before it was destroyed by a Muslim invasion in the twelfth century.

The gradual, but quasi-total, disappearance of Buddhism in India can be attributed to the disappearance of the earlier royal support, both financial and institutional (Maurya under Ashoka in the third century BC; Gupta era, fourth–sixth centuries AD; and the Pala Empire, eighth–twelfth centuries AD). The development of Hinduism's *bhakti* movement in the eighth century in Tamilnadu, which we studied in Chapter 4, arose partially as a result of the spiritual challenges of Buddhism. The Chinese Buddhist monks who came to India from the fifth to the eighth centuries already spoke of Buddhist decline in the northwest of the subcontinent. The arrival of the new political regime in North India from central Asia, which brought Afghan and Persian culture to the Gangetic plains, obviously strengthened Islam. Finally, after southern India was temporarily conquered by the Sultan of Delhi, Buddhism survived only in the subcontinent in Sri Lanka and in the Himalayan kingdoms.

Although Buddha—or *Shakyamuni* (the sage from the Shakyas)—is said to have lived ca. 560–480 BC, his importance in Buddhism is not as the apotheosis of a human being, but as a spiritual principle of experience. As an archetype of the Enlightened One, he embodies a perfection that was attained over many incarnations of becoming a *bodhisattva* committed to enlightening others. The innumerable *bodhisattvas* dispense grace to the faithful. Individuals may invoke these buddhas, for instance by repeating Avalokiteshvara's Heart mantra: "Gone, gone, gone all the way over, gone with all beings to the other shore, enlightenment, rejoice!" (*Gate, gate, paragate parasamgate Bodhi svaha*). The spiritual experience of the Buddha's nature to be found in Shakyamuni inspired not only his teaching, but also his dharma body (*dharmakāya*). Already in the Indian Buddhist temples of Gandhara, Mathura, and Ajanta (Maharashtra near Hyderbad, first and second centuries), one finds seven Buddhas displayed in human form. In Sanchi (in Madhya Pradesh, first century BC) and Bharhut, Shakyamuni and his six predecessors are depicted by seven *stupas* containing their relics.[4] The belief in reincarnation explains how the "human" historical Buddha also has a glorified, unadulterated "enjoyment body" fully expressing Buddha's true nature.

By the third century, with the Mahāyāna school of *Avatamsaka* sutra, reincarnation was to be overcome by "Indra's net" (*indrajāla*), a limitless jeweled expanse manifesting emptiness (*śūnyatā*) and dependent origination (*pratītyasamutpāda*). Simultaneously, this metaphor encompasses the realities of these concepts and the interpenetration of all beings. Buddhist art is hard-put to display how this body can be infinitely small or immeasurably big. This metaphor for interpenetration, "inter-being," possesses thirty-two signs derived from an astrology older than Buddhism itself.[5] *Nirvana* has no cosmological functions in man's world since it is ageless: it represents a safe, soteriological release and liberation from rebirths. Appeals to the three refuges, Buddha, the dharma, and the *sangha* (the monastic community), certainly do resemble prayer as invoking protection. Buddha, who personally embodies *nirvana*, gave rise to a devotional strand in Buddhism accompanied by a certain "polytheism" that was opposed by the more monastic, "purer" gnostic vision. Edward Conze goes so far as to claim that there really is no difference between the Godhead in Western mystical writing and in Buddhism.[6]

The continuity and discontinuity between Theravada and Mahāyāna Buddhism is organic. What the Buddha preached in the deer park in Benares consisted of the following four holy truths, and meditation on these remains one of the basic tasks for all Buddhists:

1. What, then, is the Holy Truth of Ill? Birth is ill, decay is ill, sickness is ill, death is ill. To be conjoined with what one dislikes is suffering. To be disjoined from what one likes means suffering. Not to get what one wants also means suffering. In short, all grasping at [any of] the five *skandhas* [involves] suffering.

2. What, then, is the Holy Truth of the Origination of Ill? It is that craving which leads to rebirth, accompanied by delight and greed, seeking its delight now here, now there; i.e., craving for sensuous

4 A *stupa* is a tall, mound-like structure containing relics (*śarīra*) of Buddhist monastics, and is used for meditation.

5 Thich Nhat Hanh has described inter-being in his typical playful and accessible manner: "If you are a poet, you will see clearly that there is a cloud floating in the sheet of paper. Without a cloud, there will be no rain; without rain the trees cannot grow; and without trees we cannot make paper. The cloud is essential for the paper to exist.... So we can say that the cloud and the paper *inter-are*." Cited in David L. McMahan, *The Making of Buddhist Modernism* (Oxford: OUP, 2008), 150.

6 Conze, *Buddhism*, 39.

experience, craving to perpetuate oneself, is craving for extinction.

3. What, then, is the Holy Truth of the Stopping of Ill? It is the complete stopping of that craving, the withdrawal from it, the renouncing of it, throwing it back, liberation from it, non-attachment to it.

4. What, then, is the Holy Truth of the steps which lead to the stopping of Ill? It is this holy eight-fold Path, which consists of: right views, right intentions, right speech, right conduct, right livelihood, right effort, right mindfulness, right concentration.[7]

There are likewise four kinds of concealed suffering which a mature person must understand:

1. Something, while pleasant, involves the suffering of others.
2. Something, while pleasant, is tied up with anxiety, since one is afraid to lose it.
3. Something, while pleasant, binds us still further to conditions which are the ground on which a great deal of suffering is inevitable.
4. The pleasures derived from anything included in the *skandhas* are worthless to satisfy the inmost longings of our hearts.[8]

It should now be clear what the moral, mental, and epistemological components of the "noble eightfold path" are:[9]

· Right Belief (in the Truth)
· Right Intent (to do good rather than evil)
· Right Speech (avoidance of untruth, slander, and swearing)
· Right Behavior (avoidance of blameworthy behavior)
· Right Livelihood (some occupations, such as butcher and publican, were disparaged)
· Right Effort (toward the good)
· Right Contemplation (of the Truth)
· Right Concentration (will result from following the Noble Eightfold Path)

The purification of the mental and deeper spiritual traits of one's being is an arduous but inspiring task, one which can be undertaken by following the above precepts under the guidance of a Buddhist monk and in a monastic setting.

7 Ibid., 43–45.
8 Ibid.
9 Cf. https://en.wikipedia.org/wiki/Noble_Eightfold_Path (accessed May 28, 2018).

Thich Nhat Hanh

At first sight, the basics of Buddhism we have just presented summarily might seem to exclude prayer, at least in our Western sense, from Buddhism. In a "religion" that eschews both gods and personal prayer, how can we apply our heuristic tools of "iconic words and verbal icons"? This short chapter on contemporary Buddhism provides a critical test for our approach to the study of other faiths. To offer an answer to this question, we must turn away from Buddhism in general—for it is not a unified system, and is too vast to cover in anything like its entirety—and focus on just one manifestation of contemporary Buddhist practice: that which has arisen in the wake of the Buddhism monk and teacher Thich Nhat Hanh (b. 1926), which best exemplifies the tensions of contemporary Buddhism "abroad" and beyond its original cultural setting.

As our study focuses on verbal prayer, we are especially interested in the use of chanted invocations, which we can examine as text, as opposed to silent or non-verbal prayer and meditation. In contemporary forms of Buddhism, such chanting is found in one school of Zen (Chan) as spread in the West by Thich Nhat Hanh, a monk from the monastic milieu of Huế in central Vietnam. While Thich Nhat Hanh is only one teacher among many, his knowledge of classical Chinese (the language of the East Asian Buddhist sutras) and his early entrance into the monastery of Tu Hieu in Huế at the age of sixteen display his deep roots in Vietnamese Buddhism.[10] Furthermore, his writings are popular in the West, and made accessible by being written in English.

Nhat Hanh's master was Thich Chân Thât of the forty-third generation of the Chinese/Vietnamese Lâm Tê School (Lâm Quan branch).[11] Nhat Hanh was a poet and a novelist, as well as a social activist for peace during the Vietnam War and afterward, and his motto is "Compassion is the only answer." His teaching will help us to reflect on the status of prayer in Buddhism.

When, in 1944, Thich Nhat Hanh entered his monastery as a novice at the age of sixteen, he was given a small book in Chinese characters and told to memorize it, for it would guide him along the path of Zen (Chan) Buddhism. This book was the well-known "Little Manual of Discipline," or *Luat Tiêu*. It is divided into three parts: the essentials of the discipline to be practiced every day, the essentials of the discipline that every novice must know, and the exhortation by the Zen master Kouei Chan, encouraging adherents to

---

10 The strict monastic tradition of Zen Buddhism was codified by Master Po Chang (779–803) in his monastery.

11 In the 17th century, the Chinese monks around Nguyên Thiều established this dynamic new school, the Lâm Tế (in Chinese, Linji).

Pagoda where Thich Nhat Hanh was trained, near Hué

meditate and embrace consciousness of what is precious in their vocation. Nhat Hanh describes his reluctance to submit to this discipline, foreign to what he had absorbed in the French colonial junior high schools. [12] He was being asked to learn mental formulas to be repeated, each one appropriate to the moment of the day and manual work, in order to attain mindfulness (*samyaksmriti*), an inner vigilance over his thought, acts, and motivations. This is the monk's goal. A person who knows, one who is awakened, is called a Buddha, and Buddhism is the doctrine of awakening, a teaching of wisdom. It can only be acquired by practice, creating the conditions for *sila* (discipline), *samādhi* (contemplation), and *prajna* (wisdom). [13]

It is striking to realize what a revolution Buddhism created in India, for salvation, or awakening, is obtained neither through grace nor merit, but wisdom. This was a startling new perspective on life, for the power of properly performed sacrifices as prescribed in the Vedas had never before been doubted. Buddhism rejected the system of castes, the divinities, and all ritual sacrifices. Above all, it refused to admit the notion of self or soul (*atma*) that was the starting point of all Indian philosophy in the Upanisads.

For the Brahmins, the concept of non-self and non-soul represented a liberation from the bindings of dogma that constituted a frontal attack on their very existence. That the non-self is everywhere present means that nothing possesses any "self" (*sarva dharmas nairatmya*). This logically leads to the doctrine

12 Thich Nhat Hanh, *Clefs pour le Zen* (Paris: Seghers, 1973), 8.
13 Ibid., 10.

of impermanence (*anitya*). Since everything is in constant transformation, it cannot retain its identity. Such absence of identity is the key to knowledge. The abyss between the ceaselessly changing things and static concepts show that there exists, in inter-dependence, a principle of cause and effect that is "inter-original." This is another way of saying that birth and death of things at any moment depend on a multitude of causes. A Zen monk, Dao Hanh of the twelfth century, said: "If that is existence, all exists, even the dust; if that is emptiness, everything is emptiness, even the universe." As a novice, Nhat Hanh found these teachings daunting; even for a Vietnamese, with the necessary linguistic skills, studying Buddhist doctrine posed a challenge.[14]

> As a novice I was required to read Buddhist philosophy. I was only 16 and unable to grasp the concepts like interdependent co-arising, and oneness of subject and object. It was difficult to understand why the perceiver could not exist independently from the object being perceived. I managed to get a high mark on my philosophy exams, but I didn't really understand. I reasoned that, thanks to awareness, the finite world of phenomena could partake of the transcendent realm of consciousness. Being can only be defined in opposition to non-being, and if there is not awareness of either being or non-being, it is as if nothing exists. The deeper implications were not at all clear.

Nhat Hanh went on to study at the Bao Quoc Buddhist Institute in Huế and received full ordination as a monk there in 1949 at the age of 23. Modeling himself on the higher education that the Chinese Buddhist reformer Tai Xu (1890–1947) had received in China, Nhat Hanh and several young monks went to the An Quang pagoda near Saigon and studied at Saigon University. To support himself, he wrote novels and poems. Returning at his elders' request to his monastery in Huế in 1955, he began editing the magazine "Vietnamese Buddhism" (*Phâ Giao Viêt Nam*). Beginning with that period, Nhat Hanh wrote tracts and participated in many movements designed to reunite and renew Vietnamese Buddhism and make it into a force for peace and social work.[15] The opposition he encountered led him to nearly forty years of exile (1966–2005). Not unexpectedly, Nhat Hanh's teaching on mindfulness stressed learning how to dwell deeply in the present moment.

---

14 Ibid., 120.

15 The biographical data on Nhat Hanh in this section is taken from John Chapman, "Return to Vietnam of Exiled Zen Master Thich Nhat Hanh," in *Modernity and Re-enchantment: Religion in Post-Revolutionary Vietnam*, ed. Philip Taylor (Singapore: ISEAS, 2007) 297–341.

Beginning in 1975, he founded a monastic community in l'Yonne (Burgundy) called *Patates Douces* (Sweet Potatoes), and recommenced writing, authoring a three-volume history of Vietnamese Buddhism. Nhat Hanh progressively wrote over forty books in English and French to explain Buddhism to a non-Vietnamese audience, not to mention some 85 publications in Vietnamese. In 1982, his community moved to another village, Thenac, near Bordeaux, to have more space for the growing monastery. In 1983, he began lecturing in America and eventually founded two more monasteries on the East and West coasts in 1997 and 2000. By 1998, there were some 500 members, and about 300 meditation practice centers (called *sangha*) had grown up worldwide.

I have taken the time to present the biography of Nhat Hanh because the teaching of Buddhism in the West, especially in America, has been fraught with problems; and I want to propose Nhat Hanh as a legitimate, authentic voice for my analysis of contemporary Buddhism that follows. Even if Nhat Hanh is criticized for overly popularizing, his work is grounded in solid training in meditation and a deep knowledge of the Chinese sutras. Obviously, he is not representative of Japanese, Burmese, or Singhalese Buddhism, but there is no single teacher who is. Indeed, modern Buddhism in different parts of the world has often seemed to shake off its regional embeddedness. Nhat Hanh is representative of this updated Buddhism.[16] Like another Buddhist exile, the 14th Dalai Lama, Nhat Hanh's focus on issues of justice and peace might lead one to imagine that, in his teaching, meditation no longer takes center stage. The opposite is true. Innovation is inevitable, and, in the teaching of Nhat Hanh, "inter-being" has "replaced" the role traditionally held by the concepts of *karma* and reincarnation. It is not a question of relegating older notions such as *karma* to the sidelines, but of focusing on our mutual responsibility for the suffering of others. Systemic causes of one's condition explain the circumstances of those who are disadvantaged.

It is perhaps Nhat Hanh's well-known exercises in mindfulness, emphasizing the sacred in the mundane, that have had the greatest influence on Western Buddhism.[17] The cultural frenzy and economic beating that America and Europe have experienced recently also go a long way to explain the success of inter-being, which displays an attentiveness to the small and fragile beauty found in daily life. But does this mean that Buddhist modernism, in David McMahan's words, "has a particular investment in minimizing appeals to the

16 For an analysis of Buddhism and modernity in America, see McMahan, *Making of Buddhist Modernism*; and, for a more historical approach, see Rick Fields, *How the Swans Came to the Lake: A Narrative History of Buddhism in America* (Boston: Shambhala, 1992).

17 McMahan, *Making of Buddhist Modernism*, 216–17.

miraculous" because of a self-conscious attempt to ally itself with science and naturalism over and against Christianity's explicit appeals to the supernatural?[18] McMahan reminds us that Zen Buddhism prefers concrete images to the abstract dogmas of Christianity; but what Christianity is he referring to?[19] Certainly not the Orthodox kind. Paul Reps, in his well-known book *Zen Flesh, Zen Bones*, describes a Shinshu priest who believed that salvation could be obtained simply by the repetition of the name of Amitabha, the Buddha of Love. McMahan considers the repetition of the name of a *bodhisattva* to be a traditional religious practice associated with traditional dogma. He goes on to describe Buddhist modernism as "the reinterpretation and demythologization of traditional doctrines, vigorous world affirmation, and hybridity with western discourses of emancipation."[20] On the other hand, Nhat Hanh insists that engaged Buddhism is not a privatized spirituality, for, when we eat with mindfulness, we think of the starving; and, by cultivating inner peace, we actually do bring peace to this planet.

Is Repeating the Name of Buddha a Chant without Transcendence?

If you ask how Buddhists pray, you quickly realize that they don't, and that you have phrased your question poorly. Yet Buddhists do have invocations: they invoke the examples of their saints.[21] If the self is to be extinguished, prayer "without a self" must be different from religious traditions such as Christianity, where the self is integral to salvation. *The Chanting from the Heart: Buddhist Ceremonies and Daily Practices*, used by the monks and nuns of Nhat Hanh's Plum Village, contains recitations that vaguely resemble prayer: invocation of the *bodhisattvas*' names, invocation of the Three Refuges, and praises to the Bodhisattva of Compassion and to the Buddha.[22] That is not to say that chanting does not play a large role in Buddhism to prepare the mind for meditation or as part of formal monastic ceremonies.[23] The most common Theravada chants in Pali are:

18 Ibid., 236.
19 Ibid., 237.
20 Ibid., 252.
21 See the analysis of Hans Küng, *Le Christianisme et les religions du Monde: Islam, Hindouisme, bouddhisme*, trans. into French by Joseph Feisthauer (Paris: Éditions du Seuil, 1986), 511–602.
22 Unified Buddhist Church, *The Chanting from the Heart: Buddhist Ceremonies and Daily Practices* (Berkeley: Parallax Press, 2007), 32–35; 41; 56–59.
23 See, for example, Alex Wayman's translation and commentary, *Chanting the Names of Mañjuśrī* (Delhi: Motilal Banarsidass, 1985).

- *Buddhabhivadana* (Preliminary Reverence for the Buddha)
- *Tiratana* (The Three Refuges)
- *Pancasila* (The Five Precepts)
- *Buddha Vandana* (Salutation to the Buddha)
- *Dhamma Vandana* (Salutation to his Teaching)
- *Sangha Vandana* (Salutation to his Community of Noble Disciples)
- *Upajjhatthana* (The Five Remembrances)
- *Metta Sutta* (Discourse on Loving Kindness)
- Reflection on the Body (recitation of the 32 parts of the body)

So praise is chanted, but words found in one's heart are different from everyday words.[24]

> "Manjusri," said the God Brahma, "is what you have been telling me the Absolute Truth?" "All words are true," said Manjusri. "Are lies then also true?" asked Brahma. "They are," said Manjusri. "And why? Good sir, all words are empty, vain and belong to no point in space. To be empty and vain and to belong to no point in space is the characteristic of Absolute Truth. So in that sense all words are true."[25]

Given the antinomian quality of Buddhist teaching, the resort to chanting may be a way around the aporia of any statement, proclaiming the paradox and not trying to resolve it. This is a Buddhist variation of Dionysius's negative apophatic teaching.

Looking further afield, the *Tathâgatagarbha* sutras have recently inspired in Thailand the *Dharmakāya* movement, which sees in all beings the *dharmakāya,* the true self of the Buddha. This is the ultimate body, the Buddha Body of Reality. Initially in the Pali Canon, Gautama Buddha tells Vasetha that Tathāgata (Buddha) is the truth body or the Dharmabhuta, the one who has become truth and in which one can take refuge. After the Buddha's *parinirvana,* his physical body (*rûpakaya*) is distinct from his Dharmakaya. This is already found in the *Aṣṭasāhasrikā Prajñāpāramitā* (The Perfection of Wisdom in One Thousand Lines) dating from the first century.[26] The Yogācāra school

24 The Buddhist eLibrary website gives easy access to many of these chants: http://www.buddhistelibrary.org (accessed December 12, 2017).

25 Arthur Waley, trans., *Visesha-cita Brahma-pariprcchâ,* Takakusu XV, 50 & 82, quoted in Edward Conze, ed., *Buddhist Texts Through the Ages* (New York: Harper Torchbook, 1954), 276–79.

26 Among the early Mahayana sutras, this family of sutras number about 40 texts written in India between 100 BC and AD 600.

in the third century formalized the three-body (*trikāya*) doctrine according to which Buddhahood possesses three aspects:[27]

- The transformation body (*nirmānakāya*),
- The bliss or enjoyment body (*sambhogakāya*), and
- The Dharma body (*dharmakāya*).

In the Nichiren school of Japanese Buddhism and throughout Asia, one chants homages to the True Dharma of the Lotus, using a Mahāyāna *sutra* that portrays Gautama Buddha as one who attained enlightenment in ancient times. Kumarajiva's translation of the *Lotus Sutra of the Wonderful Law* celebrates how this law is uninterruptedly intertwined in the lives of the disciples of Nichiren. Pure Land Buddhists, on the other hand, chant the *Namu Amida Butsu* (Homage to the Amitâbha Buddha); and, in more elaborate services, the *Expanded Sutra of Immeasurable Life*; whereas Zen, Singon, and other Mahāyāna schools chant the *Prajnāpāramitā Hridaya* or Heart Sutra in morning offices. The soteriology of Amidism is considered compatible with Zen Buddhism and should not be identified with any given school of Amidism.

Repentance ceremonies involve paying reverence to the Buddhas and *bodhisattvas*. Dhâranîs, extended mantras, are often used as invocations in morning services in Zen monasteries. Roshi Kapleau interprets these formulas as:

> A *dhāraṇī* is an extended mantra, a rhythmic sequence of sounds that express through their unique spiritual vibrations an essential truth transcending duality. The power which such a formula possesses to evoke invisible forces when chanted by a person having a sincere heart depends to a certain extent on the sound itself, but even more on the state of mind of the chanter... uttered by a being with pure faith, a concentrated mind and an open heart.[28]

Perhaps the most well-known Buddhist chant in the West is the Vajrayâna school's *Om Mani Padma Hum*, a mantra of six syllables expressing the *bodhisattva* of Compassion Avolokitesvara, or Guanyin in Chinese. It is also called the mantra of great compassion (*mahākaruṇā*) which enables the approach to

27 Asanga treats this at length in his *Mahāyānasaṃgraha*; see Etienne Lamotte, trans., *La somme du Grand Véhicule d'Asaṅga (Mahāyānasaṃgraha)* (Louvain: Bureaux du Muséon, 1938), 2 vols., 266–345.

28 Roshi Philip Kapleau, *The Merging of East and West* (2013), cited in https://fr.wikipedia.org/wiki/Dharani (accessed December 18, 2017).

Avolokitesvara. Here the distinction between prayer or invocation is hard to make; or at least we lack the words to describe the veneration that implores such compassion.

From the very beginning, Buddhist chant was the cause of suspicion. In the *Cîtassara Sutta* (A.iii.250), Buddha lists the five dangers of reciting the *Dhamma* using musical intonation. The five dangers associated with chanting all involve destroying concentration. Clearly this did not much restrict the use of chanting; Dôgen (1200–1253) defended chanting by claiming that since there is no separation between metaphor and reality, liturgies can be celebrated intimately, by which he means that in liturgy one must listen and speak with one's whole body-mind, "listen with eye and see with ear." Accomplished in this way, chanting is to experience the non-dual reality.[29]

So the purpose of Buddhist invocation is not the same as that of Hindu prayer, if only because the praises do not have the same destination. Here one seeks to awaken *inner* compassion and wisdom, and one radically rejects all worship based on fear or, even worse, propitiation of statues in view of personal profit. One tries to pull into one's heart energies of mercy and purity, declaring one's intention, as in the Golden Chain prayer for Amida, wherein one asks to be part of a link of pure deeds that stretches around the world. So addressing Amida Buddha is a means to transform our inner lives in the image of Amida's compassion in which we place our trust. At the same time, one lists all good intentions sought: helping the hungry, the sick, and all those who seek the other shore where they will realize *nirvana*, "Namo Amida Buddha." Chanting the *Amitâbha* (or *Sukhâvatîvyûhas*) *Sutra* or the *Ksitigarbha Sutra* is done with the same intention:[30]

> At that time the Buddha told the Elder Shariputra, "Passing from here through hundreds of thousands of millions of Buddha lands to the West, there is a world called Ultimate Bliss. In this land a Buddha called Amitabha right now teaches the Dharma....
>
> ...
>
> Shariputra, what do you think? Why is this Buddha called Amitabha? Shariputra, the brilliance of that Buddha's light is measureless, illumining the lands of the ten directions everywhere without obstruction, for this reason he is called Amitabha.

29 See John Daido Loori, *"Symbol and Symbolized" Mountain Record: the Zen Practitioner's Journal* 25, no. 2 (2007); and cf. https://wiki2.org/en/Buddhist_chant (accessed December 18, 2017).

30 Cf. http://www.amitabha-gallery.org/plchant.htm (accessed December 18, 2017).

...

> Moreover, Shariputra, the life of that Buddha and that of his people
> extends for measureless, limitless *asamkhyeya kalpas*; for this reason he
> is called Amitayus (of Infinite Light). And Shariputra, since Amitabha
> realized Buddhahood, ten *kalpas* (aeons) have passed."

At first glance, it might seem that the devotees of Pure Land Buddhism
were avoiding the strenuous and lengthy meditation associated with Zen
Buddhism. But such an assessment would be unfair, since these invocations
and contemplations of different Buddhas' holiness are very traditional. In the
reflections of the Yogācāra school, Akshobhya and Amitābha represent wisdom and compassion. In the Golden Light Sutra (*Suvarṇaprabhāsa Sūtra*), one
also finds Amogasiddha and Ratnasambhava completed by Vairosana in the
center.[31] These five *Dhyani* (meditation) Buddhas are part of the *dharma-kāya*
embodying the whole principle of enlightenment. Louis de la Vallée-Poussin
has argued that this clearly popular devotion does, in fact, have its roots in
Buddhist philosophy, albeit in a cosmological form.[32] Amitābha and Amitāyus,
around the first century in certain milieu, began to eclipse the historical Buddha. Hence Buddha in human form rests on the Vulture Peak, a mountain
near Benares that is still part of a universe mixing good and evil. Buddhists
conceive of a blessed land, Sukhāvatī—analogous to the Brahmanic land of
bliss or land of the setting sun situated in the West—known as the western
pure land of Amitābha.

Sakyamuni had explained to Ananda that meditation on the sun reveals
the kingdom of Amitabha where one is born miraculously in a lotus to listen
to the teachings of Buddha, and later to be born radiant sons of Buddha.
This was rendered possible by a vow made by a monk, Dharmākara, in ages
past to the Lord of all the world, Lokesvararaja, that, if he, Dharmākara,
became a Buddha, it would be to govern a world exempt from all suffering.
And, he added, "If my 'field' cannot be a land of blessing, I'd rather never
become a Buddha." After many aeons of charity and meditation, Amitābha
is the last reincarnation of this monk. To arrive in this land of bliss, it suffices to say the name of Amitābha, no matter what one's life has been like.
What is more, there are future Buddhas applying to us the merits of their
good actions—such as Maitreya (the twenty-ninth), who will return to earth
from the Tushita heaven. This Buddha follows the historical Buddha (the

---

31 R.E. Emmerick, *The Sūtra of Golden Light: Being a Translation of the Suvarṇabhāsot-
tamasūtra* (London, Luzac and Company Ltd., 1970).

32 Louis de la Vallée-Poussin, *Bouddhisme* (Paris: Beauchese, 1935), 266–73.

twenty-eighth), himself preceded by twenty-seven earlier Buddhas. These future Buddhas are accompanied by Tārās (Savior or Stars), ready to visit this earth and even hell to escort souls to paradise.

Hans Küng finds in this quest for the Pure Land an opening for an anthropology that expresses the dignity of man.[33] How? Nāgārjuna's (second century) doctrine of emptiness (*shūnyavāda*) had made emptiness the key to a new paradigm where "becoming" meditating on being and nothingness was baptized the middle way (*mādhyamika*). This doctrine was proclaimed using a fourfold dialectic. Thus it is in reality; that it is other; that it is both thus and other; that it is neither thus nor other. Whereas, in the Pali canon, the word *shūnyavāda* (the doctrine of emptiness) rarely appears, emptiness has become a means of illumination both epistemologically and cosmologically with the *Madhyamika* school. Entering the void allows one to escape suffering. But, if Nāgārjuna considered the void negatively, like the Greek philosopher Pyrrho, who prescribed suspension of speech and judgment and the practice of impassibility, the *Yogācāra* school understood the void in a positive manner: all beings and all realities express the same absolute.[34]

In the wake of the eighth-century "Hindu" philosopher Shankara, corrected by Rāmānuja's "qualified monism" (*viśiṣṭādvaita*), subsequent Buddhist philosophers said that all negation contains an affirmation. Thus, while clearly not a God, an unconditioned transcendence became another paradigm of Mahāyāna Buddhism. The void therefore took on a positive meaning: ineffable, unspeakable, that which neither appears nor disappears. Beyond personhood and beyond being, this Absolute is an absolute negation, a life force, a mindset or *plēroma*, of the highest reality.

The atheism of Buddhism seen in this light needs to be qualified by its cultural context. If in a polytheistic Asian context where both gods and men are thought to be regulated by their karma, the void that originally designated the absence of soul comes to mean that absolute without attribute that is inherent in all things, making *samsāra* and *nirvana* identical.[35] Identifying one's own emptiness with the Absolute provides liberation. And the *nirvana* of the Theravadin here comes to mean the absence in a void, an absence of reality, one's own being forever extinguished, at rest, while, at the same "moment," the metaphysical reality of Buddha penetrates all manifestations. In Theravadin Buddhism, *dharma* had designated an eternal truth that saved mankind from the world of suffering. This new paradigm of *dharma* references the

---

33 Küng, *Le Christianisme*, 525.
34 Ibid., 530.
35 Ibid., 534.

dharmakāya, the body of the dharma teachings.[36] This symbol of the ultimate transcendental reality includes Buddha's teachings, his illumination, and the reality he experiences. David Chappell concludes that this Buddhist doctrine allows not only expressions of respect and veneration, but also of prayer and supplication.[37] That having been said, Chappell immediately remarks that the term *dharmakāya* has taken on so many other meanings in Mahāyāna schools that its usefulness has been criticized. This has the effect of throwing one back to one's own personal ascetics and meditation. Nonetheless, *nirvana,* the void, and *dharmakāya* are manifestation of divine qualities. These three, together with the original Buddha, constitute an impersonal "God," in which one may take refuge but to whom one does not pray.

The term Zen, or Chan, the school of Buddhism that appeared at the end of the eighth century, designates a tradition that took the seated position used in meditation as the basis of Buddhism. The *Lankavatara Sutra* of Gunabhadra (AD 394–468), once translated into Chinese, became the basic text of Zen. In the southern Chinese school of Zen, Chen Houei (AD 668–760) established an authoritative history of the tradition of Zen Buddhism involving a succession of patriarchs.[38] In this school, sudden illumination was cultivated, while, in the northern Chinese school of Zen, gradual illumination was the hallmark. This was the school of Bodhidharma, later called Chan. It was the monk Huian Sou (AD 668–752) of the northern school who, while developing the doctrine of the non-reference of words, introduced the use of *kôan,* dialogues with a master to provoke doubt, and then to progress in practice.[39] From the eighth century, five southern schools flourished. It was Po Tchang (AD 739–808) who created a monastic rule of life that broke off from that of the monasteries of the *Vinaya* tradition. While Chinese in origin, Zen traditions in Vietnam, Korea, and Japan do not differ radically one from another.

---

36 Hiuan Tsang's (Xuanzang) *Vijnaptimâtratâsiddhi,* which Louis de La Vallée-Poussin translated and annotated in two volumes (Paris: Geuthner, 1929), 703–16.

37 David W. Chappell, "Comparing Dharmakaya Buddha and God," in *Spirit within Structure: Essays in Honor of George Johnston,* ed. E.J. Furche (Allison Park, PA: Pickwick, 1983), 189.

38 See Jacques Gernet, trans., *Entretiens du Maître dhyâna Chen-Houei du Ho-Tsö (668-760)* (Hanoi: EFEO, 1949). Bernard Faure, "Chan/Zen Studies in English: the State of the Field," cf. http://www.thezensite.com/ZenEssays/Miscellaneous/ChanZenStudies.htm (accessed November 9, 2017).

39 Nhat Hanh, *Clefs pour le Zen* (Paris: Seghers, 1973), 163-203, has translated 43 kôan and poems of Tran Thai Tong (1218-1277), first king of the Vietnamese Trân dynasty, who later became a monk and monastic author.

Monastic Life

Life in a monastic setting in central Vietnam is always organized around a common finality: meditation.[40] The superior is assisted by monks responsible for administration, for the gardens, the granaries, the library and the sanctuary, the reception of lay and monastic visitors, the recitation of sutras and other ceremonies, and the relations between the monks. Every monk, by rotation, is given certain tasks, whereas the novices serve as attendants to the superior. Twice a month in the Buddha sanctuary, there is a review of observance of the two hundred and fifty rules of the *bhikkhus* (monks) and the fifty-eight rules of a *bodhisattva*. The novices participate in this recitation. They also follow the six principles of communitarian life:

- To live together under the same condition
- To observe the same rules
- To master one's tongue so as to avoid disputes
- To share one's belongings
- To share different points of view
- To create harmony among opinions to maintain the joy of communitarian life

The monks rise at 4:00 AM and have 15 minutes to wash, dress, and make their beds, before going to the meditation hall and taking the lotus posture while a monk uses the meditation bell to chant a prelude:

> The fifth division of the night has begun already, and the door of Reality is open.
> I wish that everyone would be on the way/platform of *Prajna*, Wisdom.
> Let every one of us enter deeply into the doctrine of the three vehicles and realize the harmony between the two truths.
> May the Sun of Marvelous Wisdom rise and dissipate all dark clouds.

During the meditation period, the large bell is struck regularly. After meditation, the monks gather together in the sanctuary to recite the sutras. Breakfast consists of a rice soup, vegetables in vinegar, and soy sauce, which is eaten in silence. After breakfast, the "Heart of the Prajnaparamita" is recited. The monks then disperse for their appointed tasks before returning at 11:30

---

40 The sketch summarized below is from Nhat Hanh, *Clefs pour le Zen*, 139–47.

AM to rest. Lunch is at noon; the monks go to the refectory in procession. From 2:30 until 5:30 PM, each monk returns to his corvée; later, at 7:00 PM, the recitation of sutras begins. At 8:00 PM, the monks study and practice Zen. After this last session of meditation, which can last late into the night, the monks sleep. Twice a year, the fifteenth day of the fourth lunar month and the fifteenth of the seventh lunar month, are periods of retreat and intense meditation. The monks who have been living in isolation return to their monasteries of origin to participate in this retreat. Certain monks live as hermits in small huts alone and do not go abroad; novices assist them by providing a link with the monastery, bringing water, fruit, rice, and vegetables.

There is, of course, no way to describe what occurs in the heart of a monk during meditation; but the basic "program" is outlined in the authoritative texts of the school of Vijnanavada. This *meditation paradigm* is the framework used for meditation during the hours of "sitting" in immobile silence. Nhat Hanh describes what is being accomplished during these hours as purification. Zen adopted in its own way the Yogācāra ("Yoga as Practice") school's view of an interior lens for deconstructing human experience through a rectified epistemology and psychology. (This resembles the ascetical teaching of St Gregory of Sinai [1260–1346] concerning the altar of the heart; his contribution to the *Philokalia* had a great impact on Eastern Christian monastic practice.) Yogācāra is considered the third turning of the Buddhist wheel of doctrine (*dharmacakra*), but not in contradiction with the Pali *nikāyas* or *agamas*.

Beginning in India with its founding text, the *Samdhinirmocana Sūtra* ("Explanation of the Profound Secrets"), Asanga (AD 300–370) and his half-brother Vasubandhu first formulated these teachings. In contradiction to the Madhyamaka school, affirming the existence or non-existence of any ultimate reality, Yogācāra claimed that only the mind can hold any ultimate reality. By dint of meditation, Xuanzang promoted meditative practices directed toward the *bodhisattva* Maitreya. He visited the Tushita heaven at night to receive instruction from Maitreya.[41] While Xuanzang (AD 602–664), after ten years of study and translation in India, later said that the Madhyamaka position was true, the alternative mind-only school was useful for novices to understand the conventional processes of their minds.[42]

Vasubandhu's description of the eight kinds of consciousness, the three natures, and emptiness, systematizing the thought of the Yogācāra, allows one

41 See E. Obermiller's translation, "The Doctrine of Prajnā-pāramitā as exposed in the Abhisamayālamkāra of Maitreya," *Acta Orientalis* 11 (1932): 1–2.

42 It seems that, in his presentation summarized below, Nhat Hanh relied partially on Hiuan Tsang's (Xuanzang) *Vijnaptimātratāsiddhi*.

to realize what is meant by "representation only" (*vijnapti-mātra*). The critical evaluation of consciousness was to be the product of prolonged meditative experience. *Vijnapti-mātra* (mere representation of consciousness) designates three aspects of the world as it appears in our consciousness that are denied also in three ways: that this consciousness is not the absolute mode of all reality; that individuals are not a transformation of any absolute consciousness; and that individuals are only illusory appearances of some monistic reality. So emptiness is an absolute absence of the distinction between subject and object. The novice studying these texts learns, through meditation, how our mind (falsely) constructs reality. Needless to say, the crucial relation that any theism finds between a personal God and human beings has no place here, even if non-dualism of the "Hindu" sort shares certain features with that of the Vijnanavada's refusal of duality.

Nhat Hanh's presentation of Vijnanavada serves to establish the close reliance of Zen meditation on the Vijnanavada teaching concerning the classification of *dharma*, things that can be conceptualized.[43] These fall into five classes:

- The eight kinds of knowledge (*citta*)
- The fifty-one states of knowledge (*catasika*)
- The eleven physical and physiological phenomena (*rupa*)
- The twenty-four relational phenomena (*citta viprayuta-samsaka*)
- The six unconditioned phenomena (*asamkrta*), which display six categories

These classifications make up the hundred "things" or *dharmas*. For the Vijnanavada, all sensations, perceptions, thoughts, and knowledge arise from the storehouse of consciousness (*alayvijnana*) whose unconceptualized nature is the *tathata*, the great wisdom and perfect mirror. The eight *vijnanas* fall into three categories:

1. Knowledge of objects (*vijnaptir-visaya*), such as sight, touch, hearing, taste, and smell, centered in the *manovijnana*
2. The *vijnana,* or discrimination between self and non-self, which gives rise to the activity of thought (*manas*)
3. The basic or *alaya vijnana*

The fundamental *vijnana* is the basis of all manifestation of knowledge of subject and object. Any *vijnana* contains both the subject and the object

---

43 Nhat Hanh, *Clefs pour le Zen,* 120–36.

of its knowledge, as well as its proper nature (*svasamvittibhaga*). This world of consciousness and knowledge is composed of dependent things which, because of their inter-dependence (*paratantra*), have no real identity. They carry with them an illusion-imagination called *vikalpa*. If one destroys this discrimination, this *vikalpa*, knowledge becomes pure and can reveal the *tathata*. This is their spiritual program. In their perfect (*nispanna*) nature, the true nature of the *vijnana* of which Vasubandhu speaks is nothing other than the *tathata,* or the "illuminating nature of knowledge," in which the five *vijnana* of our sensations become the source of miraculous wisdom. The *manovijnana* can become the wisdom of marvelous inspection. When the *manas* becomes the wisdom of non-discriminating nature, the storehouse (*alaya*) becomes the "wisdom of the great and perfect mirror." Henceforth the *alaya*, at the base of all being and non-being, conserves the essences and energies of the *dharmas* in the form of seeds (*bija*). This revelation is obtained by meditating on the interdependent nature of things (*paratantra*), which provokes a transformation of the *alaya,* neutralizing the roots of our latent tendencies or passions (*anusaya*). This process of illumination is laid out in the *Lankavatara Sutra*, systematized by Vijnanavada. It is not the phenomena themselves that disappear in the purification, but any discrimination-imagination involving them. So Nhat Hanh concludes that Zen is not the study of Zen; Zen is direct contact with the reality of life.[44] Why talk about music, he quips, when one can listen to it?

Some of the teachings of Nhat Hanh as one finds them at Plum Village may appear disturbingly simple. For example, the four mantras of True Presence:

1. I am here for you.
2. I know that you are here, and I am happy.
3. I know that you are suffering. That is why I am here for you.
4. My dear one, please help me.

However, if one takes the time to look at the events of Nhat Hanh's remarkable biography—for example, the time he led a pilgrimage of a hundred of his Western Buddhist *sangha* back to Vietnam in 2005—one realizes that he is wholly serious in his intentions.[45] When one reads of how he was able to counsel the veterans of the second American/Vietnamese war, one can only be impressed by his deep compassion.[46] In retreats for reconciliation and

44 Ibid., 135–36.
45 Chapman, "Return to Vietnam," 237–41.
46 Fields, *How the Swans Came to the Lake*, 357–58.

healing with American soldiers, Nhat Hanh guided these veterans, showing them how to release their obsessional guilt for having murdered innocent children through "at the very moment" saving other children who otherwise would have died. I witnessed firsthand how much sympathy he had to offer others. This was also the fruit of his non-discrimination meditations.

Just as the *bhakti* movement in India brought the ardor of prayer center stage, the extinction of self on which early Buddhism focused was supplemented by liturgical chanting. This chanting is certainly a form of invocation focused on the Buddhas and the *bodhisattvas*. What have we learned about prayer in terms of the Christian anthropology of prayer presented in our introduction? While the Buddhist understanding of self (*ātman*) cannot be identified with the notion of soul for it is transcendental (*adhiātman*), the continuing question of the extinction of self and its assumption of a Buddha nature seems to have been favored by invocations. To whom these invocations are addressed is a delicate issue. Perhaps the easiest way around the question of theism in Buddhism is to say that these "prayers" are addressed to Buddha, who has achieved enlightenment. But Buddha's intervention as teacher is different from that of the Trinity in Christianity; although the cosmos was created *ex nihilo*, this "void" in Buddhism resonates with a dialogical quality that it does not possess in Christianity. On the contrary, here we have a dialogue, not between the Creator and the created, but at the interface between a man and the knowledge arising from the storehouse of consciousness (*alayvijnana*) whose unconceptualized nature is the *tathata*, the great wisdom and the perfect mirror. Enlightenment is certainly favored by invocational affirmations, but is sought as a statement beyond any cognition; any conceptualization of enlightenment is an obstacle to it. That having been said, the devotion of Buddhists as they chant their prayers or recite their *sutras* resembles nothing as much as the ardor of Hindu *bhakti*.

CHAPTER 6

Prayer in Its Own Right: An Assessment

WE COME NOW TO THE CONCLUDING CHAPTER IN THIS volume. How has our Christian anthropology of prayer helped us in our exploration of the prayer traditions of other faiths? In our conclusion, we need to assess the extent to which we have been able to access the practice of prayer in its own right by using the experience of Christian prayer as a guide. The search for such a method was motivated by our dissatisfaction with social science approaches, which, while having merits of their own, in general tend to devaluate the very reality of such dialogues with God. Simply put, we are trying, through this approach, to treat prayer with the respect it deserves. When we speak about prayer in its own right, we are investing it with the values it articulates in its dialogues with the divinity, yet these change in the religious context of each invocation. We may have treated prayer with great respect, but we have not made our task any simpler.

Since the early nineteenth century, the Christian approach to the prayers of non-Christians has evolved. We no longer speak of pagan prayers to demons. Instead, we try to understand the theology that is put forward in each kind of invocation, expressed in terms that are different from those of Christian theology, but which merit a special consideration because of certain shared features: theism, the primacy of veneration of the beloved, humility through asceticism, attention to the revelation of certain words used in these prayers, etc.

Using the model of the Axial Age (Jaspers' *Achsenzeit*), the distinction between religion and culture is one way of clarifying the religious preoccupation with personhood and self (Foucault's *le souci de soi*). The new sense of transcendence was both anthropological and soteriological. In a collection on self and self-transformation, David Shulman and Guy Stroumsa have compared the different approaches toward such deliberate mutations of selfhood.[1] Concerning the place of Christianity among these new world religions, they wrote:

1 David Shulman and Guy G. Stroumsa, eds., *Self and Self-Transformation in the History of Religions*, 8.

None were as insistent and successful in this pursuit as the Christians. Jesus Christ himself had undergone the most radical of all transformation: the Son of God had become man, incarnated in a mortal body. The new theology entailed a new anthropology. If Christ suffered in his body, the body of a man could no longer be considered an appendix to the real self, as it had been, by and large, in Greek philosophies. In contrast to other movements, Christianity offered salvation to all: anyone could model a life after that supreme exemplar and be saved through self-transformation. Ritual purification became identical to moral progress, and constant spiritual exercise, *askèsis*, became the condition *sine qua non* for the ascent of self. In this striving one was not alone: spiritual direction may not have been a Christian invention, but its development in early Christianity is certainly unique. Acting as a *khalifa* of Christ on earth, as it were, the ancient (the elder, *ho gerōn*) in the Egyptian desert played a crucial role in the efforts of the monk to reconstitute the self. In that sense, a living model of an already accomplished self-transformation. . . . Between the second and fourth centuries in the Roman Empire, it is in the domain of religion rather than culture that a radical change occurred. . . . Transformation in self transforms all contexts for selves.

Still, why write a volume on prayer from the specific perspective of Christian anthropology? What are the advantages of abandoning the axiom of neutrality adopted by social scientists? I am not the only person who, while researching religious experience, found that the discipline's deliberate under-interpretation blocks access to the very subject—prayer. Discussing the nature of rituals, Don Handelman writes that no level of social reality exists prior to the exchange and the interactions of specific individuals.[2] Therefore, "no assumptions need to be made immediately about how social-cultural order and ritual are related, neither about meaning of signs and symbols that appear within a ritual, nor about the functional relationships between rituals and social order." For Handelman, ritual expands the world for the people participating in it, allowing them, through introspection, to see things that they had not yet seen.[3] Answers to questions such as to whom "first honor" (*mutalmei* in Tamil) is attributed in South Indian rituals should not be immediately interpreted in terms of

---

2   See Don Handelman and David Shulman, *Siva in the Forest of Pines: An Essay on Sorcery and Self-knowledge* (Delhi: Oxford University Press India, 2004), and Don Handelman and G. Lindquist, eds., *Ritual in Its Own Right: Exploring the Dynamics of Transformation* (New York and Oxford: Berghahn, 2005).

3   Handelman and Shulman, *Siva in the Forest of Pines*, 12.

political meaning. From the native point of view, this kind of precedence is a blessing by the deity of a person's power before that of his public identity.[4]

In these closing pages, I will rapidly review some of the more recent publications in religious anthropology that provide a *Sitz im Leben* necessary for more detailed studies than the one I have provided here. I contend that, between highly detailed ethnographic studies such as my *From Cosmogony to Exorcism in a Javanese Genesis* and a broad comparative study of prayer and ritual illustrating various kinds of self-transformation, such as what Shulman and Stroumsa have provided, there is room for a confessional comparative approach to prayer.[5] Comparison is often better performed without relativism. The "hidden ear of God" leads us to suppose that many of mankind's invocations should be taken seriously, even if one comes to them as a Christian. The status of the name of God, *Elohim*, Allah, *Isvara*, is often the best point of departure.

From Cosmologies to Theistic Monotheism: Methodological Issues

As understood in this book, religion has founded a primordial and universal mode of knowledge expressing a given person's spiritual culture, i.e., his beliefs. I reject the common social science approach which claims, *mutatis mutandis,* that cosmology and sociology can explain the religious institutions with a positivistic epistemological realism inherited from Emile Durkheim (1858–1917), although the holism of his sociology has remained a permanent contribution.[6] There is clearly more to religion than just piety. As is to be expected, many contemporary studies of Christianity outside of Europe focus on the contradictions of an unspoken and unavowed appreciation of non-Christian prayer and ritual by people who have recently acquired a certain Christian culture.[7]

---

4 Ibid., 117.

5 Stephen Headley, "The Mirror in the Mosque"; Shulman and Stroumsa, *Self and Self-Transformation.*

6 For an overview of the emergence of social science at the "expense" of theology, see John Milbank, *Theology and Social Theory: Beyond Secular Reason* (Oxford: Blackwell, 1990), and, for the school of thought that Milbank helped create, see James K.A. Smith, *Introducing Radical Orthodoxy: Mapping a Post-Secular Theology* (Grand Rapids, MA: Baker Academic, 2004). See also Joel Robbins, "Anthropology and Theology: An Awkward Relationship?" *Anthropological Quarterly* 79, no. 2 (Spring 2006): 285–94.

7 See Fenella Cannel, ed., *The Anthropology of Christianity* (Durham and London: Duke University Press, 2006); and her *Power and Intimacy in the Christian Philippines* (Cambridge: Cambridge University Press, 1999); Lorraine V. Aragon, *Fields of the Lord: Animism, Christian Minorities and State Development in Indonesia* (Honolulu: University of Hawaii Press, 2000); Adeline Masquelier, *Prayer has Spoiled Everything: Possession, Power, and Identity in an Islamic Town of Niger* (2001). Other studies introduce a more pragmatic linguistic perspective: Aurore Monod Becquelin and Philippe Erikson, eds., *Les Rituels du Dialogue*

That being granted, to use Maurice Leenhardt's expression, divinity "is pitched at ground level" and is imminent and empirically observable.[8] One can try to understand prayer without trying to explain it away by all sorts of external analyses. Second, since that experience of God or divinities is extremely varied, prayer will remain both an inclusive catch-all category and never a unitary homogenous one. A third and still more decisive reason why the concept of prayer cannot fully feature the claimed communion through words between man and God is because man himself is not the same from one culture to the next and sometimes not even from one generation to the next. If Western individualism is now exported worldwide, the constituents of personhood still vary dramatically from culture to culture. Man, being human, may be construed radically differently, which means that prayer differs not only according to the divinities addressed but also according to the humans who are praying, invoking, and supplicating the divine.

Theo-linguistics in any religious setting requires a vision of the spirits, ancestors, or divinities to which prayers are made. And the difficulty is not just the multiplicity of destinations of prayer. Nowhere is a definition of divinity more crucial than in monotheistic prayer, where God has all the initiative of speaking toward men.[9] How does God come toward his creature, putting words on his lips? In a monotheistic context, for Christians, prayer is understood as a dialogue initiated by the Creator of man, incarnate, crucified, dead, and buried before rising from the dead and ascending into heaven. St Ignatius of Antioch, writing to the Romans, makes this point: "Now that Christ is with the Father, he is more visible than he was before."[10]

The person structured by Christian monotheistic prayer, to use Leenhardt's terms, was shaped in Europe before being revised into modern individualism.[11] There are atemporal values of Christian faith—for instance, forgiveness and

---

(Nanterre: Société d'éthnologie, 2000); Webb Keene, *Signs of Recognition: Powers and Hazards of Representation in an Indonesian Society* (Berkeley: University of California Press, 1997); idem., *Christian Moderns: Freedom and Fetish in the Mission Encounter* (Berkeley: University of California Press, 2007); David Mosse, *The Saint in the Banyan Tree: Christianity and Caste in India* (Berkeley: University of California Press, 2012). The collection "Anthropology of Christianity" at University of California Press, directed by Joel Robbins, continues to publish good studies in this vein. See also M. Engelke and M. Tomlinson, eds., *The Limits of Meaning: Case Studies in the Anthropology of Christianity* (New York and Oxford: Berghahn, 2006).

8 Maurice Leenhardt, *Do Kamo: La personne et le mythe dans le monde mélanésien* (Paris: Gallimard, 1947), 3.

9 Abraham Joshua Heschel, *God in Search of Man: A Philosophy of Judaism* (London: Souvenir, 2009).

10 St Ignatius of Antioch, *Epistle to the Romans*, ch. III.

11 Leenhardt, *Do Kamo*, 4.

compassion—that imitate those displayed by Christ on the cross. These have been transmitted without interruption since the first century A D and are still well received. Nowadays, Christians' sense of their own selves, transformed by modernity, finds certain aspects of their faith incomprehensible. Certain prayers require sharing spaces of belief where notions of shame and honor, to give two examples, have since volatilized in a secularized culture. This becomes more complex when we compare Christian and non-Christian prayer. Leenhardt shows, in his work *Do Kamo* (1947), how unlike modern Europeans a person from small-scale tribal societies with his "decentered personage" may be. Although Leenhardt's ethnographic data are drawn from the Canaque of New Caledonia at the beginning of the twentieth century, the cultural differences at stake here do represent an unprecedented change in human and cultural relationships. Cultural anthropologists have documented them worldwide. This was sketched out by Louis Dumont in his *Essais sur l'Individualisme* (1963, ch. 6), where, turning the focus on Europe, he describes the Christian origins of the modern individualism. Today, fifty years later, the status of personhood in Western Europe has never been more ambiguous and debated. That being said, any comparative anthropology of prayer is obliged not only to study the prayers and their changing status institutionally, but also to understand the drift of the notion of personhood behind the *orans* who says the prayers.

The issue at stake in prayer is that of the separation of subject and object. This has been the foundation of European epistemology since Duns Scotus (ca. A D 1266–1308), who introduced the distinction between our imagination of external objects, which takes place in the mind of the beholder, and their mental treatment as representatives of reality. The partners in any invocation possess a very different status. In India, a thousand years before Duns Scotus, Bhartrhari's fifth-century "grammatical" philosophy analyzed ritual and attributed meaning—and hence representation of reality—not to words but only to the higher level of complete sentences (*vākyasphoṭa*), making them the initial and primary level of signification.[12] So the problem has been with us for a long time. Late medieval scholastic religious psychology constrained the imaging subject with imagined objects, while, with René Descartes, the individual's *cogito* was made the basis of his personal ontology. Prayer called

---

12 Bhartrhari is dated to the fifth century AD. His *sphota* or holistic view of language was rejected by the later composite position of the Mimamsa School for whom each word had denotive meaning. For Bhartrhari, sound cannot be distinguished before the whole word is heard. In the same vein, his sentence-holistic view of meaning meant that the meaning of an utterance is known only after the entire sentence (*vākyasphoṭa*). See Madeleine Biardeau, *Théorie de la Connaisance et Philosophie de la Parole dans le brahamisme classique* (Paris: Mouton, 1964).

this ritual use of language into question. Participation and communion became endangered categories in a univocal ontology.

Only beginning with Marcel Mauss's *Essay on the Gift* in 1924 did the European post-Enlightenment tradition discover that "there exists, above all, an intertwine of spiritual ties between things which are to some degree soul, and individuals and groups that treat each other to some degree as things."[13] Karl Polanyi formalized Mauss's observation that, in "tribal" cultures, law, economy, society, and religion all belonged to the same sphere and did not separate domains of cultural understanding.[14] This led Dumont to re-evaluate exchanges of values that would seem to separate the giver (the subject) from the given (object).[15] For Dumont, the relation of subject and object is part of a larger whole located outside the relationship itself, which is jeopardized in Western societies when the individual is raised to the status of a supreme value. In his study of the exchange system of the Aré-Aré (Solomon Islands), Daniel de Coppet showed both empirically and ethnographically how the subject's image, breath, and body are circulated.[16] He identifies three movements (return, linked succession, and stop), three forms of the subject's participation in the objects "exchanged." The relational logic of the passage of objects between subjects is confounded and of limited value, for "linear causality and the principles of non-contradiction and excluded middle . . . (are) inadequate for a logic of substances."[17]

Unexpectedly, this advance in the anthropology of exchange theory occurred precisely at the time when theologians like John Milbank and other members of the Radical Orthodoxy movement were reformulating the philosophical and theological focus on the person in terms of his ability to participate in the other.

From the above sketch, I conclude that the study of prayers as texts is insufficient if it does not involve their "orality."[18] Paradoxically, only thus could

13 Marcel Mauss, *Essay on the Gift*, first French edition 1923–24 issue of *L'Annee Sociologique*, 163. English translation, *On Prayer* (New York: Durkheim/Berghahn Books, 2003).

14 Karl Polanyi, *The Great Transformation: The Political and Economic Origins of Our Time* (New York: Rhinehart, 1944).

15 Louis Dumont, *Homo Aequalis I. Genèse et Epanouissement de l'Idéologie économique.* (Paris: Gallimard, 1977); *Essai sur l'individualisme. Une perspective anthropologie sur l'idéologie moderne* (Paris: Editions du Seuil, 1983).

16 Daniel de Coppet, et al., *On Relations and the Dead: Four Societies Viewed from the Angle of their Exchanges* (Oxford: Berg, 1994), 62–63.

17 Ibid., 3.

18 Even Clooney, whose interest is in texts, admits that the repetition inherent in meditating on texts bears comparison with the exchanges in an oral conversation; see his *Theology after Vedanta: An Experiment in Comparative Theology* (Albany, NY: State University

the two interlocutors remain mutually invisible, silent, auditively speaking, undecipherable yet in communication.[19] They "speak" to each other on the basis of a preceding relationship of mutual confidence, hence faithfulness. To say that persons praying are different from one another, different enough to change the contents of their prayers, is self-evident. What matters to people praying is that they share distinct experiences of a common value, participation, even sometimes communion, with one another and, above all, with their "Lord." Thus, in this dimension of participatory prayer, communion is a shared desire to be with the other that leads to an ever-deeper participation through prayer. For Christian ascetic theology, the clearest case of what we have just described is called *theōsis* or deification, where the resemblance of the *orans* to the image in which he was created is gradually restored through prayer.[20] Thus, although the creature continues to be separated from his Creator by an abyss, he nonetheless becomes "God-like," partaking in the glory of God before whom he stands, whose light is reflected on his face and whose mercy he lyrically celebrates in his prayers. Obviously this *terminus ad quem* eludes description.

The Transmission of Prayer from Israel to Christianity

If, from the outside, invocation appears totally incomprehensible, one may ask why people who engage in prayer rarely inquire into why they do so. Let us take an etymological approach, for the meaning of the word "prayer" (εὐχή, "euchē") in Greek is surprising.[21] The earliest meaning of this word is the solemn vow one takes to perform a sacrifice. As Emile Benveniste puts it:

---

of New York Press, 1993), 170.

19 See Laine Berman's *Speaking Through the Silence: Narrative, Social Convention and Power in Java* (New York and Oxford: Oxford University Press, 1998).

20 For an inversion of roles between God and man through fusion, see Isabelle Nabokov, *Religion Against Self: An Ethnography of Tamil Rituals* (New York: Oxford University Press, 2000), 8, where she gives seven references for the Indian examples of these kind of ontological transformations. For Handelman, the Indian god Siva can be less than god: "No two-ness comes into existence as god's presence among living beings acts to curve cosmos away from further evolution, differentiation and difference, all of which rupture the relationship between god and human beings" (Handelman and Shulman, *Siva in the Forest of Pines*, 218–19). He is a "tensile" god: "*Cit* [awareness], is clearly differentiated from *ātman*, 'self.' *Cit* . . . is not and cannot be aware of its opposite *a-cit* (or *a-sat*, 'non-being'). God's self, if he has one, can be located right here, in this very lack of awareness and in the astonishing, far-reaching changes it consistently generates, including hidden form." In the sorcery Handelman studies, objectification is present in sorcery but also in sacrifice, "which enables the cosmos to turn freely through itself, feeding itself, knowing itself, healing itself, taking itself away" (*Siva in the Forest of Pines*, 214).

21 See Benveniste, *Le vocabulaire des institutions indo-européennes*, vol. 2, 225.

> As an anticipated offering, this act is based on the principle of an ever
> increasing reciprocity, also known from other institutions: what is offered
> is called a superior gift; so the promised being is ... by advance acquired
> by the divinity.[22]

Here we find again the notion of credit that de Certeau reads as the
foundation of belief in the Indo-European languages. Thus θύω ("thuō" in
Greek), "to sacrifice" or to honor a god with a sacrifice composed of prayers
and things offered, originally meant to produce smoke. From the meaning of
vow evolved the notion of declaring one's intention, something one desires
to ask the gods and to share with them.

A similar corpus of prayers displays a faith that is ineluctably convergent.
The transmission of an understanding of the praxis prayer from Israel to
Christianity will illustrate this point. In Hebrew, the word *dabar* means both
account or commandment, but also a thing or its reality. Since God created
by his word, action and word cannot be dissociated. Do words really realize
what they mean? Deuteronomy admits that this is a question:

> Now what I am commanding you today is not too difficult for you
> or beyond your reach. It is not up in heaven, so that you have to ask,
> "Who will ascend into heaven to get it and proclaim it to us so that we
> may obey it?" Nor is it beyond the sea, so that you have to ask, "Who
> will cross the sea to get it and proclaim it to us so that we may obey it?"
> No, the word is very near you; it is in your mouth and in your heart
> so that you may obey it. (Deut. 30:11–14)

The people of Israel characterized themselves as the hearers of the divine
word: "Has any other people heard the voice of God speaking out of fire, as
you have, and lived?" (Deut. 4:33). Further, the Lord took the initiative to
speak to his prophets, such as Isaiah:

> Is [true fasting] not to share your food with the hungry and to provide
> the poor wanderer with shelter—when you see the naked to clothe him,
> and not to turn away from your own flesh and blood? Then your light
> will break forth like the dawn, and your healing will quickly appear;
> then your righteousness will go before you, and the glory of the LORD
> will be your rear guard. Then you will call, and the LORD will answer;
> you will cry for help, and he will say: Here I am. (Isa. 58:7–9)

22 Ibid., 237.

So also Jeremiah the prophet, forewarning Israel that Nebuchadnezzar would conquer Jerusalem (586 BC), said:

> You understand, O LORD; remember me and care for me.... [Your words] were my joy and my heart's delight, for I bear your name, O LORD God Almighty. (Jer. 15:15–16)

In Christianity, prayer took on a new dimension because Jesus of Nazareth not only dialogued with his disciples, but is yet more, as Hebrews puts it:

> In the past God spoke to our forefathers through the prophets at many times and in various ways, but in these last days he has spoken to us by his Son. . . . The Son is the radiance of God's glory and the exact representation of his being. . . . (Heb. 1:1–3)

John the Evangelist begins his Gospel with an awareness of this decisive new aspect of dialogue and communion with God:

> In the beginning was the Word, and the Word was with God, and the Word was God. He was with God in the beginning. Through him all things were made. . . . The Word became flesh and made his dwelling among us. We have seen his glory, the glory of the One and Only, who came from the Father, full of grace and truth. (John 1:1–3, 14)

Of course, many other approaches to prayer exist beyond the one applied here. Fabio Giardini attempted a systematic "psycho-theology" of Christian prayer by addressing how the mind develops attentiveness and awareness in prayer, making of prayer a form of both knowing and loving.[23] Thus prayer becomes an ascent, and, through worship, a communion. This approach is stimulating, but it necessarily ignores many of the anthropological issues that have preoccupied us here.

Abandoning Prayer in Univocal Epistemology

The praxis of prayer is impossible to envisage inside an individualistic world-view. Individuation attempts to reject sets of values transmitted by institutions. Values coming from outside the individual's own world-view have less chance

23 Fabio Giardini, *Pray without Ceasing: Toward a Systematic Psychotheology of Christian Prayer Life* (Fowler Wright Books Ltd., 1998).

of being taken seriously. Here it makes little sense to pray as one's ancestors were taught. When, in the thirteenth century, Europe began turning away from a theology of communion, of participation between creator and creature, what emerged was a sort of "onto-theology." Its object was God, but God who was considered less a person than an abstract category of being. Certain contemporary philosophers (J. Milbank, J-L. Marion), in their effort to return to Aquinas, affirmed God's existence, his being as creator, only by analogy to man's. For human existence, "to be" or "is" have different meanings. Duns Scotus effaced this distinction, using the verb "is" for both God and man, irrespectively. His "phantasm," his representation of being, was not dependent on revelation in the experience of communion but on an epistemological concept. Duns Scotus thus confounded two kinds of existence within the same representation, as formulated "univocally" by the individual, with its own autonomous metaphysics. This means that God is a subject in our minds prior to any experience of him as creator of our being. The "advantage" of this viewpoint is that human existence is granted full autonomy. A creature need not be understood to be created by God, to have received his being from God in the gift of creation. From this point of view, one can no longer ground epistemology on what is revealed in the book of Genesis (1:26), where man is said to be created *ex nihilo* in the image and resemblance of God. This critical epistemology gradually spread *mutatis mutandis* over the following four centuries from theology to philosophy, to ethics, to political science (in the category of citizen), and later to social sciences generally. It became the foundation of Enlightenment skepticism concerning any anthropology of prayer, and the impossibility of dialogical communication became self-evident.

There exist two ways to escape from this dead end. One is to practice a close reading of ascetical and patristic sources for an understanding of invocation. The other is to confront European philosophy head-on, as in the Radical Orthodoxy movement, in order to return to an understanding of liturgy before it was "conceived of" as impossible. Over the last twenty years, theologians and philosophers like Catherine Pickstock and John Milbank have been dialoguing with contemporary atheists and agnostics on the *aporia* of univocal ontology.

In contemporary Western European culture, and not just legal culture, protection from the other is fundamental. The contemporary affirmation of self implies a degree of alienation from the other. Personhood is not based on interpersonal communion but on a temporal atomization of the dimension of communication, plotting out strategic positions in the outside world. To go back to the patristic theology of St Maximus, the spatial-cosmic dimension of otherness, of difference (*diaphorà*), is explained as a result of the fall subsequent to the creation of mankind *ex nihilo* by God.[24] Death (*diaíresis*, division), linked to decomposition (*diàspasis*), exists because communion and otherness do not coincide. Though both space (*diàstéma*) and time are part of creation, time remains finally directly dependent on God. As Fr Georges Florovsky pointed out:

> "Time is reckoned from the creation of the heavens and the earth," as St Maximus the Confessor said. Only the world exists in time, in change, succession, duration. Without the world there is no time. And the genesis of the world is the beginning of time.[25]

To return briefly to Western European philosophy, Descartes took onto-theology's epistemology a step further, for, if Duns Scotus's epistemology of solitary interior representation of the outside world precedes the constituting of self, then all that Descartes's *cogito ergo sum* can reveal is "immanent" space contained within the individual's mental vista. Beings who are immanent in this space are esteemed more coherent than if viewed in the multiplex time, because such a representation can preserve interiority while distancing difference and multiplicity. This impurity of such complexity should not contaminate the monadic solipsistic self-presence. A certain nihilism appears underneath this fragile metaphysics.[26] Instead of communal liturgies celebrating the place of the creator amongst his creatures, subjectivity is devoid of the desire to participate in the celebration of this difference. Reality, otherness, is measured, calculated, and matter is eventually defined as a feature of extension, i.e., space can be distinctly, clearly calculated and our grasp of this shallow reality of the other is incapable of distinguishing the finite from the infinite.

The Risks of Comparing Prayers

In Chapter 1, we saw that various theologians, including Pickstock and Bulgakov, attempted to deal with prayer "in its own right." Is that the case with recent Catholic studies attempting to situate Christianity amongst others religions?[27]

24 St Maximus, *Ambigua*, no. 67 (Paris-Suresnes: Edition de l'Ancre, 1994), 356–63.

25 Georges Florovsky, *The Collected Works of Georges Florovsky. Volume 3: Creation and Redemption* (Belmont, MA: Nordland, 1976), 43.

26 See, in the monthly review *Esprit* (no. 403, March–April 2014), "Notre nihilisme," which deals with the contemporary obsession with values and the triumph of nihilism.

27 Jacques Dupuis, *Vers une Théologie Chrétienne du Pluralisme Religieux* (Paris: Cerf, 1999); *La rencontre du Christianisme et des religions. De l'affrontement au Dialogue* (Paris: Cerf, 2002); and J. Ries, *Les chrétiens parmi les religions. Des Actes des Apôtres à Vatican II* (Paris: Desclée, 1987).

Questioning the meaning of contemporary religious pluralism in God's plan
for humanity today may involve an exploration of God's covenant, revelation
as Word, saving mediation, and entrance into the kingdom before embarking
on the question of whether prayers can be shared and practiced together with
persons of other faiths.[28] Julien Ries's study provides a useful historical overview
of the last 2,000 years of religious confrontation before asking to what extent
a Christian can expect to find legitimate revelation in non-Christian religions.
My own approach, while not lacking in theological underpinnings due to its
anthropological slant, has tried to clear the playing field by first of all inquiring
into what constitutes prayer. If the category of revelation is brought to the fore
too soon, it seems too abstract to permit the kinds of comparisons I have made.

Catholic priests like Jacques Dournes and Raimundo Panikkar redefine who
is foreign to the Gospel in order to find their way back to Christianity after a
prolonged experience of a tribal and "non-Christian" culture such as India.[29]
After Leenhardt, these two figures exemplify an effort to situate Christianity
in the eyes of those who are not Christians. Finally, it is a missionary endeavor.

Closer to my perspective are the influential studies of the Jesuit Walter
Ong. In his *The Presence of the Word* (1967), he retains a Catholic understanding of revelation (the Word became flesh) while treating the incarnation as
belonging to the domain of Sensorium.[30] For Ong, the word is not inert, but
lives and endures as does a sound.[31] He is the Word of God by the fact that
he is Son. The Word of God for Ong is reciprocating man's response to God
as he approaches the Father "in his name." As St Paul says, "faith comes from
hearing the message, and the message is heard through the word of Christ"
(Rom. 10:17). Man enters into communication and participates in the life of
others through sounds and words.

But what of silent invocations? Can they be studied? There exist surveys
of languages of "unsaying"; for instance, Michael A. Sells's *Mystical Languages
of Unsaying* (1994) deals with the historical figures of Plotinus, John Scot
Eriugena, Ibn 'Arabi, and Meister Eckhart. The orality of written scripture is
everywhere important, for scripture was a spoken word long before it was
ever written down, as William Graham has shown in his *Beyond the Written
Word* (1987). The Vedic hymns studied above in Chapter 4 illustrate this amply.

28 Dupuis, *La rencontre du Christianisme*, chs. 9–10.

29 J. Dournes, *Au plus près des plus loin, Projet pour la mission* (Paris: Aubier, 1969) and
Raimon Panikkar, *The Unknown Christ of Hinduism: Towards an Ecumenical Christophany*
(London: Darton, Longman and Todd, 1981) and his *Vedic Experience*.

30 Ong, *Presence of the Word* (Minneapolis: Univ. of Minnesota Press, 1967).

31 Ibid., 12–13.

A local ethnography such as Sam D. Gill's *Sacred Words* (1981) classifies the types of prayer by ceremonial use corresponding to an indigenous Navajo typology. The closer one is to the facts concerning the execution of oral rites, the better one can grasp their distinctions between good and evil, which are often at the heart of their intentionality.

If I have entitled my approach "prayer in its own right" and compared Christian prayer with Hebrew, Muslim, Hindu, and Buddhist prayer, it is because prayer tends to get lost in the multitude of understandings of Asian spirituality. Selva Raj and Corinne Dempsey, editors of *Popular Christianity in India* (2002), chart the ongoing emergence of syncretic cults, which, on the ground, are normal, even if they provoke negative reactions from their ecclesiastical superiors, who attempt to distinguish between what is acceptable acculturation and exaggerated introductions of Hinduism into Christianity. While this quest for normative dogmatics is quite legitimate, if one contrasts two books like Michel Fédou's *Regards Asiatiques sur le Christ* (1998) and M. Stephen's *Christian Theology in the Indian Context* (2001), one sees that the transmission of a rich cultural heritage, whether European or Indian, involves such a stretch, such a grand *écart*, that taking on board the ever-changing and ongoing local experiences of Indian Catholics has proved daunting. While their Hindu cousins change their "cherished" divinity (Sanskrit *ishta-devatā*) several times in a lifetime, should Indian Catholics change patron saints in the same manner? Questions like this arise explicitly and pervade Indian Christian community life.[32]

The challenge of any such synthesis/syncretics may, in part, explain why an anthropologist like David Mosse relies on a historical assessment of how Catholicism took root in the extreme southern part of Tamilnadu, allotting the lion's share of his work to examining the strategies used to accumulate a strong local identity through local alliances with royalty. This leaves little room for the kind of understanding of prayer I have put forth here. Mosse provides an analysis of the first Catholic missionary in Tamilnadu, South India—the Italian Roberto Nobili, who arrived in Madurai in 1606. As a pragmatic rationalist, Nobili and his recent converts tried to preserve a dual representational economy where "'the cultural' was the realm in which the relationship between signifier and signified was contingent and changeable; whereas idolatry involved the fusion of meaning and semiotic form."[33] Customs were defined as "civil and thus the mediator between idolatry and culture became ranked castes."

---

32 Cf. Selva J. Raj, *Vernacular Catholicism, Vernacular Saints: Selva J. Raj on "Being Catholic the Tamil Way"* (Albany: SUNY Press, 2017), and Christine Mangala Frost, *The Human Icon: a Comparative Study of Hindu and Orthodox Christian Beliefs* (Cambridge: James Clarke, 2017).

33 Mosse, *Saint in the Banyan Tree*, 6.

Nobili did not imagine that he could learn from South Indian religion, for he considered that these superstitions reflected a failure of reason. Nobili would go on to reconstruct "shreds of divinely bestowed truth from degenerated, local texts and practices."[34] As a Thomist, his method was to separate out the rational from the irrational as incompatible with revelation. Once separated from reason, universal truth could not lie in specific semiotic forms.[35]

Webb Keene, in his study of the Protestant missions in eastern Indonesia, esteemed that this separation of belief from language, of words from the things they designated, would permit the notion of individual agency and allow "Christian moderns to emerge."[36] It is not certain that this has occurred in South India as predicted, for Mosse concludes that "Christianity took root not as a conserved religious tradition but through the innovation beyond the mission center involving the search for the miraculous and creative inference from the basic mission teaching. Some innovations would have failed; others, being socially relevant, became public."[37] This, for Mosse, does not mean that syncretism is inevitable:

> Catholics may adopt "Hindu" ritual and aesthetic forms (but not images) along with shared attitudes to sacred power; but elements from clearly distinct provenance are not mixed.... Hindus worshipping at Catholic shrines (or visiting them for exorcism) do not try to give Christian saints Hindu identities or bring their own ritualists to mediate.... The success of the Jesuit Madurai Mission in the rural periphery (in contrast to its failure in Brahman centers) evidently had much to do with the way Catholicism was articulated through an indigenous religiosity.... On the Tamil plains ... in the late 1600s, rulers of previously peripheral regions sought affiliation to status-enhancing cults with overarching cosmologies in place of localized clan deities to legitimize their expanding power within larger state systems.[38]

Mosse claims that Nobili was searching for an expression of the Christian faith "beyond the social," by which he refers to the Jesuit notion of personal interiority, beyond the "civil" claims of caste behavior. He then calls our

34 Ines G. Županov, *Disputed Mission: Jesuit Experiments and Brahamanical Knowledge in Seventeenth-Century India* (New Delhi: Oxford University Press, 1999), 133.
35 Mosse, *Saint in the Banyan Tree*, 7.
36 Keene, *Christian Moderns: Freedom & Fetish in the Mission Encounter* (Berkeley: University of California Press, 2007).
37 Mosse, *Saint in the Banyan Tree*, 13.
38 Ibid., 14–15.

attention to the fact that Mauss had identified a parallel to the emergence of the Christian person (*la personne morale*) as the locus of moral evaluation in the appearance in India of *bhakti*, that is to say religion devoted to a chosen, cherished Lord (*Isvara*, one's own personal *ishta-devatā*). So, for Mosse, the Jesuit distinction between spiritual individual and social persons controlled by caste could already be found in Indian devotional sects, where, in acts of piety, one's caste falls away, as we saw in the *bhakti* poets in Chapter 4. The fact that this does not occupy greater space in Mosse's analysis can be explained by the definition of conversion he uses, which leads on to the discussions of the "production" of Catholic religion in South India. The nascent Catholic churches became the object of political-economic investments; the temples and pilgrimage sites were patronized by the new mode of royal statecraft, where rights, services and "first honor" were produced in much the same way as at the Hindu *kovils* (temples), thus integrating them into local sacred geography and pantheons.[39] For Mosse, "Catholic religion is not a trans-historical global phenomenon introduced into 'local cultures' by missionary agents, but a contingent and at times unstable category of thought and action . . . that does not however fail to point beyond itself to a transcendent truth."[40]

Even if one admits the complexities of conversion, should one envisage a nearly total "transformation," a domination of world religions over local ones?[41] To historicize this worldwide religious "evolution," Robert Hefner cites the five stages outlined by Robert Bellah.[42] Heavily influenced by Max Weber, Bellah described "traditional" religions that so completely structured the self that it became difficult to distinguish between self and cosmos, and between traditionally religious and more modern societies. Indeed, since the word/concept of society itself is a modern one, should we suppose that Judaism, Christianity, Islam, Hinduism, and Buddhism challenge the status quo, always questioning the local cosmologies? Does the so-called "transcendental tension" of monotheisms really encourage social reform by providing opportunities for private personal thought and action? Is this where their rationality lies? Are the prophets Jeremiah, Isaiah, and Ezekiel really only participating in *intra*-denominational competition to control the doctrines of the first and second temple in Jerusalem?

---

39 Ibid., 268.

40 Ibid., 269.

41 Robert Hefner (ed.), *Conversion to Christianity. Historical and Anthropological Perspectives on a Great Transformation* (Berkeley: University of California Press, 1993), 3–46.

42 Robert Bellah, "Religious Evolution," *American Sociological Review* 1964, vol. 29(3): 358–74. Cf. p. 361.

Another question raised by our study of prayer is whether religious ration-alization really clarifies faith by canonization of scripture and institutional-ization of doctrine. Hefner shows that believers' rituals and prayers do not simply embed formal truths.[43] I wonder whether a comparative history of missionary activity, Muslim or Christian, would really show that the "power" of these faiths derives from the *control* of religious knowledge and identity over time and space. The reading of the two volumes of Saiyid Athar Abbas Rizvi on the spread of Sufism in India gives the impression of a largely charismatic diffusion occasionally supported by local rulers who patronize Sufi poets and build their *dargah*.[44] Islam did not always have an authoritative "culture and cohesive religious structure." Much of its strength during the "weaker" periods of the caliphates derived from the fact that its coherence is not due to internal constraints but to its ability to incorporate outside cultural influences.

As David Parkin and I showed in *Islamic Prayer Across the Indian Ocean, Inside and Outside the Mosque* (2000), there is a trope that implies that prayer outside the mosque in a "Muslim" country will always be a source of com-petition between Islamic monotheism and the local spirits that were there before Islam arrived. Robin Horton's study of conversion in Africa discussed by Hefner describes a two-tier system with local spirits and higher gods, which sometimes embraced several overlapping ethnic and territorial boundaries.[45] For Horton, conversion involves incorporation of the self-same spirits into a larger social order that promotes a reformulation of local indigenous religions, but not necessarily its disappearance.

Exclusive religious adherence supposedly introduced by Islam and Chris-tianity, and the *self-identification* implied in that conversion, is dubbed a moral economy. But are these really "ready-made formulas for a revitalized social community"?[46] The historical process was rather longer and more compli-cated than that. Garth Fowden, in his study of the consequence of Constan-tine's conversion and the subsequent introduction of state-sponsored mono-theism in late antiquity, describes a movement from empire to commonwealth on the basis of a shared missionary monotheism, Christian and Muslim.[47] And, in the 800s, the early Abbasid Muslim caliphate achieved what Con-stantine, during his lifetime four and a half centuries earlier, had attempted

43 Hefner, *Conversion to Christianity*, 18–19.

44 Saiyid Athar Rizvi, *A History of Sufism in India* (New Delhi: Munshiram Manoharlal, 1978–83), 2 vols. André Wink gives a very different vision of the making of the Indo–Islamic World in his *Al Hind*.

45 Hefner, *Conversion to Christianity*, 20–21.

46 Ibid., 29.

47 Fowden, *Empire to Commonwealth*.

to initiate: the coincidence of multi-ethnic universal rule and universal faith.

A second issue: if the system after conversion remains two-tiered for several generations, are the local spirits really subordinated to those in the higher cosmos? It should be questioned: have "they" reduced this so-called "higher" Christian macrocosm to issues of membership and its boundaries, its relation to political power and the controlling of the beliefs of the laity? Was St Paul's vision of an inclusive covenant based on the pretentions of monotheism and not on the family of God preached by Jesus of Nazareth? While trying to understand the role of transcendence in empire building is relevant, weren't the truths these world religions announced first brought down to earth— "pitched at ground level," to use Leenhardt's expression—in the daily prayers of those whose immediate needs preceded the efforts of those seeking to build a long-lasting civilization with political power? When the latter faced the armies of neighboring civilizations and their own different religious practices, sometimes alliances were made, as Fowden has shown in his *Before and After Muhammad: The First Millennium Refocused.*[48] The study of syncretic practices throws a different light on these cleavages; dhimmitude did not always lead to the extinction of Christianity or Judaism under the caliphates.

The Hidden Ear of God: Accessibility and Indifference

To return to the issues raised in Chapter 1, when St Ephrem the Syrian distinguished the "visible ear of humanity" from "the hidden ear of God," what was he trying to tell us? Was he saying that God hears everyone's prayers? Was he describing something that normally we cannot imagine, that seems therefore unreal to us, as prayer itself often does? Prayer is like a musical instrument; unless we practice it often, it goes flat, discordant because it lacks implication on our part. If one's heart does not tell one to rise early to pray, then the prayer one makes at the end of the week in a congregation on Sunday risks being primarily audible to the "visible ear of humanity." The "doctrine" of ascetical experience, the vocabulary of ascetics, was forged through years of "failed" prayer, as argued by Shulman and Stroumsa. The earliest "sentences" of the desert fathers, their *apophtegmata*, were spontaneous words of advice addressed to their disciples living in nearby hermitages after all-night solitary vigils and prolonged fasting.[49]

---

48 Recently, in his *Before and After Muhammad: The First Millennium Refocused* (Princeton: Princeton University Press, 2014), Fowden analyzed, *inter alia*, the cross-fertilizations of exegetical traditions between Islam and Christianity, between Roman law, rabbinic Judaism, patristic Christianity, and Islam.

49 See the standard alphabetical collection (i.e., by the name of each monk) translated

The silence and solitude with which they surrounded their prayer required an experienced guide in order to avoid boredom and discouragement. The twenty chapters of the first thematic, systematic collection of these ascetic adages or *apophtegmata* were organized around the anthropological profiles, descriptions of the life of prayer, that were later found *inter alia* in Evagrius of Pontus (AD 345–399) and John of the Ladder (seventh century), an abbot at the Monastery of the God-Trodden Mount Sinai (St Catherine's).

The vocabulary of the prolonged efforts at prayer by these anchorites was voluntaristic: "Give your blood and you will receive the Spirit" (Longin, sentence 5, *Apophtegmata*). The only way to attain the depth of listening that made prayer intelligible was compunction (in Greek, *penthos*). Thus Abba Matoès (sentence no. 2) said, "To the extent that man approaches God, to such an extent he will see himself as a sinner." And he who knows he is a sinner does not judge his brother.

This deep inner honesty that one is seeking in prayer, if attained, allows two kinds of sadness to be distinguished: the first leads to recoiling from the sight of one's own faults and the weakness displayed by others; the second sadness leads to profound discouragement and depression (*acédia*). Still, for a valiant repentant who perseveres, compunction prepares the path to joy. Along the way, the repentant may stumble, even collapse, but his guide, his elder (*geronda*), shares the pain of these failed prayers and allows him to pick himself up and continue along the path of poverty and patience, permitting one to endure until such time as the temptations that impede prayer volatize.

So then, within this Christian ascetical arena, what is prayer? Prayer is a work of the soul that must be accompanied by manual labor. While endlessly making baskets or ropes, an activity so mechanical that it can be done even in the darkness of night, man hides his life in silent repetitive prayer. As Paul Evergetinos (d. 1054) said, one hides one's life like a man burying seed in the earth in order to harvest a hundredfold. In order to be alone (*monos* in Greek) with God, says Abba Zaharias (sentence no. 1), one does violence to oneself in all things. The path is arduous. As another anonymous saying runs, "If you are proud, you are the devil. If you are sad, you are his son." But the wisdom given to the one who prays commands silence and the relinquishment of self-judgement. On his deathbed, Abba Bessarion (no. 11) said, "The monk should become like the cherubim and the seraphim, only eyes."[50] The life of prayer, which is identical

from the Greek by Benedicta Ward, *Sayings of the Desert Fathers* (Kalamazoo: Cistercian Studies, 2005). Cf. also S. C. Headley, *Du Désert au Paradis: Introduction a l'acétisme orthodoxe* (Paris: Cerf, 2018).

50 Henri Brémond, *Les Pères du Désert* (Paris: Gabalda, 1927).

to an ascetic life, is a therapy allowing one to reject, indeed to vomit out, all that lies in the depth of the psyche, polluting it, and to modify the balance of one's psychic energies through simple humility and purification.

This freedom to pray at all times, to ignite the fervor in one's heart, broadens considerably our understanding of oral invocations. Here prayer is a silent and *hidden* activity of the inner man; in a monastic context, the Greek word for meditation (μελέτη, "meletē" in Greek) actually designates a broader form of prayer (otherwise εὐχή, "euchē," or προσεύχομαι, "proseuchomai" in Greek). What the monk in the desert is cultivating in the depths of his heart is a secret activity, a sensitivity that embraces both thoughts and desires, feelings and interior words, filling both his mind and heart and through which he is constantly able to stand in communion before God. As a contemporary hermit near the monastery of St Macarius at Wadi Natrun (southwest of Alexandria) said, when you pray continually with a depth we are at pains to imagine, God becomes your *friend* and speaks, dialogues, with you in your prayer as might a friend.

So prayer is an activity that is both simple and multiple. The *orans* struggles with all his strength to live an interior life "according" to God. And this is not marginal. Henri Brémond wrote, in his *Les Pères du Désert*, that it was the ascetical fathers who had the broadest and deepest influence on Christian life and civilization.[51] Keeping guard over one's heart permits one to avoid the dangers of the memory of past sins, to reject destructive thoughts and images through unabated prayer, through depending constantly on grace. One must admit one's unconsolation. One throws oneself and one's weakness before God. In God's presence, one cries out in prayer, "Save me!" The freedom to do this efficaciously for Christians comes from the habit of constantly accusing oneself, of cultivating a deep humility that allows one to avoid ever justifying oneself. Seeing the beauty of God's creation and all the miracle of life, one is led to reject one's superficial exterior *persona* in favor of this person who stands before the truth of God. That person's confident prayer is indeed a "laborious rest," fending off the blasphemous and sensuous thoughts that would interrupt one's compunction and deprive the words of prayer of their meaning, of their silence. As Abba Theodore of Phermé (ca. fourth century) said after seventy years of *ascesis*, the monk never rests. These friends of God have known the great suffering and ever-greater joy in prayer.

So why does St Ephrem place the "hidden ear of God" at the center of the act of prayer if not for the obvious reason that, without His ear, there can be no prayer? I have insisted, perhaps to the annoyance of the reader, that

---

51 Cf. Fowden, *Empire to Commonwealth*.

prayer, before it is saying, is listening to the words one may use to address God. For that reason, it is to be treated with a maximum of respect. In this attention, Christian "silent" prayer, such as we find it described in the fourth- and fifth-century desert fathers, captures this discretion. Prayer requires more sobriety than many people imagine, and, while Christians do not have any monopoly on sobriety, those who traverse the great dramas of life have this special kind of privacy spontaneously, instantaneously. Thirsting after contact with God, some enter the deserts of their own hearts and, as pilgrims, cross through many arid regions to reach an oasis of peace and real prayer. The difficulty of such prayer is epitomized in the most ineffable prayer of all prayers pronounced by Christ trying to overcome the ultimate crisis of his own "life." Such is the foundation of Christian prayer, stepping off from the prayer of Jesus described in the garden of Gethsemane:

> "My soul is overcome with sorrow to the point of death."... Going a little farther, he fell with his face to the ground and prayed, "My Father, if it is possible, may this cup be taken from me. Yet not as I will, but as you will." (Matt. 26:38–39)

We can now understand why prayers in Judaism, Christianity, and Islam end in "amen" (ἀμήν, "amēn" in Greek, or, as in Arabic, 'āmīn—"so be it"). As an affirmation, the *amen* indexes one's faith with great seriousness. Indeed, the Hebrew word for faith (*èmunah*) comes from the same root as "amen" (root: *aleph-mem-nun*). For all three religions, "amen," as a verbal root, means *to be firm, confirmed, reliable, faithful, have faith,* believing one can be heard by God. Often, "amen" refers to the preceding words of the speaker and expresses affirmation. A solemn "so be it" concludes prayer. In Judaism, the response to a blessing being recited is to say "amen," and Christians adopted that practice. In Isaiah 65:16, one reads "the God of truth"; in Hebrew this is "the God of amen." Jesus often used "amen" to put emphasis to his own words (also translated "verily"). In the Gospel of John, Jesus introduced important messages saying, "Verily, verily, I say unto you," which derives from the Aramaic "*āmēn.*"

The need to affirm a truth proclaimed in prayer or heard listening to one's teacher has full resonance in all three monotheisms, showing us that they have something in common. Truths come to life in the ears of the faithful, unless one refuses and flees to attempt deicide. Amen.

آمين

INDEX

STEPHEN C. HEADLEY (1943–) is an Orthodox priest (Moscow Patriarchate) who studied theology at St. Vladimir's Orthodox Seminary (New York) and l'Institut St. Serge (Paris). After a BA and MA in oriental studies at Columbia University (1965, 1969), a diploma in Sanskrit philology at the EPHE (4th section, Paris; 1972), and a doctorate in social anthropology at the EHESS (Paris, 1979), he did research at the CNRS (Paris) from 1981 to 2008. Currently, with two other priests, the author serves in the Orthodox parish in Vézelay (France). His most recent books are: *Du Désert au Paradis: introduction à la théologie ascétique* (Editions du Cerf, 2018) and *Christ after Communism. Spiritual Authority and its Transmission in Moscow Today* (Orthodox Research Institute, Rawlings, NH; 2010). The two subsequent volumes of his *Theological Anthropology* yet to appear are: *Rivers of Ritual: An Anthropology of Alternative Rites* and *After Secularization: A non-European Perspective.*

www.ingramcontent.com/pod-product-compliance
Lightning Source LLC
Chambersburg PA
CBHW022006080426
42733CB00007B/497